Juice Guru

Juice Guru

Transform
Your Life by Adding
One Juice a Day

BOOST VITALITY, INCREASE LONGEVITY & STAY SLIM

Steve & Julie Prussack
with additonal recipes by Chef Babette Davis

Robert
ROSE

For complete cataloguing information, see page 240.

Disclaimer
The recipes in this book have been carefully tested by our kitchen and our tasters. To the best of our knowledge, they are safe and nutritious for ordinary use and users. For those people with food or other allergies, or who have special food requirements or health issues, please read the suggested contents of each recipe carefully and determine whether or not they may create a problem for you. All recipes are used at the risk of the consumer.

We cannot be responsible for any hazards, loss or damage that may occur as a result of any recipe use.

For those with special needs, allergies, requirements or health problems, in the event of any doubt, please contact your medical adviser prior to the use of any recipe.

Design and production: Daniella Zanchetta/PageWave Graphics Inc.
Editor: Judith Finlayson
Recipe Editor: Tracy Bordian
Copy Editor and Indexer: Gillian Watts

Cover image: Assorted fresh juices © iStockphoto.com/Monticello
Author photographs: Steve and Julie Prussack by Violet Schrage; Chef Babette Davis by Dino Mosley
Fruit & vegetable illustrations: © iStockphoto.com/Pingwin (*except* celery © iStockphoto.com Kathy Konkle)

Juice photographs: Nothin' But the Greens © iStockphoto.com/Phasinphoto; Ginger Citrus Spice © iStock photo.com/Naito8; Pomegranate Punch © iStockphoto.com/Gojak; Wheatgrass Cleanser © iStockphoto.com/ Kirin_photo; Redhead Supreme © iStockphoto.com/Poplasen; Easy as ABC © iStockphoto.com/Violleta; Holy Basil Supreme © iStockphoto.com/AlexPro9500; Tropical Turmeric © iStockphoto.com/Nata_Vkusidey; Big Blue © Shutterstock.com/Jane Rix; Magic Mango Juice © iStockphoto.com/5PH; Watermelon Straight Up © iStockphoto.com/Wiktory; Carrots Alive © iStockphoto.com/AnjelaGr; Pineapple Express © iStockphoto.com/ Pavel Hlystov; Pear Me Down © iStockphoto.com/5PH; Classic Green Smoothie © iStockphoto.com/Olga Miltsova; Strawberry Açai © Shutterstock.com/Anna Hoychuk.

The publisher gratefully acknowledges the financial support of our publishing program by the Government of Canada through the Canada Book Fund.

Published by Robert Rose Inc.
120 Eglinton Avenue East, Suite 800, Toronto, Ontario, Canada M4P 1E2
Tel: (416) 322-6552 Fax: (416) 322-6936
www.robertrose.ca

Printed and bound in Canada

1 2 3 4 5 6 7 8 9 MI 24 23 22 21 20 19 18 17 16

· ·

This book is dedicated to you, our reader. You are about
to embark on a journey with us that will help you become
healthier and improve your life on multiple levels. We honor
your commitment and thank you for joining the Juice Guru
community. We are here with and for you.

Steve and Julie

Contents

Acknowledgments

We would like to extend our deepest gratitude to the following people who made this project exceed our expectations:

Our literary agent, Marilyn Allen, for her tireless representation and passion for bringing our vision to light.

Juice Guru Advisory Board members Thomas Lodi, MD, and Gabriel Cousens, MD, for their careful review of and support for our work.

Jameth Sheridan, MD, as well as the "Father of Juicing," Jay Kordich, and Linda Kordich, for a lifetime of inspiration, support and wisdom.

Our parents, for their loving support of our dreams.

Our editors Judith Finlayson and Tracy Bordian, with the assistance of nutritionist Doug Cook, for pushing us to make this book a powerful statement on the benefits of daily juicing.

The designers, the team at PageWave Graphics, especially Daniela Zanchetta.

Bob Dees and the rest of the Robert Rose team, for a tradition of publishing stellar books that exceed the quality of others on the market today.

And finally, a special thank you to Fate, for reuniting us after 20-plus years apart so we can share a life together and spread the message of health and juicing to our friends and family.

Introduction

If you picked up this book, you are interested in juicing and wondering how it could improve your life. We used to be just like you. Our lives needed a boost. We weren't sure why our energy was so low, why it was so hard to focus, why our moods were erratic, why it was so hard to lose weight and why we had such a hard time getting into better shape. We both have stories of how we came to juicing and how it changed our lives, but our stories are very different.

In 1984, when big hair was cool and Michael Jackson was king, we were both 15 years old, living in New Jersey. We met and fell in love at a high-school dance. From that point forward—through the rest of high school and into college—we were a couple and best friends. We did everything together, including eating an unhealthy diet of pizza and other nutrient-deficient fast food. We never imagined eating anything green, and juicing wasn't even remotely on our radar.

Our love was strong, but as happens to so many young couples who find themselves in long-distance relationships (we attended different universities), we agreed to "see other people" and slowly lost touch. In the blink of an eye more than 20 years sped by. Those two decades included a marriage and divorce for each of us, and a son (Eli) for Julie. As fate would have it, we found each other again in southern California on Halloween in 2009. Just like that, the magic was back. We married in 2012.

Julie remembers that it was very easy to fall in love with Steve all over again because he looked the same to her as he had 20 years earlier, thanks to his long-term healthy lifestyle, which included daily juicing. Unlike many men in their forties, Steve appeared to have the energy and vitality of a twenty-something. It was as if time had stood still while they were apart.

But Steve hadn't always been this way. By the time Steve graduated college, his unhealthy lifestyle had already caught up with him. He was an overweight smoker with high cholesterol and elevated blood pressure. He felt winded after climbing a flight of stairs. By the age of 25, he had reached a breaking point. He couldn't hide the fact that he felt much older than his years and wondered if life was downhill from there. Steve wanted a solution, and that's when he discovered juicing (see the Juice Guru Story, page 13). Steve turned his life around and has since maintained his healthy lifestyle and weight. He has never needed prescription medications to maintain his blood pressure or cholesterol levels or for anything else.

On the other hand, during the years they were apart, Julie had managed to maintain a relatively healthy diet, although she wasn't eating fruits and vegetables in substantial quantities. A lawyer by trade, she spent years juggling the demands of her busy career and motherhood. At the age of 40, she was tired and still carried about 10 extra pounds left over from her pregnancy. She also suffered from chronic acid reflux, for which she sometimes took medication.

After they first reunited, Julie refused to even taste Steve's green juices. Steve never pushed, but quietly guided and led by example. It was a slow progression, but today (and for the past several years), Julie enjoys daily juices—even of the deepest green. The first thing Julie noticed after she began regular juicing was that her acid reflux disappeared (it's been gone since 2010). She also lost all of her excess "baby weight" and now has no trouble maintaining her high-school weight. (In 2012, she turned the gown she wore to Steve's high-school prom in 1987 into her wedding dress, without a single alteration to the size.) Julie has also gained a vibrancy she hasn't felt in years.

Juicing has given us both a new lease on life. And we are passionate about spreading the word. It is our mission to show the power of prevention through juicing so you will not only live longer but live well for longer.

Steve and Julie Prussack

How to Use This Book

Part One of this book will explain daily juicing—why it's a unique approach and how it works. It will also give you all the information you need on the benefits you will gain as a daily juicer.

In Part Two you'll dive right into making Daily Juice a habit for life. We'll give you step-by-step guidance on how to make juicing a part of your daily routine, based on current research on how best to create new habits and stick with them. And we'll walk you through some of the minefields that might threaten to take you off track.

Part Three will give you the lowdown on ingredients, along with 100 recipes—everything you'll need to make Daily Juice an irresistibly delicious part of your daily routine. We also sprinkle celebrity chef Babette Davis's incredibly delicious pulp recipes throughout the book so you won't need to waste any vegetables and fruit through the juicing process.

So, read on ... the rest of your life starts now.

The Juice Guru Story

When I was growing up, juicing in itself was a strange idea. I hardly even drank the bottled kind! When I was in college, I lived on fast food (like most students). After I graduated, I took a good look in the mirror and realized that I was feeling (and looking) old before my time. More important, there was a history of cancer in my family and I didn't want to repeat the habits that led to disease and suffering. I knew I had to make a change.

One day, I wandered into a used bookstore in New York City and came across a book called *The Juiceman's Power of Juicing,* by Jay Kordich. On the cover was a photo of the author looking youthful, healthy and vibrant. Sure, I had seen him on late-night infomercials that ran during the 1990s, but at that point the idea of juicing seemed kind of crazy to me. On a whim, I picked up the book and thought I'd at least give juicing a try. Perhaps it could be just the thing to restore my youthful energy.

I purchased a juicer and began making the recipes in Jay's book. I soon found that not only did the juices make me feel better and boost my energy levels, but I also started to lose weight. I began to make healthier food choices. After living on fast food for so long, this was quite a concept. My college friends had always teased me, asking, "Steve, do you *ever* eat salad?"

Drinking fresh juice and eating healthy foods helped my body to purify. I remember how it felt when my body started to change—it seemed like my engine was becoming "cleaner." Although I had quit smoking a decade before, regular juicing seemed to be removing the toxic residue from my body. One life-changing day when I was drinking fresh juice, the tips of my fingers opened up and a tar-like substance that smelled like nicotine was discharged. I couldn't help but wonder what this substance would have done to my health if it had stayed in my body. That fear drives me to this day.

Those experiences taught me the true meaning of an expression I learned in elementary school: "You are what you eat." My passion intensified, and I knew I wanted to dedicate the rest of my life to spreading this message.

When I reunited with my high-school sweetheart, Julie, I shared my passion for juicing with her. She caught on. Together we started a digital magazine related to health. This evolved into Juice Guru, which allowed me to produce the first (and only) juicing-related radio show on the world-wide syndicated iHeartRadio network. We also created free digital programs related to helping people get started with juicing.

Photos: Upper left: Steve and Julie Prussack; lower right: Chef Babette Davis.

I wanted to spread the message further, so in 2013, Juice Guru launched an accredited juice-coaching school that certifies coaches to lead their own juice programs in their communities, as well as virtually on the Internet. We have worked with some well-known celebrities and CEOs of major corporations, teaching them how to develop the juicing habit. We are now working with juice bars to help train owners and staff to take their knowledge about the benefits of juicing deeper so they can better support their communities. Most recently, we began producing an online juicing-related television show so we could continue our mission of spreading the message about juicing and how to maintain an optimal lifestyle.

Juicing and achieving and maintaining good health have become the central focus of our lives. It is a wonderful life, and we are thrilled to be able to share so much of it with you. Take this journey with us. You'll soon discover that the secret to restoring your former healthy self isn't too difficult and is well worth the effort.

Part 1

Daily Juice: A Glass a Day Keeps the Doctor Away—and Then Some

Chapter 1
What's It All About?
Daily Juice: All the Benefits, None of the Pain

Juicing has seen an exponential rise in popularity in recent years, even attracting mainstream attention. In fact, that's likely the very reason you picked up this book. In metropolitan areas, juice bars have become almost as common as Starbucks, and fresh juices threaten to overthrow Frappuccinos and macchiatos with their trendy "cool" factor. Celebrities boast about juicing. It's written about in magazines, blogs and books. You may even have heard your friends talking about juicing at the office, gym or salon, or during the daily pickup from school.

And with good reason—regular juicing is one of the most reliable methods for keeping lean, healthy and fit while maintaining your youthful vitality and looks. It's no secret that fresh fruits and vegetables are essential for becoming and staying healthy. But did you know that a glass of fresh juice is one of the most effective means of delivering that energizing nutrition to your body? Fruits and vegetables are highly nutritious, and by transforming them into juice you can consume way more nutrients in a single sitting than you could ever eat in their original state, significantly amping up your nutritional intake.

Juicing may be hot, but it's not new and it's not a fad. Over the past century, juicing has been used in many European countries as a preferred method for alleviating disease. And more and more Western doctors are recommending juicing as an indispensible part of a safe and effective preventive care program. If we're lucky, juicing is a trend that will stick.

Juice Guru Philosophy: *Drink Your Vitamins*

Fresh juice is like a magical liquid multivitamin pill—rich in vitamins, minerals, enzymes, phytonutrients and other good stuff—that is quickly utilized by your body. And, unlike the isolated vitamins in capsules or pills, the countless nutrients in freshly pressed juice come directly from whole-food ingredients. There is no danger of toxicity, over-accumulation or imbalance, as there may be with manufactured supplements.

Anyone Can Do It

Possibly the best thing about Daily Juice is that anyone can do it. There are relatively few hurdles to overcome and you can quickly achieve results. By following our protocols, you will improve every area of your life (even your sex life!) without having to change who you are or how you spend your time.

Daily Juice empowers you to change your life without changing major elements of your lifestyle. You can wake up, enjoy your Daily Juice and then meet your best friend for lunch, have a special dinner with your partner, or join your friends at the bar for the big game, all without skipping a beat.

It's Not About Fasting

Until now, in the juicing world the emphasis has been on juice *fasting* (also known as juice cleansing, feasting, detoxing or dieting). Juice fasting is when, for a period of time, you consume nothing but fresh juices, and it has gained traction in our culture as something of a health craze. Fasting can be a bit daunting, since it requires a fair amount of planning for successful implementation and you can't eat solid food. But if you want to lose a great deal of weight or are looking to support your body while it is healing from an illness, juice fasting is an exceptional tool. In fact, Steve's first book was about juice fasting. This book is *not* about juice fasting.

It's About Making Juice a Daily Routine

Rather than telling you how to fast for days or even weeks on nothing but juice, this book will demonstrate how just one well-timed fresh juice a day will transform the quality of your life. And we take it one step further than other books on the art of juicing. We will help you apply the science of habit-creation to easily make juicing a daily pattern that you will stick with for life.

A Lifetime Habit

We have had incredible results working with clients, using nothing more than a juice a day and the protocols in this book. We will show you, step by step, how to make juicing a habit for life—one that you will work hard to keep because of how incredible you feel. Your body will thank you, as will your mind and your spirits.

The Daily Juice Protocol

The Juice Guru Daily Juice protocol is this: Drink one 24- to 32-ounce (750 mL to 1 L) freshly pressed juice first thing in the morning on an empty stomach, and wait 20 minutes before eating anything else. That's it … unless you are looking to lose weight, which we will get to shortly. Having your juice first thing, on an empty stomach, allows for rapid digestion. And waiting 20 minutes before eating anything else ensures quick assimilation by your body of the valuable wealth of nutrients.

A Unique Approach

Daily Juice has several major advantages over other juicing programs for the average person. Most important, you won't be depriving yourself as you would on a diet or juice fast. Daily Juice is an *addition* to your daily routine that provides long-term results and won't require life-changing adjustments. You will realize many of the incredible benefits of juicing with very little change to your lifestyle, and you can easily maintain those benefits for life.

Case Study: Tyler's Story
Better Focus and Peak Performance

Tyler Polon is a 13-year-old student who was recently accepted into the National Junior Honor Society. He is also a competitive hockey player. Like most high-achieving kids, Tyler was looking for something to give him an edge. As he told us, "Surprisingly, I found that edge in juicing."

Tyler's father, a graduate of the Juice Guru Certification Program, decided to bring juicing to his family with a view toward improving everyone's health. Since juice fasting is not appropriate for growing kids, he started juicing first thing every morning. Tyler noticed that his sleep improved after only a couple of days of Daily Juice, and that after a week, his mind had become clearer and he had much more stamina than usual. "The juices make me feel more alert and vigilant in school, and they fill me up more than a traditional breakfast," he explained. "In hockey, the juices give me more energy and increase my stamina tenfold. Overall, the juices make me feel better, and they have helped me clean up my diet."

Tyler started slowly with sweeter juices—which are generally more palatable for kids and novice juicers—but he quickly moved on to green juices. "We started with sweeter juices (mostly apple with some ginger) as a means of boosting energy for hockey games," he told us. "Now I incorporate kale, spinach, ginger, parsley, celery, cucumber, apple and sometimes carrots. In fact, my juices have become almost all green vegetables. I don't really have a favorite. It's important to me that I can focus and perform at the highest level possible. I'll drink just about anything if I believe it is healthy and will give me an advantage." Tyler explained how juicing also helped him clean up his diet: "Consuming more fruits and vegetables made me more conscious of other foods I was eating, and that steered me away from junk food."

Juice Guru Philosophy: *The "Break-Fast" Solution*

We call the Daily Juice protocol a "break-fast" solution for several reasons. Consider this: Every night when you go to sleep, you actually fast for about eight hours. You may not have thought about it this way, but that doesn't stop your body from taking full advantage of the interval. While you sleep, your body takes a break from digesting (and, of course, other energy-draining tasks such as walking, running and working) and gets down to the important business of cleaning itself out and repairing, renewing and rejuvenating your cells. When you eat your first meal of the day, you are breaking that fast, which is why this meal is called breakfast.

Consuming a freshly pressed juice to break your nightly fast has several advantages. First, it extends the overnight cleansing process, bringing vital nutrition into your body without forcing it to stop its repair work to do the heavy lifting of digestion. Second, juicing on an empty stomach ensures that the nutrients will be absorbed quickly, because there will be little or no insoluble fiber or other substances in your system to slow down or prevent absorption. Third, by having juice first thing in the morning you get all your servings of fruits and veggies out of the way for the day, allowing you to live your life as you please—within reason, of course.

Take a Digestion Break

Your stomach spends six to eight hours breaking down solid foods before your cells can even begin to absorb the nutrients. Juice, on the other hand, is essentially predigested by your juicer, which extracts the nourishing liquid from the solid fibers. As a result, juice spends as little as 15 minutes in your stomach before its nutrients are available to feed your hungry cells. And relatively little effort is required on the part of your digestive system to extract the nutrients. Your juicer does the hard work of breaking down the plant cells and liberating nutrients, such as minerals, carotenoids and polyphenols, that are otherwise bound to the structural components of your fruits and veggies. That leaves you with plenty of energy to spare.

Timing Is Key

Timing is key. Every client with whom we've worked has noticed a profound difference in both the quantity and quality of benefits they enjoy from drinking their Daily Juice first thing in the morning, as opposed to with a meal or on a full stomach. And you will too.

Not only is Daily Juice enjoyable to drink, it is loaded with the vitamins, minerals and phytonutrients your body needs. Consider this: 1 cup (250 mL) of cooked sliced carrots provides 47 mg of calcium, 367 mg of potassium and a vitamin A equivalence of 26,000 IU (International Units). In comparison, one cup (250 mL) of carrot juice provides significantly more vitamin A equivalence (45,000 IU) and more minerals: 57 mg of calcium and 689 mg of potassium.

An Addition to Your Diet, Not a Replacement

If you search your local bookstore or the Internet for information on juicing, most likely you will come up with books and programs for juice fasting. These programs come in all shapes and sizes and with many different names. They are known as *reboots*, *cleanses*, *fasts*, *feasts*, *fresh starts*, *flushes* or *detoxes*. The basic idea behind a juice-fast program is to drink only juice for a period of time—from three days to as long as three months—to help your body achieve specific results, such as heal from an illness, reduce and/or eliminate medications, cleanse your system of stored toxins or lose weight.

That all sounds good … in theory. It's true that juice fasting can be a phenomenal way to achieve all of those goals. But if, like the average person, you are simply looking to gain energy and health, the thought of not eating solid food for days or weeks may send you running for the door. It's sad but true: traditional thinking around juicing has created extremely high barriers to entry. In fact, many who try an extended juice fast find they need to do so at a costly retreat to do it right. As a result, most people are too turned off or overwhelmed by the thought of juicing to enjoy its benefits. They may dabble in a juice or two or even attempt a cleanse for a few days, but ultimately the commitment needed to continue may seem too intense to allow the average person to benefit from regular juicing.

Daily Juice is different. Daily Juice requires very little change to your lifestyle, yet it allows you to enjoy many of the benefits of a cleanse. There is no "diet" associated with the Daily Juice protocol, although you will likely find yourself naturally craving healthier foods. Unless you are inclined to overindulge in junk or fast food or you otherwise follow an unhealthy diet, you don't have to stop enjoying the foods you love. You don't even have to stop drinking other beverages you enjoy, such as coffee and tea. But don't be surprised if you no

---

Juice Guru Philosophy: *Want to Lose Weight?*

If you want to lose weight, we recommend one extra step in your Daily Juice routine. Consider not consuming any food until lunch, or perhaps have a midmorning snack of fruit, a smoothie (see pages 212 to 223) or another healthy food (see page 21). In other words, swap your traditional breakfast for a 32-ounce (1 L) glass of Daily Juice. You will be surprised to find that you are less hungry than you might think. A large serving of fresh juice, particularly one that is rich in leafy greens (see pages 110 to 127), is extremely nourishing and will satisfy your hunger well into the afternoon.

longer need or want them. And there are no barriers to Daily Juice, once you make the relatively small effort to turn it into a habit. Best of all, the effects are long-lasting, since the habit you create today will ensure that Daily Juice remains a part of your healthy routine for the rest of your life.

The Answer to Yo-Yo Dieting

Another major advantage of Daily Juice is that it puts an end to harmful yo-yo dieting. Also known as weight cycling, yo-yo dieting is a cycle of gaining weight, losing weight and then gaining it back again. Studies suggest that this pattern can be extremely harmful to your body. Some studies show that weight cycling may increase the risk for certain health problems, including high blood pressure, high cholesterol and gallbladder disease. Other studies indicate that extreme weight cycling can even damage the heart. But these physical effects aren't the only negative fallout from yo-yo dieting. Attaining a slim figure, only to lose it, is likely to have an emotional impact. Increased feelings of life dissatisfaction and mental distress are common among yo-yo dieters.

Healthy Snack Options

If you are looking for a midmorning snack other than a fruit or a smoothie (see pages 212 to 223) to keep you going after your morning juice, this quick list will help. These delicious low-calorie, high-nutrient snacks will satisfy hunger and provide balance. They are also easily digestible, so they will not make your body work too hard.

- 1 sliced apple served with 2 tbsp (30 mL) almond or other nut butter for dipping
- 1 cup (250 mL) raw coconut water
- 1 cup (250 mL) coconut or nut-based probiotic yogurt
- 1 standard bag (2 oz/60 g) dehydrated kale chips (if you make them yourself, sprinkle with sea salt and nutritional yeast, which has a naturally cheesy flavor)
- ¼ cup (60 mL) raw or dry-roasted pumpkin or sunflower seeds
- ⅓ cup (75 mL) raw or dry-roasted almonds or cashews
- ½ cup (125 mL) carrot sticks served with ½ cup (125 mL) hummus for dipping
- ½ avocado (sprinkle with nutritional yeast and sea salt for a delicious taste, and if you like it spicy, add just a pinch of cayenne to the mix)

A Weight-Cycling Scenario

You may be surprised to learn that juice fasting can play a part in the weight-cycling scenario. At a recent Juice Guru webinar event, we surveyed more than 200 people who had tried various juice reboots, cleanses or detoxes to find out how long it took, on average, for them to gain back the weight they had lost. Our results, while surprising to many novice juicers, were consistent with what we have come to learn about the effects of juice fasts. One hundred percent of those cleansers gained back all—or even more—of the weight they had lost, within five to ten weeks. In other words, juice fasting (when done incorrectly) acts like just another fad diet.

The 200 juice fasters in our survey are not alone in their inability to keep off the weight between juice fasts or periodic diets. This is a common problem among dieters. In fact, Steve struggled with this problem for years. Since his mid-twenties, Steve has enjoyed a healthy whole-food, plant-based diet. He also routinely juice fasted several times a year for optimal health. But Steve found that, between fasts, his weight consistently fluctuated by eight to ten pounds (3.5 to 4.5 kg). His frustration with this weight cycling and its psychological toll ultimately led him to research and develop the Daily Juice protocol in this book.

Juice Guru Philosophy: *Daily Juice Helps to Sustain Weight Loss*

Daily Juice solves the problem of periodic dieting, including juice fasts, as it did for Steve. Working with our clients, we have found that one large glass of juice a day, consumed according to the protocol outlined in this book, can help sustain any weight loss achieved through dieting. For example, 46-year-old Rob (see page 30) reports that with Daily Juice, he easily maintains his ideal weight, even through periods of less exercise. And Daniella (see page 35), a rising opera singer, reports enjoying using Daily Juice to help keep her weight down for her frequent public performances.

Who Can Benefit from Daily Juicing?

The short answer is *everyone*. Daily Juicing provides you with an incredible amount of nutrients that digest rapidly and assimilate efficiently into the cells of your body. With Daily Juice you will absorb more nutrients every day than most people do in a week. You can't overdose, and the natural nutrients in your juice won't become toxic or otherwise harmful, as can happen from over-supplementation of isolated nutrients in the form of pills, capsules or powders.

Daily Juice is also an excellent choice for those who cannot enjoy the benefits of fresh juice during a fast, such as children, teens, pregnant women and the elderly. For children and teens, Daily Juice floods their bodies with vital nutrients that boost their immune systems and help them stay healthy and able to attend school rather than staying home sick with a cold or the flu. Children who drink juice daily can also gain an advantage in the classroom from increased focus and energy (see page 18). And Daily Juice can give you and your family the energy to thrive at extracurricular activities, including sports, arts and social activities.

Elderly adults can benefit from the nutrients in Daily Juice to keep healthy, strong and sharp—all without the side effects and potentially harmful interactions of prescription medications. And pregnant women can give their growing babies the nutrition they need for proper development, as well as gain the energy necessary to make it through an otherwise tiring pregnancy.

(see page 18)

Juice Is All You Need

Juicing is an extremely effective way to replace energy-boosting crutches such as caffeine with vitality-building nutrients that help to maintain harmony in your body. Among other benefits, it pumps your body full of nutrition and supports your natural healing mechanisms.

Juice Guru Philosophy: *Big Rewards for Small Effort*

Daily Juice tears down the traditional high barrier to juicing for the average person who isn't already ill: having to give up eating for days or weeks in order to realize the many incredible benefits of juicing. With relatively small effort, you will seem to age more slowly and with increased vitality, and greatly enhance the lives of everyone you love by including them in your new juice-a-day habit.

Case Study: Chef Babette's Story
Ageless at 65

My name is Babette Davis, and I'm the executive chef and (very hands-on) co-owner of the Stuff I Eat restaurant in Inglewood, California. I am also the chef behind the mouthwatering pulp recipes in this book. I definitely have to be in tiptop shape both physically and mentally to get through the countless hours I spend on my feet preparing meals, serving my customers and otherwise managing a popular restaurant. I'm actually up by 4:00 a.m. most mornings and sometimes don't end my day until after 8:00 p.m. In addition to that, I'm 65 years old.

I can honestly say I never thought that I would be where I am, doing what I do, at my age. In my forties I suffered from a host of ailments, including asthma and eczema. My digestive system was a mess. And I required a number of medical procedures including shoulder and carpal tunnel surgery, to correct nerve and other damage, and two hernia operations. I also suffered from a lack of good health and energy.

Over the years I cleaned up my diet. First I became a vegan and then I began to incorporate more raw foods, including whole fruits and vegetables, into my diet. With these changes I saw tremendous benefits to my health and energy levels. But as I continued to get older and my career became more demanding, I realized I needed something more to help me through my day. I found the answer in Daily Juice.

I have been juicing in accordance with the Daily Juice protocol for a year now. I enjoy a 24-ounce (750 mL) juice first thing in the morning and sometimes squeeze in another one later in the day. The results? Well, as anyone who knows me can tell you, I look and feel amazing and certainly defy my age, although the truth is, that was not my intention.

When I first started juicing, it was all about taste. It's fun and exciting to be able to blend your own custom juices (my favorite is a combination of apple, cilantro, lime and ginger). But very soon after I began my Daily Juice routine, I noticed that incredible changes were happening to my already relatively healthy body. As I said, I'm 65, and I never get sick anymore—not even a cold. And unlike most of my peers, I do not have a single chronic condition. I've heard the rhetoric regarding fruit sugar, blood sugar issues and diabetes. Yet despite the fact that my Daily Juice is mostly apple, I have no diabetic or pre-diabetic tendencies to speak of, and I have never experienced the "crash" associated with high sugar levels.

But the most significant change I've noticed since starting on Daily Juice is my increased energy and fitness levels, which logically should be declining as I age. When I drink a juice first thing on an empty stomach, I feel instant energy. I juice immediately before my daily workout, and I'm having the most energetic workouts I've ever experienced. For example, in the past year I created a pushup challenge for myself, adding a few every day. Today I can do 65 pushups in a row—one for every year of my life. I have incredible muscle mass and strength in every part of my body, and my energy and stamina are significantly greater than they were in my thirties.

"Senior citizen" is simply not in my vocabulary. I look at Daily Juice as my preventive medicine for life and a way to stay virtually ageless and full of life energy. I may not choose to continue being so hands-on at my restaurant indefinitely, but there's no question that I will be able to do so for many years to come.

Chapter 2
The Benefits of Daily Juice

Now that you have the lowdown on what Daily Juicing actually is, let's explore why you should do it. Why exactly is drinking a glass of freshly made juice every day such a potent addition to your good health? Why is juicing so effective at changing our day-to-day experience of how we feel in our bodies?

The answers to these questions are fairly straightforward. Basically they break down to one simple fact: freshly pressed juice is packed with nutrients that help to increase your energy, clarity, focus and good health.

Juice Is Nutrient-Dense

Whole fruits and vegetables contain a wealth of nutrients. Studies show, for instance, that a fruit as basic as the apple provides anticancer, anti-asthma, immunity-boosting and cardiovascular benefits, and it can even help regulate your blood-sugar levels. All that and it tastes great too! No wonder our moms told us "An apple a day keeps the doctor away." Now imagine consuming all the vitamins, minerals and phytonutrients in *four* apples and half a bunch of kale (one of today's most popular "superfoods") every day—as you can by drinking a serving of Apple Lemon Kale Juice (page 204)— and you'll begin to see where we're going with this.

The fact is, fruits and vegetables are the preeminent source of many natural vitamins and minerals, as well as hydration. They also contain a range of phytonutrients. These include antioxidants, such as lycopene and beta-carotene, and organosulfurs, which may be hard to find or unavailable in other foods. These substances have been shown to protect your cells from cancer damage and/or slow the process of aging, among other benefits.

Defining Nutrient Density

Nutrient density is the amount of nutrition in a food compared to its caloric load. The most nutrient-dense foods will give you a hefty nutritional bang for a relatively low caloric price tag. For example, 1 cup (250 mL) of kale— an exceptionally nutrient-dense vegetable—delivers over 1,000% of your daily requirement (DV) for vitamin K, almost 100% of your DV for vitamin A, over 70% of your DV for vitamin C, a good dose of phytonutrients and at least 16 other vitamins and minerals, all for the low, low price of just 36 calories!

A Powerful Nutrient Cocktail

Phytonutrients, vitamins and minerals are found in abundance in freshly pressed mixed juices, for three reasons. First, each ingredient—for instance, carrots—delivers specific nutrients. Carrots are particularly high in beta-carotene, which converts to vitamin A in your body, as well as antioxidants known as polyacetylenes, which inhibit the growth of colon cancer cells.

Second, when you combine a number of fruits and/or vegetables, you are expanding the range of nutrients, enabling you to consume a wide variety of nutrients in a single juice. So, for example, if you add apples to your carrot juice, you'll also receive a good dose of polyphenols, which have proven anti-asthma benefits and help to regulate your blood-sugar levels.

Third, you can consume the juice—and the associated nutrients—of a large amount of ingredients in just one drink, giving you a powerful dose of concentrated nutrition. Think of it this way: If you laid out side by side the ingredients for a Green Giant (page 113), for example, the fruits and vegetables would overfill a large serving tray. You certainly couldn't eat all that produce in a single sitting (at least, not without some difficulty). But you can easily drink the 3 cups (750 mL) of the juice they yield in a matter of minutes. Even better, this combination of ingredients tastes great too.

And because juice requires a minimal amount of digestion, that nutrition is delivered almost immediately to your cells, quickly and efficiently. We like to say that your juicer does much of the digestive work for you, separating the fiber from the juice. The juice is more easily digested than the whole food from which it is extracted.

Juice Guru Philosophy: *Stripping Away the Fiber*

Generally, it's better to eat a whole food than to isolate any part of it or artificially process the food. For example, it's better to eat a whole orange than to extract its vitamin C or to process that fruit into marmalade. Nature makes perfect foods, with thousands of nutrients that interact with each other and affect thousands of metabolic reactions in our bodies. Science has yet to even identify all these nutrients, let alone understand their various interactions. What we do know with certainty is that the closer our food stays to its natural state, the better.

Having one fresh-pressed juice every day is the exception. It is minimally processed and removes only the fiber. A high-fiber diet is important to your good health and we are certainly not saying that Daily Juice should replace high-fiber foods in your diet. Rather, Daily Juice should be an addition to what you eat every day—a superior way to obtain the nutrition you need and would not otherwise get. Fiber isn't itself a nutrient, nor is it absorbed by the body. Removing this bulk—just once a day—allows you to squeeze the nutrients from a tremendous quantity and variety of fruits and vegetables into a single juice, as well as to reduce them to a form that is more quickly absorbed by your body.

The Power of Phytonutrients

Phytonutrients refers to thousands of nutrients that are found only in plants, and especially in fruits and vegetables. Phytonutrients aren't essential for keeping you alive, unlike vitamins and minerals, but research shows that these little powerhouses are critical in helping to prevent disease and to keep your body working properly. Phytonutrients are the substances that give some fruits and vegetables their vibrant colors and distinctive flavors (for example, orange carotenes and green chlorophyll); they also protect plants from pests and other dangers.

Every fruit and vegetable contains an abundance of phytonutrients. But, since there are thousands of them, no one fruit or vegetable can contain them all. One of the major advantages of Daily Juice is that you can include a rainbow of fruits and vegetables in your juice every day. This will help to keep you healthy and disease-free.

Living with Daily Juice

Now that we've given you a taste of why, let's explore some of the more tangible benefits that you can expect from Daily Juice.

More Energy and Vitality

Soon after beginning your Daily Juice habit, you should notice a surge in your energy level and a feeling of well-being. In fact, an especially strong green juice can almost give you a euphoric "high." But unlike the jittery high you get from coffee, sugary sodas or so-called energy drinks, the powerful rush you feel from a fresh juice will not be followed by an energy crash. It's also a focused energy that allows you to think clearly.

How can juice make you feel so energized? The short answer is that juices are full of high-quality nutrition. A properly nourished body has a greater capacity for thinking and feeling than one that is nutrient-deprived. Healthy bodies experience a smoother stream of consciousness and a much higher output of energy.

Drinking juice also aids the body's digestive process. Your body absorbs the nutrition in a liquid more quickly, and you benefit from the resulting rush of energy. Think of it this way: with Daily Juice you'll be getting more key nutrients in that morning glass of juice than most of your friends will get in a week or more from a normal diet.

Better Rest

Juicing may also help you get a better night's sleep and further ensure that you have the energy you need for the day. In a study published in the *European Journal of Nutrition* in 2012, researchers found that daily consumption of tart cherry juice over just a seven-day period greatly increased the production of melatonin—a molecule critical to regulating your sleep/wake cycle—in study participants. This resulted in longer and more restful sleep. In an age of overscheduled lives and precious little downtime, Daily Juice can help you get the rest you need to thrive.

The Biology of Juicing

For a deeper exploration of why juicing helps to keep you energized, here is a short lesson in molecular biology.

Enzymes + Easy Digestion = Energy to Spare

There is one key to understanding why fresh, raw juices give you sustained energy. Juices contain an abundance of active enzymes and thus require fewer of our own enzymes to digest.

What Are Enzymes?

Enzymes are highly specialized proteins that are responsible for every action in our bodies. This covers everything from replicating DNA to converting oxygen into carbon dioxide to creating new memories. Enzymes don't actually perform chemical reactions in our cells, but they do act as necessary catalysts that speed up those reactions. Every movement you make, every breath you take and physical sensation you experience requires enzymes. They are present in all living things. And they are essential for the proper functioning of our bodies.

Two Types of Enzymes

Enzymes come in two varieties, metabolic and digestive, and each type does a different job. Metabolic enzymes are used to help build, repair and maintain all of your body's organs and tissues. Digestive enzymes (found in fresh juices) break down the food you eat into nutrients your body can absorb.

Juice Is Easy to Digest

One reason why fresh juices boost your energy is that your body is spared much of the arduous job of having to secrete digestive enzymes to break down what you have consumed. The juicer has already done that for you, leaving you with an easier digestive job that takes no more than 20 minutes. This is an even bigger deal than it sounds, considering that, of all the processes in our bodies, digestion generally uses the most energy. Any help we can get from our food to aid in that process is invaluable for our overall energy levels.

In addition, living plant foods have plenty of their own enzymes. Many people believe that the living enzymes in fruits and vegetables greatly aid in the digestive process. In 1943 the physiology laboratory of Northwestern University established the "law of adaptive secretion of digestive enzymes," based on its own studies. This law holds that if some of your food is digested by enzymes found in the food itself, your body will secrete fewer of its own enzymes. Bromelain, for instance, which is found in pineapples, has been used for centuries in South America to aid digestion.

And by consuming these ingredients raw, rather than cooking them at high temperatures, the enzymes are likely to remain intact and active. When your food is easily digested, your body can put its energy toward more important tasks, such as healing and rejuvenation.

The Traditional Breakfast

Take a moment to think about what you ate for breakfast this morning. Did you have a big meal, with bread, pancakes and/or eggs? If so, think about your energy level afterward. Chances are you felt sluggish, sleepy and not exactly peppy. Even if you ate a lighter breakfast of cereal, it likely took some time for you to feel on top of your game.

There's a reason for this. According to a study conducted by the Mayo Clinic, it takes six to eight hours on average for food just to pass through your stomach and small intestine. The average transit time through your large intestine, where it is further digested, s about 33 hours for men and 47 hours for women. And that's for just one meal!

This is part of what makes Daily Juice so valuable. Because juice is easily and quickly digested, you get the nutrients you need considerably faster, which boosts your energy levels and keeps them there.

Sharper Focus and Greater Productivity

Ever experience foggy-brain haze? You know, that unproductive state that generally occurs after lunchtime and can last well into the afternoon? Sometimes it strikes even earlier and, on occasion, can last all day. There are many factors that could be causing this decline in your focus and productivity levels, but one major factor may be your nutritional intake.

Not surprisingly, drinking fresh juices every day provides your brain with a rainbow of nutrients to help keep it sharp and on top of its game. Virtually every person we have started on Daily Juice (ourselves included) reports having a significantly clearer mind and greatly increased productivity. This is as true for kids in school as it is for adults at work. Here's why.

> **Nutrients for Brainpower**
>
> Beets, carrots and spinach contain iron, folic acid and zinc, all of which improve the oxygen-carrying power of blood and thereby increase brainpower, concentration and memory.

Nutrition: Your Brain's Best Friend

Brain chemistry and nutrition are inextricably linked. Without proper nutrition you cannot have healthy brain function. Each and every nutrient has a role to play in cognition and perception, and all are essential to living a life in focus rather than in a fog. According to recent evidence, in some circumstances proper nutrition can help to manage and prevent mental health problems such as depression, attention deficit hyperactivity disorder (ADHD) and Alzheimer's disease. For instance, a 2015 study done under the auspices of the University of Wollongong in Australia concluded that daily cherry juice is helpful in treating dementia, because of

Case Study: Rob's Story
Regaining Positive Attitude and Staying Fit

I have been an optimist for most of my life, priding myself on seeing the positive in any situation, no matter how bleak. But the past two or three years have been the toughest stretch of my life, one that included a difficult divorce from the mother of my two children. For the first time I can remember, I was overcome by feelings of depression, defeat and hopelessness. When I thought I had hit rock bottom, something else would happen and the floor would drop out from under me again. That wasn't like me, and it certainly wasn't a feeling I liked. But I felt overwhelmed by it and couldn't escape, no matter what I did.

In trying to figure out how to recover my positive outlook and my life, I stumbled on the idea of juicing. It's popular and I seemed to be hearing about it everywhere. But having lived on the standard American diet for most of my 46 years, I have to admit that the idea of juice cleansing—consuming nothing but juice—was a bit much for me. It also didn't seem realistic, given my extremely hectic schedule as a working single dad. That's when I learned about Daily Juice, and a new chapter of my life began.

I followed the Juice Guru's protocol, and my attitude and outlook on life changed. From just one morning juice I got immediate positive energy to start my day and keep me going well into the late afternoon. Within the first week of juicing, I started feeling better on the inside. And it didn't take long for people to notice a difference in my appearance, energy and attitude. I was back to being myself in no time. It was awesome!

Having achieved my initial goal, I kept juicing because I loved how it made me feel. That alone would have kept me a Daily Juicer for life, but I started seeing additional results that were just as incredible. I started losing excess weight without the need to exercise on a regular basis. I do love to exercise—don't get me wrong—but with my new position as a single dad, it just wasn't realistic to work out as often as I used to. But Daily Juice seemed to make up for the gap. I felt and looked slimmer, and it didn't take long for my son to comment on the reappearance of my abdominal "six-pack."

I have been juicing now for several months. If I stop juicing for a day or two it isn't catastrophic, but I can definitely sense a difference: I feel a little sluggish and less alert. As soon as I reintroduce Daily Juice into my diet, I have an instant feeling of positive energy. When I say "instant," I really mean it—within minutes I feel the energy and positivity rush. As a result of adding fresh juices to my diet, I have also found that my taste buds have changed. My eating has become much healthier, even though I haven't had to make an effort to go on any particular "diet." I just started removing unhealthy foods because I felt better without them. I also lost my sweet tooth, and I can't say I miss it. I've always had a healthy appetite, and when I'm bored, I tend to eat. Now when I reach for something, it's a healthy snack like a piece of fruit, which was never my go-to snack before.

My standard juice is based on the Juice Guru Daily Classic template recipe (see page 108): kale, celery, parsley, ginger and cucumber. I love it, and prep to cleanup time isn't long at all now that it's become a habit. And it's well worth it. I'm definitely in a better place mentally than I was before Daily Juicing. It was exactly what I needed, not only for me but also for my children, who depend on me. It is truly amazing what a little change can do.

– Rob Polon

its abundance of a flavonoid known as anthocyanin. And a 2006 study published in the *American Journal of Medicine* concluded that regularly drinking fruit and vegetable juices may play an important role in delaying the onset of Alzheimer's disease.

Many scientific papers have been published that detail the relationship between certain nutrients and different aspects of brain function. The B vitamins, for example, aid in producing energy for brain cells, balance brain biochemistry and improve abstract thought. Vitamins C, K and E, among many others, also have key roles to play in good brain health. Vitamin C helps to cleanse your brain of heavy metals, can improve your mood and is believed to help protect against Alzheimer's and Parkinson's diseases. Vitamin K is believed to also protect against Alzheimer's disease and to improve memory. And research shows that vitamin E, which contains tocopherols (compounds known to have antioxidant properties), is necessary to prevent dramatic loss of a critically important molecule in the brain, keeping your mind healthy and sharp. Leafy greens are particularly good sources of vitamin E.

Daily Juicing is one of the best ways to ensure that you consume both the variety and quantity of brain-boosting foods necessary to give you the clarity and focus you need to thrive in whatever you do in life. You'll notice the difference as soon as you get deep into your juicing practice. It's fascinating to learn that scientific studies are supporting what daily juicers already knew!

Get Your Essential Fatty Acids Here

You may not think of juices as having much fat content, but fruits and vegetables do provide essential fatty acids (EFAs). EFAs have beneficial qualities and thus are different from those many other fats that people shy away from. Because your body cannot manufacture essential fats, which are critical for good health, you need to get them from food.

EFAs are essential for optimal brain development. They are also essential to the brain's performance, because they coat the neural pathways, allowing electrical impulses to flow between the brain and the rest of the body as messages are transmitted back and forth. It's like oiling your brain for optimal performance. Without these essential nutrients, your brain simply cannot communicate as effectively with your body's systems, including your immune system. A lack of EFAs has also been associated with "feeling blue," as well as other emotional and mental disorders.

Berry It Up

Research shows that blueberries and strawberries can significantly improve the learning capacity and communication functions of the brain. We don't typically use berries as a base for our juices because they yield little bang for your buck when it comes to quantity. But they make an excellent high-quality addition to your juice or smoothie. Try a Goji Chia Smoothie (page 221) to get some brain-boosting benefits.

The Mighty Trio

Three fruits and veggies in particular have recently proven themselves to be powerhouses for clear thinking: spinach (and other leafy greens), blueberries and grapes.

Leafy greens such as spinach contain large amounts of B vitamins and high-quality vitamin E. A study conducted by the Rush University Medical Center in Chicago and published in 2015 followed more than 950 older adults, both men and women, for 10 years. After a battery of cognitive tests, the researchers found that those who consumed one to two servings of leafy greens every day had the cognitive abilities of a person 11 years younger, compared to those who passed on those vegetables.

Another study, published in the *Journal of Agricultural Food Chemistry* in 2010, found that drinking 2 to 2½ cups (500 to 625 mL) of blueberry juice every day may significantly improve memory and help to slow down cognitive decline associated with aging. In this study, the cumulative learning score for participants who drank berry juice was significantly improved after 12 weeks, as was their recall of word lists. Blueberries are brimming with antioxidants that act to protect nerve cells from oxygen damage, known as "oxidative stress." Our brains are susceptible to oxidative stress as a result of toxins, stress and other negative factors in the environment. This stress can lead to degenerative changes in the brain, decline in cognitive functions and, ultimately, diseases such as Alzheimer's. Consuming large amounts of foods high in antioxidants, such as blueberries, protects your brain from stress and decline.

Similarly, Concord grape juice contains a potent phytonutrient called resveratrol. A study published in the *British Journal of Nutrition* in 2009 demonstrated an increase in scores on verbal learning tests for older participants with memory decline (but not dementia) who drank 1 cup (250 mL) or more of Concord grape juice a day for several months.

This is just a minuscule window into the mind-boggling world of fruits, vegetables and their juices and their impact on brain and body processes. And these same powerful nutrients are known to improve health and longevity overall. Blueberries, for example, have been shown to reduce oxidative stress in virtually every system of the body. They also provide powerful anticancer benefits. Including this mighty trio, along with other fruits and vegetables, in your Daily Juice will help provide you with overall good health and a sharp mind.

Kale, parsley, spinach, broccoli and watercress are great sources of EFAs that can easily be incorporated into your Daily Juice. But EFAs can be found in nearly every fruit, vegetable and leafy green, so your brain is covered no matter what you juice. If you want to take it a step further, you can even soak chia or flax seeds—which are particularly high in EFAs—in water until they gel, and then mix them into your juice. However you do it, Daily Juice will give you that essential boost of fatty acids your brain is craving.

Juice Satisfies *Real* Hunger

There is a definite difference between the hunger we believe we experience each day and the real hunger of our bodies. If the body is not provided with adequate nutrition, it feels as if it is starving. The fact is, most people right now are actually starving for nutrition. The diet of most Westerners largely comprises nutrition-devoid processed foods. Less than 88% of adults worldwide report eating the recommended daily allowance of fruits and vegetables, and if you consider the recommendation for leafy greens, that percentage climbs well above 90. Even among those who do eat the requisite quantity, many do not get enough variety in their produce to fully meet their nutritional needs.

When your body feels that it is starving, your metabolism slows down in order to keep you alive on the little provided. As a result, it will burn less fat. The feeling of being hungry—or, more accurately, nutritionally unsatisfied—will also likely drive you to eat even more of the heavily processed foods (such as bacon and eggs or a jelly donut) you think you need to satisfy your hunger. This vicious cycle wreaks havoc on your waistline.

Freshly pressed juices are raw and unprocessed. Ounce for ounce, they contain more nutrients than other foods, so they are infinitely more satisfying for your body. By flooding your body with this much nutrition first thing every morning, you start the day satisfied. Your body won't be searching for more sustenance, and you are far less likely to take it in the form of a jelly donut. Any remaining "hunger" you think you are experiencing for those fattening, non-nutritious foods is nothing more than cravings. With regular juicing, you can expect these desires to fade or be replaced in part by healthier cravings.

Crave Healthier Foods

Have you ever wondered why you crave certain foods? So do scientists and researchers. While the answer is not yet completely known, at least one reason relevant to this discussion is clear. Like any habit, good or bad, many of our cravings—for food, cigarettes or you name it—are largely psychological. In particular, cravings for less than optimal foods are, in part, a result of cues in our environment.

What does this mean exactly? Well, think back to the last movie you saw in a theater. Did you instantly get in the popcorn line on arrival? If you are like most people, you probably can't remember a single movie you've seen in a theater that didn't involve munching on a bag of popcorn. Research conducted at the University of Southern California and published in

> **Keep Your Mind Sharp**
>
> Considering that you have to eat or drink up to 2½ cups (625 mL) per day of a number of fruits and veggies to realize their significant brain benefits, we can glean three guiding principles for keeping a sharp mind. It's important to (1) eat a variety of different plants, (2) eat lots of them, and (3) do it every day. With Daily Juice, you've got the bases covered.

the *Personality and Social Psychology Bulletin* suggests that moviegoers can't help themselves. As part of the study, customers entering a theater were given either a fresh bucket of popcorn or one that was a week old. The researchers found that habitual movie-popcorn-eaters ate the same amount of popcorn during the film regardless of whether it was stale or fresh, while the others ate less of the stale stuff. This was true whether the participants were hungry before the film or not.

Importantly, these kinds of habitual cravings become more acute when you give your body the same thing every day (or on a regular basis). For example, if you get into the habit of eating a jelly donut for breakfast every morning, you will tend to go for a donut tomorrow morning almost automatically. The good news is that this translates to juicing too. Once you've been juicing every day for a period of time, your mind and body begin to crave the healthier foods in the juice. And that's not just theoretical; we have seen it time and time again in those with whom we work. That's why, with the addition of juices, your overall diet will improve as well, leading to further weight loss as you substitute more and more nutrient-dense foods for those that are calorie-rich and less nourishing.

Your Best Health Insurance Policy

In 2012, the United States spent an average of $8,915 per person on health care, for a total cost of $2.8 trillion. That amount represents the costs of treating disease with doctor visits, tests, treatments and prescription medicines—once you're already sick—as well as the cost of insurance to help you cover it all. But shouldn't we be approaching health care in a completely different way? Wouldn't we be wiser, both as individuals and as a society, to invest in the *prevention* of disease?

Benjamin Franklin said it best centuries ago: "An ounce of prevention is worth a pound of cure." He was speaking in the context of fire prevention (his statements ultimately led to creation of the first ever U.S. fire station), but this sentiment certainly works in the area of disease prevention. And it's one with which we, and many researchers, agree.

Aside from significantly reducing cancer risk (see page 39), a diet rich in fruits and vegetables can lower blood pressure, reduce the risk of heart disease and stroke, lower the risk of eye and digestive problems, and have a positive effect on blood sugar. A 2015 study published in *Food and Nutrition Resources*, for instance, found that daily consumption of orange juice, as an addition to a healthy diet, can help prevent metabolic and chronic disease.

Juicing Meets the Challenge

Squeezing so many servings of fruits and veggies—eight or more every day—into our already overcrowded diets is a tall order for most people. But consuming just one 24- to 32-ounce (750 mL to 1 L) juice in accordance with the Daily Juice protocol will get that number of servings into your body before you even leave the house in the morning. Do this every day and you'll give yourself and your family the best insurance available against disease.

Case Study: Daniella's Story
A Healthy, Vibrant and Energetic Pregnancy

I'm about to become a second-time mom. My first child, Maia, is already nine, so I'm almost ten years older than I was the first time I was pregnant. You might think that my energy level could be a problem the second time around, being older and having another child to run after. But I am more energetic during this pregnancy than I was with Maia, and the reason is Daily Juice.

I actually started Daily Juicing almost half a year before I got pregnant. I learned about the idea from Juice Guru after I was encouraged by Steve's first book, *The Complete Idiot's Guide to Juice Fasting*, to complete my very first juice fast. After reading the book, a good friend and I drank nothing but green juices for an entire week. I lost weight, gained tons of energy and felt lighter, healthier and cleaner than I had in years. I wanted to continue feeling that good and actually didn't want to ruin it by eating food again, but I obviously couldn't sustain a fast indefinitely. So I visited the Juice Guru website and learned about the idea of Daily Juice. I've been hooked ever since. My weight loss stuck (until I became pregnant, that is) and my energy was through the roof. This helped me balance raising my daughter with the challenges of being a professional opera singer.

I have continued juicing every day throughout my pregnancy to ensure that my baby gets all the nutrition he needs for healthy development and growth. I drink a large juice every morning. My favorite during the pregnancy has been a combination of ten carrots, three oranges and some ginger—which, by the way, helps naturally with morning sickness. With Daily Juice I have easily maintained adequate iron, calcium and magnesium levels, which many women lack in pregnancy.

Most important to me, I've never felt that overwhelming feeling of exhaustion that most women experience, not in the first trimester and not now that I'm in my final weeks. And I look forward to continuing with Daily Juice to help me deal with the lack of sleep I am sure to experience with my new baby!

– Daniella Podobea

Lower Cholesterol

In a study published in *Biomedical and Environmental Sciences* in 2008, 32 men with high cholesterol levels consumed three to four shots of kale juice every day for three months. That's the equivalent of 30 pounds of kale—the same amount the average American would consume in an entire century. Every one of the participants dramatically lowered his "bad" (LDL) cholesterol and boosted his "good" (HDL) cholesterol, to the same extent as would an hour of daily exercise seven days a week. Those were some potent shots!

Reduce Risk of Heart Attack and Stroke

The largest and longest study conducted to date on the health benefits of fruits and vegetables, the Harvard-based Nurses' Health Study and Health Professionals Follow-Up Study tracked the health and dietary habits of almost 300,000 women

Beet Juice Lowers Blood Pressure

In a 2013 a systematic review and meta-analysis of randomized clinical trials (with a total of 254 participants) published in the *Journal of Nutrition* concluded that supplementation with beet juice was associated with a significant decrease in systolic blood pressure.

Reduced Rates of Cancer

The European Prospective Investigation into Cancer and Nutrition (EPIC) study, released in 2010, concluded that people who ate a large number of servings of fruits and vegetables (more than five) every day had an 11% lower incidence of cancer than those who ate less than one serving. Given that 1.5 million cancers are diagnosed every year in the United States, the EPIC study suggests that 121,000 of those cancers could be prevented by nothing more than an abundance of apples and kale. What's more, the study included very low-nutrient vegetables such as iceberg lettuce. It would be interesting to see the results with superfood cancer-fighters such as cruciferous vegetables (for example, kale and broccoli) and berries.

and men, beginning in 1976 and 1986 respectively. Among their findings was that people who averaged eight or more servings of fruits and vegetables a day were 30% less likely to have a heart attack or stroke. And the higher a participant's average daily intake of fruits and vegetables, the lower his or her chance of developing cardiovascular disease.

Juice Is Detoxifying

A Safer Fix

The benefits of a diet high in fruits and vegetables have been proven by countless studies. Let's face it, fruits and vegetables are a much safer "fix" than prescription medications. The expected side effects of prescription medications kill approximately 106,000 Americans every year.

One of the benefits of fresh juices is that they can help to naturally cleanse your body of stored toxins that may cause disease. Fruits and vegetables contain countless compounds that your liver, as well as your cells, uses to detoxify your body. No matter how healthy your regular diet may be, your body is exposed to toxins every day. They are in the air we breathe, the water we drink and the food we eat, which is likely to be sprayed with pesticides and fertilized with chemicals.

We simply can't avoid exposure. If you make poor food choices as well—let's face it, who doesn't from time to time?—you add to this substantial toxic load. For example, foods fried in oils such as sunflower oil are known to contain aldehydes. These organic compounds have been scientifically linked to neurodegenerative diseases, cardiovascular disease and some types of cancer. Prescription and over-the-counter drugs can also significantly add to the mix of toxins in your body.

Your body is pretty effective at ridding itself of these and other toxins through the processes of elimination and sweating. But your body's cleansing process can become overtaxed and have difficulty keeping up; toxins can build up over time and accumulate in your blood and tissues. These toxins affect the structure of cells and can cause chronic fatigue, premature aging, headaches and digestive problems, among other ailments. If your body is unable to eliminate toxins through the liver and kidneys, lungs, nose and mouth or through the skin, it will store them—first in your fat cells, possibly leading to cysts and tumors. Ultimately your body may store excess toxins in your muscles, blood and other body tissues, leading to serious and sometimes life-threatening disease.

You can assist your body's natural processes of elimination by creating the right conditions, and Daily Juice can help with this work. Having a Daily Juice first thing in the morning on an empty stomach gives your body extra support for detoxifying and repairing your cells. Many ingredients in your juice, from apples to parsley, contain nutrients known to aid in the detoxification process. The simple act of drinking them fresh in the morning boosts your body's ability to clean itself out.

Apples, for instance, contain a flavonoid called phlorizidin, which may help stimulate bile production in the liver, and pectin, which can help rid your body of food additives and metals. The unique combination of phytochemicals found in beets makes this root vegetable a potent liver cleanser and blood purifier. Gingerroot assists in detoxification in a different way, producing a healthy sweat that is particularly helpful when recovering from colds and flu. And the vitamin C in lemons is a potent antioxidant that neutralizes free radicals, which can damage your cells. These are just a few examples of the many ingredients that help make your Daily Juice a powerful detoxifying elixir.

In addition, your body goes into a natural detoxification mode every night while you sleep. A 2013 study published in *Science* suggests that even the brain cleanses itself of toxins during sleep. After a good night's sleep, Daily Juice can help you deepen your detoxification and get your day off to a great start, infusing your body with a wide range of valuable nutrients and helping to build you up the right way.

Juice Is Anti-Inflammatory

Inflammation has become a key topic in the field of health. We're not talking about the kind that occurs after you bump your head or the swelling caused by an infection. That type, known as acute inflammation, is your body's beneficial and natural response to an immediate trauma.

On the other hand, chronic inflammation occurs silently within the body and can remain undetected for years. Your body slowly loses its ability to turn off the inflammatory response and starts damaging its healthy tissues. Chronic inflammation is

A Finer-Tuned Athlete

Want to reduce pain and inflammation caused by your daily exercise routine? Try including a cup (250 mL) of cherries in your next juice. A recent study published in the *British Journal of Medicine* found that athletes who drank 12 ounces (375 mL) of tart cherry juice per day for eight days had significantly less pain and loss of strength in their muscles than participants who drank a placebo. The significant antioxidant and anti-inflammatory powers of cherries are responsible for these benefits.

known to be a primary factor in a number of chronic diseases, including heart disease, arthritis, Alzheimer's disease, immune disorders such as lupus, and even cancer. It is triggered or aggravated by many factors, including foods that contain dairy, sugar, refined carbohydrates, gluten or saturated fat.

Natural Anti-inflammatories

A wide range of fruits, vegetables, herbs and roots—including many most often used in juicing—have natural anti-inflammatory power. These foods are known to be rich in nutrients such as flavonoids, carotenoids and the antioxidant vitamins C and E, which regulate inflammatory events in your body. Drinking a freshly pressed juice every day will naturally decrease inflammation throughout your body, helping to keep you disease-free.

At the top of the list of anti-inflammatory foods is ginger, which contains extremely potent compounds called gingerols. Studies show that regular consumption of ginger reduces pain and increases mobility in people suffering from osteoarthritis or rheumatoid arthritis. You can add ginger to almost any juice for added spice and for potent protection from chronic inflammation.

Blueberries are also powerful fighters of chronic inflammation and arthritis. In a study published in the *Journal of Experimental Medicine* in 2015, researchers found that children suffering from juvenile idiopathic arthritis who drank blueberry juice daily, in addition to the prescription medication

Anti-Inflammatory Fruits and Vegetables

Here are some other "juicy" fruits and vegetables that rank highly on the anti-inflammatory list:

- **Celery** – reduces inflammation of the blood vessels and digestive tract.
- **Cantaloupe** – reduces overall inflammation in the body.
- **Lemon** – protects against rheumatoid arthritis.
- **Pineapple** – reduces overall inflammation in the body.
- **Kale** – reduces the risk of chronic inflammation throughout the body.
- **Cucumber** – inhibits the activity of pro-inflammatory enzymes.
- **Spinach** – reduces excessive inflammation, particularly in the digestive tract.
- **Beets** – inhibit the activity of pro-inflammatory enzymes and regulate inflammation in the cardiovascular system.

All five of the core ingredients in the Juice Guru Daily Classic template recipe (see page 108) are on this list, making it a potent elixir to assist you in combating chronic disease.

etanercept, significantly decreased their symptoms as compared to participants who abstained from drinking the juice. Incredibly, the serious side effects associated with etanercept (brain effects, weight gain and infection, among others) were also greatly reduced or absent in the children who drank the juice.

Juice Boosts Alkalinity

You may have heard of the idea that some foods are acid-forming and some are alkalizing, and that to be healthy our bodies should be more alkaline. But what does that mean? The measure of acidity or alkalinity in your body is its pH factor (short for "potential hydrogen"). This is measured on a scale between 0 (most acidic) and 14 (most alkaline). On a chemical level, our bodies thrive when we maintain our natural balance, which is a slightly alkaline environment.

A diet high in meat, dairy, processed food and sugar overwhelms our internal environment and creates an acidic buildup. This can lead to weight gain, low energy, weakened bones and poor skin. The foods we eat are known to burn with oxygen in our cells to produce energy that fuels the body. This digestive process creates an internal residue that can be acid, alkaline or neutral. By providing your body with more alkaline-forming foods, you'll be able to establish and maintain a healthy acid/alkaline balance. This is crucial for good health, because acid-forming foods are inflammatory, while alkaline foods are anti-inflammatory.

When we provide our body with more fruits and vegetables, we are able to tip the balance toward a more alkaline internal environment. Both fruits and vegetables supply organic sodium, which is known to replenish our alkaline reserves and keep the internal environment slightly alkaline. Fresh juices, by providing an influx of concentrated nutrition, can help balance the acid buildup in our body.

Juicing Balances Your Hormones

Most women, at least once a month, have experienced the effects of their hormones not being completely in balance. But what exactly are hormones, and what role do they play in our bodies? And, more important, how can Daily Juicing help keep those fickle things in check?

Hormones are chemical substances from the endocrine system that act as messengers throughout your body, travelling in your bloodstream to tissues and organs. Simply put, the release of hormones is one of the ways in which parts of the body communicate with each other. Hormones affect many processes in the body, including growth and development,

> **What Is Health?**
> Dr. Thomas Lodi (see page 40) says that health is not the absence of disease. In fact, an absence of anything is not the key to healing. It is the *presence* of something—the ability to regenerate, rejuvenate and procreate.

Case Study: Dr. Lodi's Patients
An Integral Part of Cancer Treatment

Thomas Lodi, MD, is the founder and leading physician at An Oasis of Healing, an integrative medical facility in Mesa, Arizona, that helps patients and their families reestablish health after being diagnosed with cancer. The facility is founded on the notion that "disease" is the body attempting to reestablish optimal functioning. The center's philosophy of comprehensive care combines standard medical procedures for the eradication of cancer (such as chemotherapy) with proven healing traditions. The Oasis offers not an alternative to traditional cancer treatment but rather a more comprehensive, holistic and integrative approach.

According to Dr. Lodi, a truly comprehensive treatment program must address how to keep cancer from coming back once medical doctors have "got rid" of it. That's why he uses Daily Juice as an integral part of treatment at An Oasis of Healing. "The people who come to our center begin their healing journey with a thorough detoxification program," he says. The main focus of this program is to "clean the water in the aquarium" by drinking 3 to 5 quarts (3 to 5 L) of green juice per day—without eating solid food—for one to four weeks, depending on their condition. "Over the years it has become apparent that, generally, those who continue to eat healthy and drink juice daily after receiving cancer treatment and leaving the center are still with us, while the opposite is true for those who stop."

The following are just a few of Dr. Lodi's many stories about cases that illustrate how he has successfully used Daily Juice to keep clients (and their families) healthy for years:

Robert, *a 50-year-old registered nurse, came to our center because his wife had advanced Stage 4 ovarian cancer. One day, after about six weeks, he took me aside and told me: "When we first arrived, I had to take nitroglycerin four to five times a day due to chest pain (angina). I had been on medication for high blood pressure for over ten years. I also needed to use insulin for my type 2 diabetes. Even so, I still had high fasting blood glucose levels. I wanted to support my wife, so I drank green juice along with her and changed my diet. Now, I no longer take any medication. My blood pressure is normal, my blood glucose levels are normal and I have no chest pain." I explained to Robert that we call this "second-hand health." He has continued to drink one quart (liter) of green juice every day for six years and has not needed to resume taking medications. He teaches all his friends and patients to do the same.*

Michael, *a 52-year-old male, called me concerning his prostate cancer. The cancer was found early, treated and was well contained. It had not spread. He was not able to come to our center for a variety of reasons so I advised him to do a six-week juice fast and call me back. He called eight weeks later to report that his PSA [prostate specific antigen, used to detect the presence of cancer] was in the high normal range. He continued drinking juices daily and eating healthy for the next year and reported that his PSA had returned to the normal range. His wife, who had hypertension and was overweight, joined him on this journey. Not only did she lose her excess weight by the next year, but she no longer had hypertension and was medication-free.*

Anna, *a 48-year-old woman, had Stage 4 breast cancer that had metastasized to her lungs, to such a point that she required oxygen and assistance when using the bathroom. After receiving conventional cancer treatment, she was told she had three weeks to live.*

When Anna arrived at my center, I treated her comprehensively with multiple therapies, including low-dose chemotherapy. She was then put on a green juice feast for six weeks. Eight weeks later she was jogging to our center. And eight years later she was still cancer-free. Juicing remained a regular part of her day.

James, a 78-year-old man, had cardiovascular problems, including angina and hypertension. He was feeble and needed to live in an assisted-living facility. After a three-week juice feast and other lifestyle modifications, he regained much of his strength. Ultimately he was able to throw most of his medications away. He continued juicing daily for about three years, with continued improvement in his health. At that point we lost contact with him.

Dr. Lodi reports that he has "hundreds of such stories. And what we have learned is the following: 'That which is required to be restored to health is also required to maintain health.'"

metabolism, sexual function and mood. In addition to a healthy libido and overall mood (not insignificant in themselves), the proper balance of hormones in your body is important for optimal health, including things such as cancer prevention. So it's important to find a way to keep your hormone levels stable.

The fact is, the average American female (and many males) over 35 years of age suffers from some form of hormonal imbalance. With increasingly poor diets, stressful lifestyles and inadequate physical exercise, more younger men and women are developing hormonal imbalances as well. Juicing can help balance your hormones and, if you're a woman, control premenstrual syndrome (PMS), perimenopause and post-menopausal symptoms.

How Does It Work?

Juicing allows you to consume large amounts of nutrients that support hormone balance and helps you to lose excess weight, which is linked to hormone imbalance. For instance, increased consumption of magnesium—found in produce such as beets, leafy greens and watermelon—is linked to healthy hormones. Cruciferous vegetables such as kale and broccoli are also known to balance hormones, the result of a compound they contain called indole-3-carbinol (I3C). As for the painful cramping associated with PMS, especially during perimenopause, that pain is caused in large part by inflammation. Certain fruits, vegetables and roots—particularly ginger, celery and cucumber—have strong anti-inflammatory effects (see page 36) that go to the source of the pain more safely than over-the-counter drugs such as ibuprofen.

A Fine Balance
Aside from recommending a healthy diet, experts also advise women to pay close attention to both weight and exercise for keeping good hormone balance. Daily Juicing can help you lose excess weight and keep it off. And as for exercise, let's just say that it's a good thing juicing gives you all that extra energy to spend.

Case Study: Julie's Story
Balanced Hormones at Last

As noted in the introduction to this book, I enjoyed many health benefits after I started juicing. But the most incredible change was one that I least expected. For my entire adult life I suffered from severe PMS. For up to a week before my cycle ended, I experienced painful cramping, significant bloating and dramatic mood swings. It was hard to miss the arrival of my period! But since I began Daily Juice, these symptoms have subsided to such an extent that I barely even realize when my cycle is ending each month.

Bring Out Your Inner Beauty

When we think of beauty, normally we think of outer beauty. We visualize ourselves having smooth, unblemished skin, shiny hair, a slim figure and a healthy glow. Daily Juice will give you all that and more.

A green juice containing spinach, for example, is loaded with lutein (a pigment found in certain plants), which will help keep your eyes healthy, clear and sparkling. Spinach and other green foods such as broccoli, watercress and collards also contain a good amount of calcium, magnesium and potassium, minerals that are essential to the health of your nails, hair and skin. These (and other juicy fruits and vegetables) are also water-rich, so they have hydrating effects. In addition, they shift your body toward the optimal slightly alkaline environment (see page 38), which helps to clear out toxins. When your body is clean on the inside, it shows in fewer blemishes and a glow on the outside.

Carrots, cantaloupe and leafy green veggies contain high amounts of beta-carotene, which your body converts to vitamin A. Vitamin A in turn supports healthy nails, hair and skin (not to mention good vision). These same vegetables are also rich in vitamin C, an antioxidant that lowers stress, which can weaken collagen, elastin and keratin in your body. Collagen is the most abundant protein in the human body. It's what gives your skin its strength and structure and greatly aids in the replacement of dead skin cells. Your body makes less collagen as you age, but strawberries, kale, oranges, tomatoes and papaya are just a few of the many juicy fruits and vegetables that contain large amounts of collagen-boosting vitamin C.

These are just some examples of how fruits and vegetables help you to glow and shine from the inside out. But beauty is so much more than how you look in the mirror. Your inner beauty—how peaceful, energetic and confident you are—is a huge part of what makes you attractive to others. People who juice feel good. They feel alive and full of life-energy—because they are, in a very literal way. Their moods become more stable and they feel and appear vital. We think this is by far the most attractive result of juicing. The internal confidence and feel-good factor are what others will notice most about you. Ultimately it's what makes you truly beautiful from the inside out

Turn Back the Biological Clock

Aging may be normal and natural, but many factors speed up or slow down this process. Fresh juices contain the nutrients necessary to keep your cells healthy and free of damage so you can live a long life. Daily Juicing can also help ensure that you age well, with vitality, a sharp mind and a more youthful appearance.

One of the best-known villains that attack health and youthfulness is the free radical. Free radicals are molecules in the body that have a highly reactive unpaired electron. These devious molecules can cause damage to various parts of cells and cell membranes by stealing their electrons, through a process called oxidation. An overabundance of free radicals in the body will cause disease. It will also cause your body to age more rapidly, leading to tissue breakdown. This includes sagging, wrinkled skin and deteriorating cognitive abilities.

Believe it or not, free radicals are a natural byproduct of our body's everyday metabolic processes. But free radicals from the environment—from air pollution, pesticides in food, alcohol and even fried foods—add to our natural load and overburden the body's ability to break them down. The more help you can get from nutrients in your diet, the faster your cells can handle free radicals and the easier it will be for your body to build, repair and replace cells. This all contributes to a youthful appearance, healthy tissues and longevity, and it aids in the prevention of largely age-related conditions such as Alzheimer's disease and arthritis.

One of the most popular buzzwords in health these days is *antioxidants*. Antioxidants are heroic substances that combat free radicals by inhibiting oxidation. They include nutrients you've heard of, such as vitamins C and E and beta-carotene, as well as ones you probably haven't—for instance, organosulfurs, phenols, terpenes and amines. These substances occur naturally in all plants because they protect the plant from environmental damage. They also give plant foods their distinctive qualities such as smell, taste and color. For example, the capsaicin in chile peppers is a phenol, which has a quality that translates into a sensation of heat. Capsaicin is believed to

Keys to Longevity

The Daily Juice habit is an essential component in increasing the quality and quantity of your years. But for optimal health and well-being, it's best to take a holistic approach to your life. Some other proven modalities we recommend include:

- unplugging in nature
- practicing yoga
- hiking
- working out
- meditating daily
- being present in the "now"
- feeling grateful
- developing loving relationships
- eating a plant-strong diet

be a potent pain-reliever for arthritis sufferers because when it is consumed the body releases energy-relieving endorphins to handle the intensity of the pepper's heat.

Nobody questions that plant foods are the best source of antioxidants—infinitely more so than any other food or supplement. Through juicing high-antioxidant foods such as red and purple grapes, dark green vegetables and carrots every day, we have seen our clients turn back their biological clocks by 10 or more years in terms of youthfulness, energy, looks and vigor.

Case Study: Roopal's Story
Overcoming Insomnia with Incredible Energy

There comes a time in everyone's life when you are forced to take care of yourself and figure out what works—nutritionally—for you and your body. For me, that time came about six months ago. Many of my problems started with chronic insomnia. It completely took over my life and has lasted for several years. I constantly felt tired and out of energy. And it slowly started affecting not only me but my family as well. I have two young children, and my ability to spend time with them and my patience were both compromised.

After suffering for long time, seeing many doctors, undertaking hormone therapy and even taking many different medications, I met two people who helped change my life for the better. I have known Julie for some time: our sons go to school and play baseball together. But I must admit that I didn't know her well until one day, when I happened to tell her at a baseball practice about my sleep issues. I confided how tired I felt and how impatient I was growing with everyone around me. Her immediate response was to ask, "Have you tried juicing?"

I knew very little about juicing at that time, but I was willing to try anything that might help me get some rest and energy. Julie introduced me to her husband, Steve, his previous book, and the concept of Daily Juice. They focused me on the organic ingredients (very important) that would help me with energy, guided me toward the best juicer for my lifestyle and empowered me with an incredible amount of knowledge about the benefits of juicing.

I took all their advice very seriously and started juicing consistently every day. I have been juicing now for about half a year, and I can't believe how good and energetic I feel. I feel less tired (even on days when I didn't get much sleep the night before), my skin is glowing and, most important, I am finally sleeping better. I won't say I'm completely cured of my insomnia, but juicing has given me back some of the control in my life that was slowly eroding because of lack of energy. It did for me what nothing else was able to do.

Juicing also gave me the stamina to start exercising regularly. I feel confident about the way I look now, but most important, it feels good to be nourishing my body with all these nutritious ingredients, some of which I had never before tried. Despite being a vegetarian all my life, I must admit that I never came close to meeting the required daily servings of vegetables. But now, with juicing, I get all that and some more. I have even begun trying to get my kids into juices and green smoothies.

Juicing has benefited me in so many ways that I cannot imagine my life without it, even for one day.

— *Roopal Jadeja*

Chapter 3
The Daily Juice Comparison—Get Your Facts Straight

Containers of pasteurized orange juice and bottled apple juice have been around forever. Unlike freshly pressed juices, most bottled juices have lost significant nutrition, for a number of reasons. They have likely been heated to high temperatures during the process of pasteurization, possibly irradiated, and stored for long periods of time on store shelves or in refrigerators. Often they contain additives, including refined sugars. Nevertheless, if you're anything like us, your mother probably served you a glass of one of these juices at every meal, without questioning its goodness.

But ever since it became popular to take a fresh apple, press it and drink the juice directly from the source, a number of questions and a good amount misinformation have surfaced about the juice's nutritional content. This includes misinformation about the metabolic effects of sugar from freshly pressed fruit juice. The good news is that these contentions simply aren't true or are highly misleading. Some of the misinformation comes from self-proclaimed "nutrition experts" who lack credentials in the field, or from well-intentioned but misinformed bloggers. Some comes from misinterpretations of scientific studies. And some comes from ill-intentioned marketers looking to sell their products by creating confusion.

To ensure that these "myth traps" don't keep you from becoming a Daily Juicer, we've decided to tackle some of these untruths head on.

The Truth about Fruit Sugars

Top of the myth list is the idea that juicing will give you an unhealthy dose of sugar that will wreak havoc on your blood-sugar levels and, consequently, your waistline and health. This myth does come with an aura of common sense. After all, fruit contains sugar and juices often contain a lot of fruit. But the truth is, the fructose in freshly pressed juices does not have the same detrimental effect on your body as refined sugars, such as those added to soda, bottled juices and other beverages.

Sugar Fix

Take a closer took at what's on the shelves of your local supermarket. You'll discover that the majority of food products we consume every day contain an inordinate amount of sugar. Even so-called healthy food products contain an abundance of isolated sugars such as agave syrup, coconut nectar, maple syrup, palm sugar and high-fructose corn syrup. Aside from the fact that refined and processed sugars are addictive, they are also a factor in hyperactive behavior, brain fog, tooth decay and weight gain. The Juice Guru philosophy is to significantly reduce your sugar intake. But we recommend eliminating nutritionally empty or deficient processed foods, not fruit.

Fruit Sugar Is Not the Same as Table Sugar

It's a well-known fact that fruit sugar is different from other types of sugar, such as table sugar and high-fructose corn syrup. This has been confirmed in a number of recent studies, which demonstrate that fruit sugars do not cause liver damage, hypertension or weight gain the way other kinds of fructose and table sugar do. In fact, one study of 131 participants, published in *Metabolism Clinical and Experimental* in 2011, found that participants who ate a diet that included a "moderate" amount of natural fruit sugar lost more weight than those who followed a low-fructose diet.

The most illuminating evidence we've heard to date on the subject is a study published in the *American Journal of Clinical Nutrition* in 2012, which provides valuable insight into how different types of sugar are processed in the human body. In that study, the researchers first gave participants a glass of water containing 3 tablespoons (45 mL) of ordinary table sugar—the equivalent of one can of soda. Blood samples were taken and analyzed after 0, 15, 30, 45, 60, 90 and 120 minutes. As you would expect, the researchers observed an immediate spike in the blood-sugar levels and insulin of the participants (at the 15- and 30-minute marks), but about 90 minutes later the situation had changed: the participants' blood-sugar levels crashed to below their starting point. Essentially their bodies had overdosed on insulin. This decline in blood sugar caused one notable impact, according to the study: the body dumped fat into the bloodstream as though it were starving. Not good under any circumstances, and certainly not if you are looking to lose or even maintain your weight.

But does the same thing happen with fruit sugar? The researchers went a step further to find out. They *added* 1 tablespoon (15 mL) of fruit sugar, in the form of blended berries, to the sugar-water served to participants. This time the results were unexpected. Rather than creating a bigger spike in blood sugar and insulin, this addition of fruit sugar blunted the spike from the sugar-water alone. Even more incredible, there was no crash in blood-sugar levels. So, not only did the added fruit sugar fail by itself to cause excessive deviations in blood-sugar levels, it actually had the effect of offsetting the dramatic swings caused by processed forms of sugar.

It's More Than the Fiber

At this point you might think it's the fiber in the fruit that had this beneficial impact. Certainly fiber slows down digestion and the absorption of sugar into the bloodstream. But there's something else at play in this surprising reaction. The researchers repeated the second experiment using fresh berry juice instead of the blended berries. The results were nearly identical to those with the blended berries. In other words, despite containing 20% to 30% *more* total sugars than the sugar-water alone, the sugar-water with the added berry juice had the effect of preventing the steep rise and dip in blood sugar seen with table sugar alone.

How could this be? Well, it turns out there are phytonutrients in fruits that, much like their fiber, inhibit the transportation of sugars through the intestinal wall and into the bloodstream. The researchers concluded that certain polyphenols (proanthocyanidins and anthocyanins) in the blackcurrants and lingonberries they used had this effect. It seems nature has a way of making perfect foods that, when served up fresh with their various nutrients intact, protect us from individual components of that food, such as the sugar. Prior studies have demonstrated that other fruits, such as apples and strawberries, similarly contain polyphenols that lessen absorption of glucose from the digestive tract. And, as demonstrated by the 2012 study on berry juice, a freshly pressed juice retains these nutrients from the whole fruit.

Some Fruits Regulate Blood Sugar

Fruits and their juices are simply not the same as sugary treats. In fact, many sweet fruits that are often used in freshly pressed juices are known to be excellent blood-sugar regulators. For instance, apples (which serve as the base for countless juice

Fruit Juice Benefits

The Daily Juice protocol was founded on the idea of one green juice a day—we have found this to make the biggest difference in our lives. But fruit juices also offer significant benefits, from increased brain function (see page 29) to relief from arthritis symptoms (see page 38). They should not be passed over because they contain natural sugar. To balance the undeniable benefits of fruit juices against fear of sugar consumption, we recommend fruit juices as an addition to or occasional departure from your daily green or vegetable juice, rather than as a staple of your daily practice.

combinations) contain phlorizin, a polyphenol that studies have shown to decrease blood-sugar spikes by as much as 52%. Strawberries and grapes have also been found to help with regulating blood sugar.

Far from being a cause of blood-sugar conditions such as diabetes, fruits can actually help lower your risk of type 2 diabetes. In fact, in 2013 a study was published that looked at almost 190,000 participants from the Harvard Nurses' Health Study and its follow-up study. This later research, which we'll refer to as the "Harvard Derivative Study" or HDS, confirmed that consuming several servings of whole fruits every day is associated with a lower risk of type 2 diabetes.

Other studies have come to similar conclusions, but the Harvard Derivative Study is different because it looked at particular fruits and their likelihood—by themselves—to affect risk. The HDS found that people who consumed apples, grapes and blueberries at least twice a week were up to 23% less likely to develop type 2 diabetes, compared to those who consumed those fruits once a month or less. That's a pretty sizable preventive advantage!

All Fruits Are Not Created Equal

Importantly, though, when it comes to blood-sugar conditions, not all fruits are created equal. More specifically, foods are ranked by their glycemic index (GI), which measures how a carbohydrate-containing food such as fruit raises blood glucose. When it comes to GI, the lower the better. According to the American Diabetes Association, most fruits have a low GI, but there are a few notable exceptions. Cantaloupe, watermelon and pineapple are known to have a medium GI. That's why we recommend that people with diabetes or other blood-sugar issues consult a doctor before enjoying daily fruit juices, especially if they contain these particular fruits.

The Problem Is Bottled, Not Fresh Juice

Now that we've discussed why fructose found in fruits and freshly pressed juices should not be compared gram for gram with other, harmful types of sugar, we need to turn our attention to the number-one source of confusion about sugar in fruit juice.

Specifically, 2013 saw a flurry of blogs, news reports and even television shows on the dangers of fruit juices and sugar. These reports were based solely on one study that was published that year, the Harvard Derivative Study. The finding was that "fruit juice" not only failed to deliver the same anti-diabetes benefits as whole fruit but even appeared to raise the risk of diabetes. According to the study, people who drank at least one serving a day of juice had a 21% higher risk of developing diabetes than those who did not. That's a pretty scary statistic … at least, at first glance.

The significant fact overlooked by those people who jumped on the anti-juice bandwagon is that this finding related to bottled *processed* juices, the kind readily available at your local supermarket. These included products such as processed apple, orange and cranberry juice. The study did *not* look at freshly pressed juices. How do we know? It wasn't easy to figure out, since people who cited the study (or just paraphrased its findings) generally failed to note what kind of fruit juices were implicated, or even that different types of juices exist. To find out, we had to go to the source of the researchers' information.

The Harvard Nurses' Health Study and its follow-up study—on which the HDS was based—relied on participant questionnaires for their findings. These questionnaires asked how many servings per week on average each participant ate of particular foods, including fresh or frozen whole fruits. The questions were printed on a standardized form where participants were directed to fill in a bubble using a number 2 pencil. They could choose only from a specified food or drink, such as "fruit" or "fruit juices," and a predetermined range of daily, weekly or monthly servings they consumed of each. For example, for "bananas (1)," participants could fill only one bubble, corresponding to "never, or less than one per month," "1–3 per month," "5–6 per week" and so on. No space was provided to write in juices or foods not included on the preprinted form, nor was there space to explain the answers given.

As for fruit juice, the sole options available on the printed questionnaire were juices that clearly were processed. They were limited to "one small glass" of apple juice or cider, "calcium or vit. D fortified" orange juice or non-fortified orange juice, grapefruit juice, and "other juice (for example, cranberry, grape)." These are the processed juices most commonly available in any grocery store, and not the typical juice that is freshly pressed in a juicer. In particular, "vitamin-fortified" juice indicates a juice that has to be processed, not one that is pressed from fresh fruits in your juicer at home.

No Excuses

If you are a diabetic or just want to limit your intake of sugar in any form, green juices are a perfect option. We actually prefer green juices to sweeter fruit juices and find that they provide us with more sustained energy throughout the day. You have no excuse not to Daily Juice!

Fresh Juices Are Much More Healthful

There is a significant difference between fresh and processed juices (see page 55). Basically, freshly pressed juices are considerably more healthful than processed. First, many bottled juices contain added refined or industrial sugars that are not present in a freshly pressed juice. In addition, freshly pressed juices retain the vast majority of the nutrients from the whole food, with the exception of the fiber. And as demonstrated by a 2012 *American Journal of Clinical Nutrition* study, interaction of the various nutrients in the whole fruit—in this case its valuable phytonutrients—helps ensure that freshly pressed fruit juice does not cause the same fluctuations in blood sugar and insulin levels as isolated sugar.

The processes used to make bottled juices, on the other hand, kill off many of the nutrients, especially water-soluble vitamins such as vitamin C and the B vitamins, as well as antioxidants, phenols and valuable enzymes. So, unlike freshly pressed juices, they don't contain the important components of the original fruit that work in the human body to offset the effects of sugar. In particular, one article published in *Food Chemistry and Toxicology* in 2002 noted that freshly pressed blueberry juice generally retains up to 83% of the anthocyanins in the original blueberries, while processed juice can contain as little as 13% to 23% of this vital nutrient. Notably, it was this very phytonutrient that researchers found responsible for keeping sugar out of the bloodstream in the 2012 *American Journal of Clinical Nutrition* study.

Finally, and most important, not all juices contain sugary fruit—green juices with a cucumber and celery base, for example. And they are just as delicious as the sweet stuff, especially if you add some cilantro, basil or jalapeño pepper.

Another anti-juicing argument is that because juices remove fiber from fruits and vegetables, they have no place in a healthy diet. It is actually a myth to say that juices don't contain any fiber. And we'll get to that shortly. But is it correct to say that the existence of fiber in a fresh juice actually makes it a healthier drink?

The truth is, freshly pressed juices have serious merit on their own terms, even without fiber. They are one of the most concentrated source of micronutrients, phytonutrients, antioxidants and other valuable nutrients available. The vast majority of North Americans fail to consume the recommended number of servings of fruits and veggies, especially leafy greens, and Daily Juice can provide that and more.

A Natural Juicer

Think about it this way: your body is a natural juicer. Through chewing and lengthy digestion, it breaks down fruits and vegetables into their juices and the insoluble fiber, which your body (the juicer) then expels. Juicing saves you the work of chewing and digesting insoluble fiber.

The Truth about Fiber in Your Juice

Dietary fiber is the indigestible component of plant foods. Fiber is important, but it's not actually a nutrient on its own. It is a form of carbohydrate that cannot be broken down into glucose by the human body and simply passes through our system. It's important in our diet because it has many health benefits.

There are two kinds of fiber: *soluble*, which dissolves in water and becomes gelatinous as it is digested, and *insoluble*, which does not dissolve in water and is often called "roughage." Each type of fiber has different effects on the body.

Those who argue that juice contains no fiber are talking about the insoluble kind. This kind of fiber is present in the skin and pulp of fruits and vegetables. Insoluble fiber acts like an internal broom, sweeping your intestines clean to keep you regular, and because it is bulky, it slows down your digestion. In fact, removing this kind of fiber is one of the reasons for making fresh juice. A lot of digestive energy is spent breaking down the fiber to extract the healthy nutrients from fruits and vegetables, and this lengthy step is not necessary when you drink a juice.

Basically, you can consume the nutrients from a significantly greater number of fruits and vegetables each day by including a Daily Juice—*because* the insoluble fiber is removed. To understand this better, picture a plate containing two tomatoes, eight carrots, one stalk of celery, half a head of romaine lettuce and two cups (500 mL) of spinach. Given the bulk of this meal, it would be extremely difficult, if not impossible—and undesirable—to eat it all. But you can press yourself a Fresh-Eight (page 150) and easily drink the nutrients from this quantity of vegetables.

Juices Provide Soluble Fiber

While juices don't generally contain insoluble fiber, they do contain a good amount of soluble (viscous) fiber. Soluble fiber dissolves in water and is thus present in the extracted juice. Soluble fiber mixes with water to create a gel-like substance that has many health benefits. It attaches to cholesterol particles and takes them out of the body, helping to lower total cholesterol and LDL cholesterol (the "bad" kind), thereby reducing your risk of heart disease.

Soluble fiber also helps to regulate blood sugar, which is particularly important for people with diabetes. It will even aid with weight loss, as it helps to make you feel full without adding extra calories. Soluble fiber is more prevalent in fruits than vegetables. Good juice-worthy fruits that are rich in soluble fiber include apples, oranges, beets and plums.

Daily Juice Can Help Prevent Kidney Stones

In early 2015 a flurry of reports, including a segment on the popular *Dr. Oz* show, claimed that green smoothies (and, by proxy, green juices) could be dangerous to your health. The theory was that spinach and other leafy greens, as well as berries, legumes, nuts and green tea, contain a significant amount of substances known as oxalates. Oxalates, the reports contended, are instrumental in the formation of kidney stones and are possible precursors of other health conditions.

As is so often the situation, these reports apparently came from a single article, "The Green Smoothie Fad: This Road to Toxic Health Hell Is Paved with Oxalate Crystals," by William Shaw, PhD. In it the author actually compared drinking green smoothies to being poisoned over time by doses of antifreeze. Dr. Shaw peppered his article with anecdotal stories about a person or two who allegedly had high oxalate levels and also reported drinking green smoothies, and he included a lengthy excerpt from an unknown researcher at the Campbell Soup Company. But for his scientific argument, Dr. Shaw relied solely on the general connection between high oxalate levels in the human body and the formation of kidney stones, autism, fibromyalgia and a few other conditions. What he left out, however, was mention of where the majority of those oxalates likely came from.

The truth is, leafy greens, blueberries and even chocolate do contain a considerable amount of oxalates. But only a fraction of the oxalates in our bodies actually come from the food we consume. In fact, our bodies themselves produce a full

Oxalates Get a Bad Rap

Oxalates, which are found naturally in leafy greens and other healthful juice ingredients, have been accused of contributing to kidney stones. However, according to a study conducted by Dr. Gabriel Cousens, author of *Conscious Eating*, oxalates from natural foods do not build up in the body if your metabolism and digestion work properly. And Dr. Norman Walker—the pioneer of the juicing movement—found that oxalic acid from raw foods such as juice is important in maintaining a healthy bowel.

80% to 90% of the oxalates found in our urine stream. Avoiding oxalate-containing foods is not the best way to keep your overall level of oxalates down.

Then what is the cause of calcium oxalate kidney stones? According to a recent study by the British Association of Urological Surgeons, "refined carbohydrates and animal protein" are far more likely to be a cause than high-oxalate foods such as spinach. Red meat in particular is a culprit because it is highly acidic; your body resorts to stealing calcium from your bones in an attempt to neutralize that acidity, and excess calcium ends up in your urine stream, aiding in stone formation. (Although this is beside the point, that lack of calcium in your bones also likely contributes to osteoporosis.) Many other studies from around the world have reached similar conclusions. Ironically, meat and carbohydrates are some of the very foods that Dr. Shaw recommends eating in abundance to protect against these health conditions.

The fact is, studies demonstrate that a diet rich in calcium and magnesium, as well as adequate hydration, will help prevent the formation of kidney stones. And dark leafy greens and other produce used in abundance in juices and smoothies are some of the best sources of these nutrients. At the same time, these powerhouses supply a healthy dose of hydration to feed your thirsty cells.

Juices and Smoothies Are Different

Green smoothies are very popular in North America these days. Smoothies—if made fresh with the right ingredients—can certainly be an attractive, healthful dietary option. Smoothies are an easy way to increase your daily servings of fruits and vegetables, including harder-to-juice or low-yielding fruits such as blueberries and bananas. They can be quicker to whip up than a fresh juice, and cleanup is easier too.

And we do love them. In fact, we recommend that you include a green smoothie as an integral part of your Daily Juice routine. You can enjoy a healthy 8- to 16-ounce (250 to 500 mL) smoothie as a fantastic midmorning or afternoon snack. (We've included 10 delectable smoothie recipes for you to sample and enjoy.) We do highly recommend, however, that you use a good-quality blending machine to make them, such as one of those offered by Tribest, Vitamix or Blendtec. Smoothies lose nutrients through the process of oxidation, and a well-built blender will help to minimize that nutrient loss.

If It Looks Like a Smoothie, It Is a Smoothie

Recently, many individual-serving-sized blending machines have been deceptively referred to as "juice extractors" or "nutrition extractors" by their marketers. Don't be fooled. In reality, these machines are just blenders and the drinks they make are regular smoothies. While smoothies are a great addition to your diet, nutritionally they don't hold a candle to a Daily Juice.

Green Smoothies Are Beneficial

Green smoothies can be a nutritious addition to your healthy diet, as a snack or as an easier-to-make replacement for Daily Juice. If you're like most people who live on the standard Western diet, the addition of green smoothies will exponentially increase your fruit and vegetable intake.

It's All in the Process

There are different explanations for why blended ingredients lose more nutrients than juiced ingredients. Some contend that, unlike with many juicers, the friction in blenders heats up the fruits and vegetables to higher temperatures for a longer period of time, and thus destroys some of their nutritional content. The Breville study suggests a different culprit: oxidation. During the blending process, air is pushed into the cells of the fruits and vegetables, causing nutrient loss. But regardless of why, the truth is that juices are more potent than smoothies, nutritionally speaking.

Juices Are Up to Twice as Nutritious as Smoothies

Nutritionally speaking, however, smoothies are not a substitute for Daily Juice. Breville, a company that makes both juicers and blenders, recently performed a nutritional comparison study of smoothies made in a blender and juices made in a juicing machine. Several different juicers and blenders were tested, and the results were telling.

Each of the green drinks in the study was made from the same quantities of the same ingredients: kale, orange, celery, carrots and apples. There was one exception: water was added to the smoothies to allow the ingredients to combine in the blender, much like the liquids usually added to smoothies for this very reason. The green juice made in the best-performing juicer tested contained 142% more vitamin C, 73% more alpha-carotene, 109% more beta-carotene and 54% more potassium than a green smoothie mixed for 60 seconds in the leading commercial blender. When the added water in the smoothie was accounted for, the juice still had up to twice the nutrients of the smoothie. The magnesium content was about equal in the smoothie and the juice, and calcium was actually about 2% higher in the smoothie (which is certainly not significant).

This data is good for comparison purposes, but what does it mean in absolute terms? As far as your recommended daily intake (RDI) of key nutrients is concerned, the researchers found that the green juice delivered between 83% and 85% of the RDI for vitamin C and carotenes (vitamin A equivalent), more than double that of the smoothie. Of course, this study focused only on the few ingredients contained in a single drink. When you practice Daily Juicing, you will receive from your juice almost your full RDI of a variety of vitamins and other nutrients, depending on the ingredients you use that day.

And that nutrition makes it into your body more quickly and efficiently than with smoothies, because the hard-to-digest insoluble fiber has been removed. That's why you can definitely feel a difference in your immediate energy level and overall health, depending on whether you are drinking a heavy smoothie or a juice. But don't just take our word for it. Try it yourself.

Another reason why fresh juices are nutritionally superior comes down to the sheer volume of produce you can include in a juice versus a smoothie. For example, you can use an entire head of kale in one juice. An average 24-ounce (750 mL) green juice might contain an entire bunch of spinach, four to five leaves of chard, three apples and a cucumber (among other things). Even the most powerful green smoothie might include only $1\frac{1}{2}$ to 2 cups (375 to 500 mL) of greens, a banana or two, and some other fruits.

Too Much Fiber Is Not a Good Thing

If you did try to consume the amount of produce typically contained in a 24-ounce (750 mL) glass of green juice in the form of daily smoothies, the result could be detrimental to your health. Since fiber is not actually digested by the body, the digestive tract has a slightly more difficult time processing it. Typically this isn't a problem, but if you overload your system with fiber you can experience abdominal discomfort, such as gas, cramping or bloating, as your body works through the bulk.

Juicing versus Supplements

You might be wondering why you should go through the trouble of juicing when you could simply take one of the plethora of nutritional supplements available on the market. While we don't rule out including high-quality organic supplements as an adjunct to a juicing program, the science shows that supplements do not provide the same benefits as a freshly pressed juice. Nutritional supplements may contain the essential nutrients your body needs, but in most cases the body is not able to assimilate and distribute them as effectively as the nutrients from fresh food.

That is because the various components of whole foods work in tandem with one another. An apple, for example, contains thousands of phytonutrients, as well as vitamins and minerals that affect thousands of metabolic reactions in your body. Because these chemicals react with one another, there are an almost infinite number of beneficial consequences to the body. None of this can occur when individual nutrients (such as vitamin C) are isolated in a pill or powder.

Freshly pressed juices, on the other hand, are made directly from the whole foods. They fill your body with natural nutrients in a form that is easily assimilated and disseminated. And they retain virtually all of the nutrients of the whole food, which allows the natural chemical reactions that keep your body healthy and running well to occur.

Freshly Pressed versus Bottled Juice

The shelves of supermarkets and health food stores are stacked with pasteurized juices, while their refrigerated sections offer bottled juices that claim to be freshly pressed. However, processed juice—no matter what the process—is a less nutritious option than the freshly pressed variety.

Too Much for a Pill

Scientists have identified and catalogued only a fraction of the thousands of phytonutrients believed to be in natural vegetables and fruit. We could never put all those components into a single jar, bottle, tablet, powder or pill. Accessing the full range of nutrients available in whole foods is the main reason why we recommend drinking freshly pressed juices in our Daily Juice programs.

An Addition to Juice

Some high-quality powder supplements available today can be an excellent addition to your diet. They are made of only organic whole plant foods that are dehydrated at low temperatures. The best of these can enhance your Daily Juice program. They are also great when you are traveling or otherwise unable to get to your juicer.

Freshly Pressed Juices

Freshly pressed is the best way to drink your juice. The ingredients are simply put through a juicer—there is no other processing. For maximum nutrition and potency, drink fresh juice within minutes after pressing it, as the nutrients and living enzymes deplete rapidly after juicing.

Freshly pressed juices can be described by different terms, depending on the juicer type used. *Cold pressing* is one high-yielding method of producing fresh juice. Unlike juices made by other methods, cold-pressed juices can last for several days in the refrigerator with most of their nutrients and enzymes intact.

Unpasteurized Juices

Only a small percentage of commercially sold cold-pressed juice in North America is unpasteurized, although this type is gaining in popularity. If you're not pressing your own juice at home, these juices are the next best alternative. You'll find them at local orchards that feature freshly squeezed apple cider, health food stores that sell freshly squeezed unpasteurized juices, and some juice bars. These juices, which are usually created using organic ingredients, need to be kept in the fridge, where they have a shelf life of only two to three days.

Cold-Pressed Juices

"Cold-pressed" has recently become a bit of a buzzword in juicing. But cold-press juicers were actually among the original juicers. Cold pressing is a method of juicing that actually uses a press, rather than a masticating or other type of mechanism. The Norwalk juicer, which has been around since the 1930s, is the standard in this area.

Cold-Pressed High-Pressure-Processed Juices

High-pressure processing (HPP) is a non-thermal pasteurization process. It preserves and sterilizes by applying very high pressures (between 100 and 1,000 megapascals) through a water bath that surrounds the bottle of juice. Exposure times range from a millisecond-long pulse to more than 20 minutes. The purpose is to deactivate certain microorganisms and enzymes in the juice. This in turn slows deterioration by stopping the chemical activity caused by microorganisms, and it allows the juice to remain on the shelf for significantly longer. While manufacturers do not generally disclose whether they have used HPP, you can generally tell by the expiration date. These juices are often labeled as "fresh" for as long as a month or more after they have been made.

Unfortunately, inactivating the living enzymes in your juice also reduces its life force. Many juice bars and health food stores that sell refrigerated ready-made bottled juices use this technique to extend shelf life, but they may falsely label the juice only as "cold-pressed." The truth is, HPP provides a shelf life up to 10 times longer than that of fresh juice. A company may call its juice "fresh" in name or description, but a juice that can sit for up to 45 days in the fridge is certainly *not* fresh.

There hasn't been sufficient research on whether HPP juices have the same nutritional content as freshly pressed juices. But certainly HPP takes the end product much farther away from the natural state of the original juice. As consumers, we should be aware that a juice treated in this way—and which is several days to more than one month old—could not possibly be the same as a freshly made, non-treated juice. While we can recommend HPP juice on occasion, it should not make up the bulk of juices consumed if you are looking for optimal results.

Pasteurized Not-from-Concentrate Juices

Used by numerous brands, the phrase "not from concentrate" was coined in the 1980s to distinguish pasteurized juice from juice created from concentrate. Pasteurization is the process of heating juices to high temperatures (as high as 160°F/75°C) for a short time to kill off bacteria or other microorganisms that may be present. This is helpful for decreasing the chances of food-borne illness. But following our directions on how to clean your produce properly before juicing will assure a safe experience when making fresh juice (see page 81). In addition, many fruits and vegetables have natural antimicrobial properties that effectively keep your juice free of harmful bacteria, as long as you drink it soon after juicing.

The heat of the pasteurization process can destroy much of the ingredients' nutrition. Most studies on pasteurization have been done with milk, not juice, but it's clear that water-soluble vitamins, such as vitamin C and the B vitamins, are sensitive to heat and oxidation. A considerable amount of these vitamins is destroyed by the pasteurization process. According to the results of a 2005 study in *Molecular Nutrition and Food Research*, when testing the antioxidant activity of pasteurized orange juice, researchers noted a remarkable loss of antioxidant power following the pasteurization process.

Some companies add proprietary "flavor packs" containing fruit oils and essences, so the product will have the taste and aroma of freshly squeezed juice. These additives may not be toxic, but they are used to make consumers believe they are drinking a fresh juice, with the taste that nature originally intended. Unfortunately the US Food and Drug Administration (FDA) does not currently require companies to list flavor packs on a product's packaging, which means you won't know whether your carton of orange juice contains them or not.

Fresh Is Always Best

Many processed juices contain added sugars. The bottom line: keep it fresh. You'll notice right away the increased energy and overall well-being you get from consuming freshly pressed juices.

Juices from Concentrate

Many companies create a shelf-stable pasteurized juice product from concentrate. Juice concentrates are created by heating fruits and vegetables, reducing them down to a syrup and then adding water back in. Like other pasteurized juices, this process leaves us with a drink that has lost a significant amount of its primary vitamins and minerals. Often a company will add nutritional supplements to compensate, but as discussed above, you are better off consuming fruits and vegetables juiced in their whole state as opposed to isolated vitamins or minerals that have been added back in.

Buyer Beware

Be cautious when your beverage says "100% juice" on the label—you may not be getting exactly what you think. Food companies use this term for marketing purposes, but often their juices contain additives such as flavorings and preservatives. These added ingredients have no benefits for your health and in some cases can be dangerous. For example, some juices marketed as "100% natural" have been found to contain synthetic ingredients.

One company (Naked Juice, owned by PepsiCo) was recently sued when its juice was found to contain Fibersol-2 (a proprietary synthetic digestion-resistant fiber produced by a Japanese chemical company), fructooligosaccharides (synthetic fiber and sweetener) and inulin (a plant-based carbohydrate added to foods to artificially increase fiber content). Other companies use artificial food coloring to make their juices look more appealing. One company in particular, Ocean Spray, was found to be using petroleum-based dyes to color its Ruby Red Grapefruit juice. Finally, some companies add sugar to their juices in the form of high-fructose corn syrup made from genetically modified corn.

Part 2

Getting Started: 21 Days to a Lifelong Plan

Chapter 4
Can Do! The Juice Guru Plan of Action

By this point we've empowered you with a lot of information about how Daily Juice will make a difference in your life. But let's face it, knowing that fresh juice is something that you want (or maybe even need) to make part of your daily life and actually accomplishing that goal are two completely different things.

Make Daily Juice a Habit

If just making up your mind were enough, there would be no such thing as a yo-yo diet and none of us would ever need to start on another new health kick, because we'd already be in great shape. The fact is, we all have busy lives. And resolving to do one thing in the face of so many competing demands and desires is a tall order. It may seem that your various activities already fill your daily calendar—and then some. So how in the world can you fit in making a 24-ounce (750 mL) juice and cleaning up the juicer every day?

This is the same problem that underlies every juicing, smoothie, weight-loss and health program, and we are unaware of any that tackles this problem head on. Fortunately, this is a dilemma we've encountered ourselves, as have many of our clients. And it's something we've worked hard to answer. The answer is you need to make Daily Juice a habit. And don't worry—once you do, you will have tons of energy for accomplishing all your other life endeavors too.

A Helpful Routine

The word *habit* sometimes carries negative connotations. But we're not talking about those bad habits that many of us are aware we should lose. Behaviors such as snacking when you're not hungry, smoking, and watching television to fall asleep at night aren't desirable. But some habits are actually helpful. Whether you are aware of them or not, you likely perform hundreds of useful routines every day that are deeply ingrained in your behavior pattern. In fact, a recent study estimates that most of us engage in regular practices for about half of our waking hours.

Consider the following. Do you routinely wake at the same time every morning, before your alarm? Have you ever driven to work and realized that you somehow exited the freeway without realizing it? What about this morning? Can you remember showering, brushing your teeth, making coffee or feeding the cat? Do you remember performing similar behaviors before going to bed last night? Probably you can't, or at least not with any specificity. That's because they are repetitive, habitual behaviors, and they are helpful because they save you from wasting time and energy thinking about the mundane activities of your day and allow you to focus on other things.

To make your goal of a juice a day stick for good, you need to make Daily Juice this kind of helpful habit. The Juice Guru Plan of Action will help you create that habit relatively quickly and easily.

How Long Will It Take?

What do we mean by "relatively quickly"? You've probably heard that it takes 21 days to form a habit. After all, an endless stream of books and Internet sites promises that you can accomplish virtually anything by just repeating it for 21 days, from flattening your abs to building a successful relationship to ending your smoking habit. The truth is, the 21-day timeframe for habit forming is a bit of a myth. Habits generally take longer than that to create, and some take substantially longer.

In one research study, published in the *European Journal of Social Psychology* in 2009, 96 individuals performed a chosen daily task, from drinking a glass of water after breakfast to performing 50 daily sit-ups. The results indicate that the average habit takes about 66 days to develop. But, importantly, this research also indicates that the more basic the habit you are trying to develop, the more quickly it will form. It took only 20 days, for instance, for participants to make a habit of drinking water after breakfast. The beauty of Daily Juice is that—unlike juice fasts and other "diets" and health programs that often require you to drastically change everything you eat and drink—Daily Juice requires making just a single addition to your routine. And it doesn't ask that you give up anything in return.

In addition, the 2009 study did not employ established psychological techniques to help participants create their chosen habit more quickly. In this chapter we discuss and apply several of those techniques to help you develop your Daily Juice habit faster. By following the steps we lay out, you will be on the road to creating an established habit—and lifelong good health and youthfulness—in no time.

Conscious Resolve Is Important

People who *explicitly* make a resolution are 10 times more likely to succeed in their desired goals than those who don't.

Step 1: Have the (Right) Intention

The very first thing you need to do on your road to Daily Juice is to form a clear intention to make it a habit. Merriam-Webster's dictionary defines an intention as determination to act in a certain way. You might think that once you make up your mind to do something, it won't be difficult to follow through. But research shows that good intentions aren't a significant factor in habit formation if that habit will be repeated often (once a day, for example) as opposed to less often (such as once a year). Presumably this is because the dedication required to repeat a task every day needs to be considerably stronger than for a task that must be performed only periodically.

New Year's resolutions are a case in point. More than half of us routinely make resolutions at the beginning of every year. In other words, our good intentions make us habitually create a list. But how many of those resolutions do we actually keep? According to the Statistic Brain Research Institute, the average person doesn't keep their resolutions any longer than six months, no matter how strong the initial intentions. In fact, only about 8% of people who make resolutions will ultimately keep them.

Just wanting to do something is not enough. For the best chance of success, you need to be clear about what you want and why it is important to you, and you have to consciously resolve to achieve it. In other words, don't just read this book and jump right into Daily Juice. First take the time to think about your reasons for doing so, and write them down. Be specific. And, most important, know in advance that your odds of success won't be good unless you stick to your intention and follow the steps we lay out in this chapter.

Commit to the Process

To make your Daily Juice habit stick, you need to commit to the entire process—including all the setbacks you may encounter and the time you need to put into it—and not just to the end goal. A study published in *Personality and Social Psychology Bulletin* in 1999, for instance, found that students who visualized themselves studying and gaining the required skills and knowledge to do well in an exam (that is, committing to the studying process with a positive eye on the ultimate goal) did significantly better on the exam than those who only visualized doing well. Other studies have come to the similar conclusion that a commitment based on the *process*, with an eye on the ultimate goal, leads to the best chance of success.

Juice Guru Philosophy: *The Stronger the Commitment, the Better the Result*

Good intention is only the beginning. If you are like most people, you've probably intended to get healthy or lose weight by following many diets, exercise programs or healthier eating plans throughout your life. And, like most people, you've probably failed to stick to just as many. What went wrong? Why do we begin a program with the best intentions, only to gradually slide back into our old habits?

Part of the answer is as basic as how we start the process. A strong commitment, more than good intentions, will carry you through those mornings when you feel too tired to clean the juicer or your schedule is too busy to allow time to make juice. Whereas intention is defined as a determination to do something, *commitment* is a state of feeling obligated or emotionally impelled to do it.

Commitment, however, is a tricky thing. You need to commit in the right way. Our nine-year-old son, Eli, provides an excellent example of committing the wrong way. Eli has a knack for wanting to be the best at anything his friends happen to be interested in, so that he can stand out and be considered cool. This past year he expressed intentions to be outstanding at the drums, art and the Pokemon card-trading game. But, despite his apparently high level of motivation (the need for social acceptance and validation), he failed to achieve his dreams of domination with any one of these objectives. Instead he tended to coast once he'd achieved a certain level of success, or he gave up altogether once he realized the amount of work needed to really excel.

In sum, Eli lost interest in those activities as soon as he hit a substantial obstacle. Where did he go wrong? As a nine-year-old, he visualized only the glory—the admiration that comes with being an accomplished drummer or artist or the kid with the best set of Pokemon cards in school. It's important to visualize success, because that's what keeps you going. But Eli failed to consider the difficulties he might encounter along the road to greatness before he encountered them: the necessary hours of practice or the fact that he might have to give his time and attention to something other than hanging out with his friends. As a result, he was unprepared to handle difficulties as they arose and he failed in his ultimate goal of mastery.

Most of us are just like nine-year-olds when it comes to getting excited about engaging in things and then falling flat. We need to keep in mind the importance of visualizing the road to reaching our goal. After all, anything worth having or doing requires some effort, and inevitably there will be bumps along the road. If you visualize only the endpoint of success, you are likely to be completely unprepared when you hit the inevitable obstacles. And research shows that people who think like that are the least likely to succeed in the long run.

That's why we suggest that you use a two-step process for forming your commitment to Daily Juice that has been shown to be more effective. First, feel free to visualize how incredible it will be once you have established the habit—and be specific. Imagine flooding your body with nutrition first thing every morning; imagine your energy skyrocketing and your waistline shrinking; imagine glowing from the inside out. Reread Chapter 2 of this book if you need to. Or just go to your kitchen, make a 24-ounce (750 mL) green juice, drink it up, and imagine feeling that way every day. Write down how you feel, and refer to it whenever your willpower begins to wane. But don't stop there …

Journaling

As part of your strategy for overcoming roadblocks, it might be helpful to keep some kind of journal that tracks your positive results (you will undoubtedly have many). Having this document on hand allows you to flip through it when you need extra motivation. (For more on keeping a journal, see page 73).

Visualize the Process

Research shows that success takes more than visualizing your goal. You also need to be able to visualize the road you take to get there.

Success Is in the Details

Visualizing the benefits of Daily Juice is just the first step. The next step is to write down every obstacle you think you might face along the way. These will be specific to your own life, but chances are you will face some dilemmas that are common to almost everyone. For instance, you may be tempted to have coffee first thing one morning because you're sleepy. Or you might feel like skipping Daily Juice altogether because your schedule is too hectic. Or perhaps you're feeling dissatisfied— you're getting bored with the taste of your juice or your positive results are slowing down or you'd simply rather do something else. It may seem odd to think of obstacles before you even begin, but it is much better to be prepared in advance than to try to deal with these hiccups when they occur.

Develop a Strategy

Now that you've listed possible roadblocks, come up with a strategy for handling each one. Write your strategies in positive terms: "If an obstacle occurs, then I will…" In a 2009 study published in *Psychology and Health*, for instance, researchers found that participants who went through the process of writing out an "if… then" implementation plan were able to significantly increase their consumption of fruits and vegetables, as compared to participants who formulated only a general plan to reach this goal.

For example, if you know that you might feel unmotivated some mornings because you are too tired, your strategy should be: "If I feel tired, then I will remind myself that I get a natural energy boost from juice that lasts well into my workday." Be specific, so your strategies will be more easily implemented in practice, but not so specific that you don't allow yourself flexibility. Flexibility can take the form of alternative "then" statements (for variety and practicality) or an "if" statement that is broad enough to allow for several related roadblocks. For example, it's better to say broadly, "If I feel tired one morning…" than limit yourself with "If I've been out too late at a party…"

Step 2: Reprogram Your Brain for Change

Now that you've done a good job of making up your mind to commit to Daily Juice, you'll have to change your mind in order to succeed. Of course, we don't mean that you'll need a

Reaffirming Statements

The statements that constitute your strategy for addressing roadblocks should include anything that will motivate or sway you. They can consist of statements such as "If I encounter such-and-such a roadblock, then I will look in the mirror and remind myself how great I look," or "then I will get on the scale and see how much weight I have lost since I began," or "then I will reread the section of this book documenting the benefits of Daily Juice and remember that I haven't had to see my doctor in months."

Alternatively, your "then" statements could include specific actions to overcome a roadblock. For example, "If I'm dissatisfied with the taste of my juices, then I will review the recipes in this book and try a new juice with completely different ingredients and flavor profile." Or "If I feel I'm pressed for time, then I will try one of the 'Quick and Easy' recipes that use only one or two ingredients, or I will grab a juice at a local juice bar." There are so many "then" options to choose from, you should tailor each one so it will work for you.

different intention. Rather, you'll have to train your *subconscious* mind to desire Daily Juice.

The subconscious is the part of the mind that is inaccessible to the conscious mind but which affects behavior and emotions. Research shows that habit formation is much less about conscious thought than it is about what goes on in your subconscious mind. This means that to create a habit that will stick with you for life, you need to fiddle around in your subconscious to make it consistently act in synch with your conscious intentions. Among other things, you will need to change your subconscious level of commitment to the idea of Daily Juice, as well as the cues in your environment that make you prefer one action over another.

Say It Loud, Say it Clear: "I Am a Daily Juicer!"

Deep within all of us is a strong innate desire to be and to remain consistent with our choices. The stronger your commitment and the more public you are about it, the stronger your subconscious desire to stay with it will be. For example, have you ever been asked to watch a random person's things at the beach or to hold a stranger's place in line? If so, then you're familiar with the feeling of responsibility that follows from that commitment.

Consider this experiment conducted by researcher Thomas Moriarty, which took place on a New York City beach in the 1970s. A series of fake thefts (20 in total) were staged to see how people would react. In each staged theft, an actor left his blanket and possessions, including a radio, in front of an unsuspecting onlooker. Another actor subsequently grabbed the radio and ran away. Of the 20 random onlookers (one for each of the staged thefts), only four challenged the thief in any way, even verbally. This scenario was repeated another 20 times, but with a difference. This time the actor who "owned" the blanket and radio asked the test subjects to "watch his stuff" before he left, and each of the subjects agreed. An incredible 19 of them tried to stop the thief from stealing the radio, some physically.

Why do we have this subconscious need to stick with a decision once we've committed to it publicly? The simple answer is that consistency is associated with integrity and honesty, whereas inconsistency is associated with dishonesty. In the context of creating a Daily Juice habit, you can use your vigilant subconscious to your advantage by telling the world about your commitment.

Even stronger than declaring your commitment verbally or by typing words is to declare your intention in your own handwriting. In 1955 the prominent social psychologists Morton Deutsch and Harold Gerard conducted an experiment on social influence, in part to gauge the level of commitment to a decision resulting from how the commitment was made. As part of the experiment, college students were asked to record in one of three ways their estimate of the length of a line they were shown. One group was told to commit to the answer solely in their heads, a second group was instructed to write their answer on a Magic Pad and then promptly erase it, and a third group was instructed to write their answer on a piece of paper, sign it and hand it in to the tester.

The individuals in each of the three groups were then given new information suggesting that their original estimates were wrong. Each subject was then given a chance to change his or her answer. Not surprisingly, those who had written their original answer on paper, signed it and handed it in were the most loyal to that answer, even though it was obviously wrong. And those who had never written down their answer or shared it with anyone were the least committed. This study shows the fierceness with which our subconscious minds will stick to any decision we make—even a bad one—once we've written it down and taken public ownership of it.

So an important first step is to write—not type, text or email—the words "I am a Daily Juicer!" on a piece of paper. Of course, you don't need to write down these exact words; anything that in your own mind signals a solid commitment to juicing will do. In fact, the more directly the words come from your own heart and mind, the better. Studies show that the very greatest level of commitment comes from a place of acceptance of inner responsibility, rather than from outside pressures and influences. Sign your note and hang it in a visible place in your kitchen, such as on your refrigerator. Every time you juice—or reach for something other than your juicer first thing in the morning—

you will be reminded of your commitment to Daily Juice. And that's a pretty strong influence on your subconscious mind.

For good measure, you might consider sharing your handwritten declaration publicly. Take a picture of it (a selfie of sorts) and text or email it to your mom or best friend. You could also consider using the picture as the cover photo on your Facebook wall. It would certainly be harder to fall off the wagon with that level of promotion.

Finally, research shows that people are more likely to stick to a commitment if they've already put some time or money into it. So we suggest investing now in the juicer and the supplies you'll need. This should lock in your subconscious and make it that much harder for you to give up.

Pattern Interrupt:
Location, Location, Location

Habits are largely contextual in nature. And just like psychologist Ivan Pavlov's famous dogs, who learned to salivate at the sound of the dinner bell, we too create subconscious associations between our environment and our behaviors. Where you are and who you're with at any given time of the day or year will influence your actions. As we've mentioned previously, you may go through thousands of behaviors in your day that you aren't even aware are habits. And most of these are prompted largely by cues in your environment.

Think about your evening routine. Do you wind down by watching television? Do you wash up and brush your teeth? These actions, as mentioned earlier, are largely habitual. And because they are a matter of habit, you don't give them much thought. For instance, if you routinely watch television after you put the kids to bed, you may find yourself on the coach on any given night, remote in hand, without any clear, conscious memory of how you got there. This is because the same environmental cues—approximate time, location of the rooms in your house, location of the couch, the

people with whom you live, location of your remote, and so on—
are pretty much consistent night after night. Your actions have
become habits through countless repetition in a similar context.

Now imagine that today you have moved to a new house.
Everything is different. Your living room is set up differently;
the couch, chairs and television are all in different places
and the room itself is in a completely different part of the
house. Your bathroom too is in a different location, as is every
item in it, from your toothbrush to the towels to the shower.
Whereas in your old house you performed your evening routine
automatically, for the first time in a while you now have to
consider what to do with yourself and in what order. Many
of the environmental cues of your old house are gone or have
drastically changed.

Changes such as these afford you the opportunity to break
old habits and create new ones. We're not suggesting that you
sell your house in order to make a habit of Daily Juicing! But
you can create an interruption in your behavioral patterns that
will make it easier for you to lay the subconscious groundwork
for a new juicing habit.

For example, the Daily Juice protocol calls for a 24-ounce
(750 mL) fresh juice first thing in the morning on an empty
stomach. So ask yourself: what is the first thing you eat or drink
in the morning? If it's a cup of coffee, your kitchen environment
and the cues it offers likely lend themselves perfectly to this
habit. Your coffeemaker probably sits on the counter and is
easily accessible, as are all the accessories such as filters and
your choice of milk and/or sweetener.

If you moved to a new house or rebuilt your kitchen,
everything would change. Suddenly, making a cup of coffee
would become challenging because you would need to think
about where to find the necessary implements and ingredients.
This is the effect we want to tap into as you begin to set up
your life for juicing success. If the first thing you make in the
morning is coffee, then interrupt that pattern by making your
coffee tools more difficult to locate and your juicer and related
implements readily accessible. You will be working toward
creating a strong unconscious association between waking up
and drinking juice before you do anything else in the morning.

Capitalize on Your Existing Habits

Once you've made up your mind and your kitchen to encourage
your new habit, you'll need to insert Daily Juice into your
morning routine. To make this easy, you can "attach" juicing to
your existing chain of morning habits. After all, why create your
new habit from scratch when you can hitch a ride on something
that already works for you?

As we've mentioned, you've already got a morning routine—established habits that you regularly perform, more or less in the same order, every morning. These habits are deeply engrained in your subconscious mind, because they constitute your routine before leaving the house. After all, you certainly wouldn't leave the house without brushing your teeth, would you? To associate Daily Juice with these already established habits, all you'll need is a little thought, a sticky note and a pen.

First, take a moment to identify the routine task you complete just before you hit the kitchen every morning. Is it brushing your teeth? Getting dressed? Then write on the sticky note: "Make my Daily Juice," and stick it on the bathroom mirror or your closet door, wherever that final pre-kitchen task takes place. This is a cue to add Daily Juice as the next habit in your chain. (We've used this trick to start a variety of new habits, from Daily Juice to turning off the porch light every morning.) This seemingly simple step will have a profound impact on training your subconscious mind.

Step 3: Ready, Set … Habit!

If you know you're a person who can handle new tasks and habits immediately, without needing to ease in, then skip this section. Otherwise, we suggest beginning with two "baby steps" that we've designed specially to ease you into a juicing habit that will last a lifetime.

Take Baby Steps

Baby Step #1: Before you dive into your Daily Juice habit, allow a week in which to take this smaller step: eat a piece of fruit such as an apple first thing every morning, and then wait 20 minutes before eating or drinking anything else. This small addition to your routine will create a mental placeholder in your subconscious mind. By consuming fruit at the same time as you would be having juice, you accustom your mind to beginning the day with a nutritious whole food. And because you should allow fruit 20 minutes to digest before eating anything else (to avoid fermentation in your stomach), you are preparing your mind to follow the Daily Juice protocol—by waiting before enjoying your breakfast, nutritious midmorning snack or morning coffee. But, unlike juicing, there is no prep or cleanup work involved. This makes it a much easier habit to create.

This interim step can also ease you into rearranging your existing habits, such as drinking coffee or eating a big breakfast first thing every morning. If you move your coffeemaker and supplies as part of this first step, that prior habit will be on its way out before you even start to juice. If you are new to juicing,

Meet Us Where You Are

Have you already juiced at least once a week? Are you the type of person who, based on past experience and excellent willpower, will be able to jump right into a juicing habit? Then feel free to skip our baby steps and proceed to Step 4, on page 70.

you can even establish this daily fruit placeholder habit while you are waiting for your juicer to arrive. In this way, you will use the time to your advantage to lay crucial groundwork.

Baby Step #2: After a week or so of eating fruit first thing in the morning, ease into your Daily Juice habit with a week of basic juices. These juices contain only one or two ingredients (see pages 200 to 211), which allows you to ease into juicing with relatively little prep and cleanup time. This will help with transitioning to more complex juices.

Juice Guru Philosophy: *Baby Steps Are Easy*

One major reason why diets and health reboots generally fail is that for most people it is impossible to make huge, disruptive changes to their routine in one big sweep. Starting small and building up quickly can be a good way to begin a habit. As noted, it takes 66 days on average to create a habit; however, making small amendments to your already existing habits can take substantially less time. Research shows that additions such as enjoying a piece of fruit with your lunch or drinking a glass of water every morning are more easily instilled habits.

Step 4: Juice Guru's Secret Potions

The final step to becoming successful at Daily Juicing is getting familiar with how your juicer works and the manner in which to prepare your ingredients. The best way to do this is through repetition. To make juicing second nature, it helps to be consistent in the juices you prepare when you're first starting out.

Think about it this way: switching from a pineapple, grape and ginger juice on Monday to a cucumber, celery, kale and lemon juice on Tuesday, to an apple-pear juice on Wednesday even sounds exhausting. These juices require entirely different ingredients, shopping lists, preparation, juicing times and cleanup. So, not surprisingly, it's probably your quickest route to failure if you're a newbie.

Being consistent in the ingredients you use in your recipes—at least at first—will allow you to practice the basic preparation techniques needed for most juice combinations. It will also help you to get to know your juicer: how much juice it yields, whether it works better when you rotate ingredients in a certain way (for example, harder vegetables followed by softer vegetables and leafy greens), and how you need to prepare your ingredients (some juicers require fibrous produce such as kale or celery be cut into smaller pieces to avoid clogging). Consistency will also ensure that you have all the ingredients you need on hand, saving you emergency trips to purchase additional produce.

The Juice Guru Template Recipes

Consistency explains why we created two unique recipes to help our clients ease into the juicing habit. We call these the Juice Guru Classic Template Recipes (see pages 108 and 109). One template recipe has an apple base and thus serves as your basic cleansing juice (fruits have a detoxifying effect on the human body). The other has a cucumber-celery base and can serve as your core juice for building a healthy body.

These template recipes were designed to accomplish several things at once. They contain a diverse range of healthy ingredients and thus can serve as your go-to juices for a daily dose of nutrients and energy. They are also designed to help you easily incorporate Daily Juicing into your lifestyle. By shopping for the three to five core recipe ingredients weekly or a couple of times a week, you can ensure that you will always have what you need in your fridge, ready to juice. These main ingredients are also generally available year-round in any local supermarket and don't depend on seasonality.

Using these templates will also ultimately help to make your prep work seem like second nature. Most of the ingredients— apples, cucumbers, lemons, greens and ginger—are basic to a wide variety of juices. By sticking to these at first, you'll become comfortable with how to prepare and juice them in no time.

Finally, the Juice Guru Classic Template Recipes are designed to taste great too. But if you get bored, the templates give you the flexibility to change up your flavor combinations so you won't get tired of the same old, same old. They indicate the quantities you'll need to easily swap ingredients—with cilantro or jalapeños, for example—or to simply add ingredients to the core recipe. Simply throw in an heirloom tomato or a red pepper (as indicated in the template recipe) and the flavor of your juice will be transformed. Thus the template recipes grow with you as you master the art of juicing. Just keep in mind that once you've succeeded in establishing your new Daily Juice habit, you will want to mix up your juice combinations. Variety in your nutritious fruits and vegetables is the key to a lifetime of good health.

Never Get Bored

Some people fall into the trap of making the same juice all the time. Just as we have created a habit around Daily Juicing, our brain attempts to form a habit of creating the same concoction every day. Not only do you risk getting bored, your body needs variety in the vegetables and fruits you consume. Make an effort to change up your template recipes, using the variations we suggest.

Juice Guru Philosophy: *Template Recipes Make Daily Juice a Snap*

The Juice Guru template recipes (pages 108 and 109)

- taste great
- make shopping for ingredients easier
- help avoid wasting produce
- offer options for flexibility and taste

- contain a diverse range of ingredients for health and energy
- train you in basic prep work, helping it to become second nature

Chapter 5
Staying on Track

Establishing a Daily Juice habit is the first step toward getting healthier and more vibrant and energetic—and staying that way for life. But it's a well-known fact that when establishing any habit, a number of factors can either pave your way to success or derail your efforts completely. Because we want you to achieve the incredible benefits of Daily Juice, we've dedicated this chapter to managing the factors in your life that will have the greatest impact on your ultimate success.

The number-one reason why you'll keep juicing is that it makes you feel good and you won't feel that you're missing out on something else. To understand this better, take a moment to think about past diets or health programs you may have followed. Most will have been based on the idea of restriction: cutting calories overall or omitting entire categories of food. Or, in the case of a juice cleanse, maybe *everything* you normally eat or drink was disallowed. Likely, research suggests, the awareness of those restrictions made you crave the forbidden foods even more. This in turn probably led to dissatisfaction with your diet and ultimately contributed to its failure. Cravings for particular foods become much more powerful when those foods are restricted or prohibited altogether.

That's where the Daily Juice protocol has an advantage over other juicing and healthy diet plans in terms of its potential to be habit forming. Being a Daily Juicer does not require you to give up anything you otherwise eat, drink or enjoy in your life. You will likely *choose* to give up unhealthy foods and habits, once you experience the benefits of Daily Juice and begin to crave the taste of fruits and vegetables. But the crucial point is that you aren't necessarily required to. And that fine distinction makes a big difference to your subconscious mind.

Nevertheless, it is much better to plan for potential roadblocks than to struggle with them in mid-effort. In this chapter we discuss common impediments you may encounter to making Daily Juice a regular habit. Together, let's make them opportunities for success rather than obstacles that may cause failure.

Overcoming Dissatisfaction

For one reason or another, at some point you may become dissatisfied with your new juicing habit. Possibly you will no longer be noticing significant improvements in your sense of well-being, or maybe your weight loss will reach a plateau. The fact is, the largest gains in habit formation are made at the beginning. Remember the study (see page 61) that found the average habit takes 66 days to form? In that study, researchers noted that participants made greater strides toward habit formation in the beginning days and weeks and then leveled out over time.

This makes sense. Your intention to create a habit is the strongest at the beginning. And in the case of a healthy or slimming habit, that is when the pounds seem to melt off and you feel a surge of healthy energy from the abundance of nutrition your body has likely never enjoyed before. But as time goes by, you inevitably get used to feeling good; you may not notice it as much anymore. And weight loss is never consistent from week to week, or even month to month, on any diet or health program.

Keep a Daily Juice Journal

A Daily Juice progress journal is one technique for ensuring that you don't become discouraged. It can help you turn frustration into motivation. We suggest beginning this journal before you start your Daily Juice program. Everyone has their own reason for starting a new habit such as Daily Juice. Perhaps you want to increase your focus and performance at work or gain more energy to fit everything into your busy schedule. Or maybe you want to feel healthier as you age, rather than depend on prescriptions and medical intervention.

Regardless of your motivation, the fact is, you likely aren't feeling good about where you are now. Documenting that state helps to create a starting point with which you can compare your progress at a later date. For example, if losing weight or achieving a more vibrant appearance is your goal, you can begin your progress journal with "before" pictures. If you're lacking energy, write down the things you want to accomplish during your day but simply can't because you're too tired. If it's better health you're after, visit your doctor and get a physical; write down your blood pressure and other less-than-optimal vital signs and statistics. Keeping a daily progress journal as you Daily Juice will help you see in black-and-white how much you have improved.

Keep Your Eye on the Prize

It is inevitable that you will feel you have reached a plateau at some point in your Daily Juice journey. Don't give up! Even though your body is maintaining its perfect weight and you have become accustomed to the extra energy boost every day, higher levels of health and wellness are within reach. A healthy body ages more slowly than one that is less healthy, and you will find that you not only live longer but live better. Be sure to stay on track to experience all that Daily Juice has to offer.

Documenting Your Progress

Here are some ideas for what to write in your Daily Juice journal. Don't dwell on weight loss, but definitely note it whenever you happen to step on the scale. Keep track of when you have bursts of energy or feel particularly good, and note how long those feelings last. Document how long you remain focused during your day, and how long it takes you to get tired. If you're able to accomplish more in your day, write that down too. If you receive compliments from others about your more youthful, healthful or radiant appearance (which you inevitably will), record them. And if you see a very positive reflection in the mirror one morning, be sure to capture that experience too. Write down anything that enables you to see how Daily Juice is changing your life for the better.

Juice Guru Philosophy: *Journaling as Motivation*

Jotting down daily improvements in a journal serves two purposes. First, it documents your progress, which in turn makes it seem more real. Daily successes will help to solidify your commitment as you progress. More important, however, journaling your achievements can serve as desperately needed motivation for those times when you aren't seeing much progress. Reviewing your journal, seeing how far you have come and recalling times when you felt great will make it much easier to stay on track if you feel you've lost your forward momentum.

The Blender Blast Technique

On days when you just don't have time to clean the juicer or pick up something at a juice bar, we recommend the "blender blast technique." Add the usual amount of produce to your blender, plus about ½ cup (125 mL) water. Blend, then press the pulp through a piece of cheesecloth for a quick and easy juice. This trick comes in handy when you are looking for a quick cleanup after all that Daily Juice has to offer.

Change It Up

Another culprit that creates dissatisfaction can be nothing more than boredom. Perhaps you're fed up with making juice every day, or maybe you've grown tired of the taste of your juice. If it's the process of making juice that has got you down, mix it up. Try playing your favorite music while juicing—that's what we do. Make a game out of trying to beat your best time for cleaning your juicer or for making a juice from start to finish. And if all else fails, you can give yourself a break from time to time and buy a freshly made juice at your local juice bar. After one or two juices that haven't come straight out of your own juicer, you'll be itching to get back to your habit. Trust us—there is a difference.

Tired of the Same Old, Same Old?

You should never get tired of the taste of your juice. If that happens, you're doing something wrong. When the average person first thinks about juicing, he or she imagines a drink that tastes like grass or has an otherwise "earthy" flavor. Yes, juices can taste like that, but you can easily access an endless variety of flavors. Juices can taste sweet—a Lemon Drop (page 136) tastes just like an old-fashioned hard candy. Or they can be savory and satisfying like a chilled soup; for example, try a Holy Basil Supreme (page 170), which combines a green apple base with cilantro, holy basil extract and tomato. Juices can even be spicy if you add a bit of chile pepper or sprinkle in a pinch of cayenne. The point is, whatever flavor you crave, you can create in your juice. So if you begin to feel bored with your juices, the easy answer is to make something different.

Juicing with Your Partner

It won't be surprising to learn that your partner, other close family members and friends can affect your actions. They certainly have an enormous influence on your food choices. Couples often have routines and joint habits that revolve around where and what they eat and drink. And while it isn't as essential to have the support of your partner when juicing just once a day—as it would be if you completely changed your diet—it can be very beneficial for creating a Daily Juice habit.

If you live with someone, your level of commitment to and satisfaction with Daily Juicing will be much greater if you get that person involved. Sharing your Daily Juice with the person you love will create a bonding experience that will ingrain your new habit that much more deeply in your subconscious. And if you juice with a partner, you can share the job, cutting your preparation and cleanup time in half—a big plus!

If at first your partner is reluctant to join you, that's normal. Julie took a relatively long time to come around to juicing with Steve. We suggest that you create juices that appeal to your individual tastes. Suggest juices based on the fruits and veggies your partner likes and sweet, savory or spicy flavors as preferred. Start by making the juices for your loved ones so they get "hooked" without having to do the work. Soon enough, you should have all the help you need in the kitchen.

Wooing the Reluctant Juicer

If you are trying to persuade a reluctant partner to join you in Daily Juicing, we recommend staying away from green juices in the beginning. The color green plays into the stereotype of "earthy" or "grassy-tasting" juices, and the look might turn off your partner. Vibrant reds, purples, oranges and other bright colors are more attractive to the new juicer. Second, if your partner has a particular condition or ailment such as high blood pressure or cholesterol, create medicinal juices to address that problem. For example, we have made juices that feature ginger, leafy greens or beets for friends and family members who suffer from arthritis or other inflammatory illnesses.

Friends and close family members who don't live with you can also exert serious sway over your habits. The more that people around you participate in juicing, the more likely you are to enjoy it and stick with it. So we suggest you use that influence to your advantage and make juice the "it" thing in your relationships and at gatherings. The time has never been better for this concept. Juice bars dot the landscape in most metropolitan areas, and you can get fresh juices in just about any health food store as well.

Meet your friends for a juice instead of coffee on a weekend morning or after work. Make it social and you're likely to get them hooked along with you. Or invite your best friend over for a "juice cocktail." Every time you make juice, you create an opportunity to turn on someone else to the amazing taste and benefits of juicing. Just a small gesture of sharing might be enough to set someone off on their own journey to health and vitality. (We've even used this idea to get our extremely traditional parents into juicing with us.)

And don't just limit this idea to one-on-one bonding experiences. Any social get-together that might involve drinking of any sort can just as easily be done over a large glass of juice. In this way you can be socially active while staying firmly on the track to better health. Invite your friends over and, instead of a glass of wine, serve an Apple Strawberry Fields (page 138) or a Blueberry Hill (page 139). Both of these colorful juices look beautiful served in champagne flutes, and you can even add a little sparkling water for effect.

One final idea is to invite your friends over before going out for a night of social drinking. The right juice can help ward off a hangover the next day and thus impressively demonstrate the power of fresh juice. We recommend Watermelon Mint (page 131) or Cantaloupe Straight Up (page 200). These incredible fruit juices are great to make before you go to bed—or before you even start drinking—to help you feel healthy, headache-free and well-rested the next day. Full of antioxidants and phytonutrients, they help to flush alcoholic toxins out of your system and are full of hydrating water.

Juicing with Children

Kids can be a handful, and running around after them can get in the way of healthy habits. Think of the diets you may have given up on because you just didn't have time to prepare different meals for you and your children. And juice fasting is virtually impossible to do with kids. But while your kids can't join you on a fast, they can certainly join you for Daily Juice. In fact, Daily Juice is just what the doctor ordered for little ones.

Providing your kids with the right nutrition can make a huge difference in their focus and, ultimately, their academic achievement. Studies show that increasing your kids' nutritional intake can influence their cognitive ability and intelligence levels for the better. It can actually result in their being on task more often and help increase their math and reading test scores. And because well-nourished kids are healthier, they are likely to have fewer absences from school.

Now that you know how important good nutrition is for your kids' performance in school, ask yourself when was the last time your children had a full serving of leafy greens. If your children are like most school-age kids, the answer might range from "never" to "sometime last month." You can pack a full day's supply of vitamins and minerals into a single Daily Juice and then let your children move on to the business of being a kid. It's best if they have a juice first thing in the morning, in accordance with the Daily Juice protocol. But no matter when they have it, a fresh juice will give them the edge they need to be successful in every way.

Getting Kids Involved

Kids being kids, you may first need to do some work to entice them on board. After all, you wouldn't serve your children Brussels sprouts in place of french fries out of the blue and expect them to love it. First you need to get them excited about juicing. If they're young, get your kids a stepstool and let them feed the fruits and vegetables through the juicer.

Of course, for kid-friendly juicing you have to be careful about what type of juicer you are using. We recommend vertical slow juicers for little ones, with strict rules about keeping hands out of the produce chute. If the children are older, you can have them prep the produce or even get them their own manual juicer. There are wheatgrass juicers on the market that clamp onto any table, perfect for a child's height. While these are better suited to wheatgrass and don't yield as efficiently as your top-of-the-line electric juicer, they certainly do the job.

Kids love being the "chefs" of their own juice. Talk to your children about the edge they'll get from Daily Juice, in school and in life. And don't forget that kids do what you do, not what you say. By modeling Daily Juicing yourself, you will do more for your kids than you could with a 10-hour lecture.

And, of course, make sure to tailor your juices to your children's individual tastes. Start them off slowly with Real Fruit Punch (page 187) or another sweet fruit juice. If your child isn't automatically repelled by the color green, serve a Mighty Mighty Apple Juice (page 186), which includes a nice dose of spinach— you can start with mostly apple and slowly add more greens over time. The taste of the spinach gets lost in the strong apple flavor, and kids love the taste just as much as they would a cup of pure apple juice.

Juicing on a Budget

At the top of the list of reasons people have for stopping or never even beginning a Daily Juice habit is that it's just "too expensive." And that may be true—you could buy a $2,400 juicer and use only exotic produce that costs a fortune, or you could buy all your juices from a stylish juice bar. Either way it's not likely that you

Just for the Sport of It

If you have children in middle school or high school, try educating them about the competitive edge that juicing will bring to their academic and athletic performance (see Tyler's Story, page 18). Fresh juices are the perfect choice before a hard day at school. A juice before sports practice or the big game can provide the energy and focus to take their play to the next level. Your kids' classmates and teammates will definitely want to know their secret.

Juice Guru Philosophy: *Enlist Their Peer Group*

You certainly don't need a study to tell you that your kids are heavily influenced in their decisions by their peers. So, if necessary, use your children's friends to influence them on their juicing journey. We speak from experience. We had reached a point where our son was not as interested in drinking juice as he once had been. Perhaps the cachet had worn off or maybe he had become bored. But we thought it more likely that he wasn't hearing his friends talking about how they loved juices, because they obviously weren't drinking them at home. In other words, juicing wasn't popular among his friends—it was missing the cool factor. So to turn this obstacle into an opportunity, we decided to prepare Watermelon Straight Up (page 200) and serve it to our son and his best friend during a playdate at our house. As we expected, the friend loved his juice. In fact, he loved it so much that, ever since then, he has asked for it whenever he is over at our house, as if it is a special treat.

We were thrilled with the result, so we took the concept a step further. One day we prepared a large batch of the same juice and took it to school at pickup time. All the kids were excited about trying it. A couple of children mentioned that they had tried juices before—thus making themselves appear cool and in the know—and we noticed that one child, notorious for his appetite for junk food, asked for seconds. The effect on our son was immediate. His desire for fresh juice returned, and it was obvious that this was a direct result of its newfound "coolness factor."

would end up making a sustainable lifetime change. But these clearly aren't your only options when it comes to juicing. Daily Juice can be made in an extremely cost-effective way, from juicer choice (see page 86) to ingredients.

Cost-Effective Produce

Ingredients can be pricy if you aren't careful. This is one reason why we developed the Juice Guru Daily Classic Template Recipes (see pages 108 and 109). When you first start juicing, we recommend that you don't jump right into preparing wildly different juices every day. That can lead to a lot of wasted produce. For example, a recipe could call for only a few carrots out of a bunch or half a cucumber or five strawberries. If you move on to a grape, pineapple and ginger juice the next day and then an apple, lemon and cinnamon juice the day after that, the leftover produce will end up in your compost. Sticking to one of the template recipes, but mixing it up to vary the nutritional content and keep you interested, will help avoid wasting money.

You can also make your juices more economical by limiting them to just a few ingredients. We've devoted all of Chapter 13 to quick and easy, budget-friendly recipes that serve this purpose. While these recipes don't have the same diversity of nutrients as more complex green juices, take heart. The "father of juicing," Jay Kordich, cured himself of a life-threatening tumor in his twenties by drinking nothing but a juice similar to our Apple Plus (page 201), and at the time of publication, Jay is now in his early nineties! If your budget is constrained, we recommend taking a trip to your local warehouse store and purchasing organic apples and carrots in bulk.

Juicing on the Go

Another major Daily Juice habit-killer is situations that cause you to be away from home—and from your juicer and refrigerator. This applies whether you work long hours, need to travel for work, or are lucky enough to enjoy lengthy vacations every year. Juicers are heavy and not easy to transport. The number-one question we get along these lines is "How can I continue with my habit if I can't be near my juicer?" We have four ideas to help if you just can't make your juice at home.

1. Purchase fresh juices when you can't be in your kitchen to make them yourself. Juicing has become so popular that most upscale hotels and many health food stores and some health-conscious restaurants have commercial juicers to make and sell fresh juice.

2. Purchase a low-cost manual wheatgrass juicer, which can easily be taken to work or on vacation (and it doesn't make disruptive noises like an electric juicer). Such juicers are not recommended as a replacement for your regular juicer, but they are portable and can be packed in a suitcase for long trips away from home. You can purchase produce for juicing in any local supermarket.

3. Buy a small single-cup blender and make smoothies on the days when you can't make a juice. Like manual juicers, these small blenders are light and can be packed in your suitcase for a work or pleasure trip. (If you prefer juice to smoothies even while away, you can strain your smoothie through a nut bag to create a Daily Juice.)

4. Travel with a bottle of high-quality organic green supplement powder. As discussed earlier (see page 55), we don't recommend supplements as a replacement for Daily Juice. But a supplement made only of whole, organic plant foods and dehydrated at low temperatures is a great adjunct to Daily Juice, and it can stand in for Daily Juice when you're on the go. Try mixing it into freshly squeezed orange juice, if you can get some locally, or just add it to water as indicated on the bottle.

It's All Relative

If you feel that Daily Juicing is too expensive, then consider the following. According to WebMD, in their lifetimes, the average American woman and man spend $58,874 and $43,794 respectively on medications. Total yearly sales for nutritional supplements top hundreds of billions of dollars. And overall, the average American spends more than $8,000 every year on health care. The truth is, you can't put a price tag on aging naturally with health and grace and preventing disease before it starts.

Juice Guru Philosophy: *Take Juicing on the Road*

Habits are created and maintained as a result of repetition. Don't let your absence from home set you back in cultivating your healthy Daily Juice habit.

Chapter 6
The Daily Juicer's Toolkit for Success

Understanding the ins and outs of juicing can be like learning a new language. For starters, if you are new to juicing, you'll soon find out that there are many types of juicers from which to choose. It can be hard to know where to begin.

In this chapter we'll translate juicing into a language you'll understand and lay out in one convenient place the pros and cons, as well as the dos and don'ts, of juicers and juicing accessories. In other words, we will give you the necessary nuts and bolts you'll need to put the Daily Juice program into motion.

Setting Up Your Kitchen Space

To ensure success with Daily Juicing, your kitchen space must be properly set up, as well as a pleasant place to work in. It may take a bit of planning to set up the perfect environment, but—trust us—it's worth it. A clean, organized kitchen is essential. And we recommend taking the time to ensure that it is in excellent working order. This means keeping all countertops as clean and clear as possible and sweeping the floor whenever necessary. But, more important, before you begin Daily Juicing, take the time to rid your refrigerator of outdated and poor-choice foods. Throw them in the trash (where they belong). You'll need the room for organic vegetables and fruits so you can always be ready to whip up a freshly made juice.

Clear your countertop of appliances that are using up space but not serving your nutritional needs. This includes microwave ovens, soda makers and deep fryers. Make way for your juicer, blender and any other juicing accessories you'll use every day. These health-nurturing tools should occupy prominent spots as a reminder to use them. After all, they will be playing the lead role in ushering you toward a healthy lifestyle.

You should also bring life into your kitchen by including plants or flowers. A kitchen herb garden is probably the most beneficial living element you can add. You can grow your own herbs in virtually any kitchen, all year round. Fresh herbs are loaded with nutrients and they will add flavor to your daily juice. Cilantro, basil and parsley are some of our favorites. For starters, they work well in the Juice Guru Template Recipes (pages 108 and 109).

Essential Juicing Accessories

Once you've created the appropriate kitchen space for juicing, you'll need to fill it with the right accessories. These include

- a large stainless steel bowl
- a bottle of organic apple cider or distilled white vinegar
- a vegetable-scrubbing brush
- a high-quality salad spinner
- sharp knives (we recommend ceramic to avoid oxidation)
- an apple corer
- bacteria-free cutting boards
- a fine-mesh sieve (optional; see page 82)
- a 4-cup (1 L) measuring cup (optional; see page 82)
- 1-quart (1 L) glass mason jars (to hold your 24 to 32 oz/750 mL to 1 L juice)

Wash Produce Thoroughly

All produce should be washed well. When you're ready to juice, fill your bowl with water, $\frac{1}{4}$ cup (60 mL) apple cider or distilled white vinegar, and the juice of 1 lemon. Soaking will help remove the dirt and pesticide residues from your produce. And fresh lemon juice and apple cider and distilled white vinegar all have natural antibacterial and antifungal properties that help remove bacteria from your produce without altering its taste. No need for those expensive spray-on vegetable cleaners.

Place your produce in the water-filled bowl and let it rest for 2 to 3 minutes. Use a vegetable-scrubbing brush to remove any remaining stubborn dirt and grime. Transfer everything except leafy greens to a colander and rinse under gently running water. (See "Greens Are Special" on page 83 for how to handle leafy greens.) Allow the produce to drain and dry while you set up your juicer.

Keep It Handy

We recommend purchasing a large stainless steel bowl for washing produce. Keep it close to your sink and ready to go.

Wash Organic Produce Too

We recommend using only organic produce (see pages 92 to 95). Organic fruits and vegetables have less than one-quarter of the chemical and pesticide residues found on conventionally grown produce. But, according to the US Department of Agriculture (USDA), cross-contamination from conventional agriculture results in some transference. And harmful bacteria can also be a problem, regardless of whether pesticides were used in the growing process. So even if you're using organic produce, it is important to ensure that it is thoroughly washed.

Precut Dense Vegetables

Many juicers perform better if you slice up some of the harder and more fibrous vegetables such as celery, carrots and beets. For this task, a ceramic knife is an excellent choice. Ceramic knives are super-sharp, enabling your produce to be sliced without causing oxidation or further breakdown of essential nutrients. Cut your produce on bacteria-free cutting boards. Bamboo is a great choice—excellent for the environment and naturally antimicrobial. Make sure to scrub your cutting boards well with hot, soapy water after each use, to keep them bacteria-free.

Strain If Desired

The next step, of course, is juicing. Unless you are using a top-of-the-line juice press, even the best juicers will leave a fair amount of pulp in the final product. Some people don't mind the texture of pulpy juice, but we do. That's why we recommend straining your juice through a fine-mesh sieve into a 4-cup (1 L) measuring cup (for easy pouring). This step is optional, however, based on your textural preference. Pour your finished juice into a glass or mason jar and enjoy. We highly recommend using mason jars—putting your entire juice in one container with a lid enables you to take it with you on the go.

Juice Guru Philosophy: *We Like Using a Straw*

You may want to invest in reusable glass straws. Why? Like red wine and coffee, colorful fruits and vegetables may stain teeth if you aren't careful. Drinking your juice with a straw helps to keep your teeth clean, white and stain-free. Purchasing reusable glass straws is also good for the environment. And, unlike reusable plastic straws, no toxins will leach into your juice from a glass straw. (*Note:* Be sure to pick up some pipe-cleaners to keep your glass straws clean between uses.)

Recycle the Pulp

Once you have finished juicing, what do you do with all that pulp? In this book we've included some delicious pulp recipes developed by Chef Babette Davis, but another idea is to use the pulp to supplement your dog's food (this works best with the sweeter juices). About ¼ to ½ cup (60 to 125 mL) of pulp mixed into your dog's food will provide insoluble fiber to aid digestion (it will also include a smattering of leftover nutrients). Don't, however, use the pulp as a replacement for your pet's regular food, which is specifically formulated to provide everything your dog needs to thrive.

Pulp also makes excellent compost, which can be used to nourish your houseplants or garden. Some kitchen-friendly composters work very well, and plants love this naturally organic food. What a great way to create less waste!

Greens Are Special

Soaking your greens in a basin of water (preferably lukewarm) is particularly important, because it allows any soil and grit to fall off and sink to the bottom of the bowl. We also recommend using a good-quality salad spinner to get rid of the excess water. You can rinse the greens right in the salad spinner. Give it a good spin, drain and they are ready to go.

Apples Are Exceptional

Apples are a core ingredient of juicing (if you'll pardon the pun). They are brimming with a unique mix of polyphenols, most of which provide your body with excellent antioxidant benefits. Apples are also known to lower cholesterol and provide anti-asthma and anticancer benefits (particularly against lung cancer). Importantly, apples are a low-glycemic fruit, proven to help regulate blood-sugar levels, so you can use them to sweeten green juices for kids—and for anyone else with a sweet tooth.

Apples do, however, require a little extra care when prepping for juice. They are one of the few exceptions to the rule that you can juice your produce whole, from skin to stalk to seeds. Because apple seeds contain a small amount of arsenic, you don't want them in your juice. Therefore, for preparing apples we recommend investing in a dual apple corer and divider if you don't already have one. This is a low-cost item that is readily available in most housewares stores and online (for example, on Amazon). This is the fastest way to slice up your apples while making sure to remove the core along with the seeds.

Demystifying the Juicer

Daily Juice is easy if you choose the right juicer to meet your needs. But how can you know which one to choose? Because juicers can be complex, we've included some advice to help you buy the one that best fits your needs and your budget (see pages 86 to 90). The most important qualities you'll want to consider when selecting a juicer are the quality of the juice it produces, how much juice it yields, versatility in the type of fruits and veggies it can handle, and how easy it is to clean.

Juice Quality and Oxidation

Oxidation

Oxidation is what happens when you slice open an apple and it turns brown after a short time. Oxidation depletes nutrients.

When purchasing a juicer, one factor to consider is the effect it will have on the quality of your juice. Oxidation is a natural process that occurs when the juicing process breaks open the cell walls of your produce and exposes them to oxygen. Oxidation leads to the loss of valuable nutrients in your juice, so you want to minimize this process as much as possible. This is the reason why we recommend that you drink your juice right after it's made.

Choosing the right juicer can further reduce oxidation. Recall the Breville study (pages 53 to 54), which found that less oxidation occurred when using a juicer than when making smoothies in a blender. As a result, smoothies had less nutrients than juice. Some types of juicers create more oxidation (and nutrient loss) than others, because their blades spin considerably faster. Generally, less expensive machines create more oxidation, so you may have to balance price against more nutritious juice.

Does Too Much Heat Destroy Enzymes?

Less expensive juicers often have fast motors that essentially heat up your juice. High heat (above 118°F/48°C) can affect the quality of your juice by causing a breakdown in enzymes, the life force of your juice. This is the effect that also occurs as a result of pasteurization.

Some people believe that the faster juicers (such as centrifugal juicers) may also cause heat high enough to result in enzymatic breakdown. We have yet to see proof that this occurs. In fact, an informal study conducted by an online juicer distribution business suggests that no juicer heats the ingredients or the juice to a temperature that would destroy the enzymes. If you feel concerned about the heating of your juices and enzyme retention, however, we recommend that you choose a slow juicer.

Easy Cleaning

If you are juicing every day, you don't want to spend a lot of time cleaning the juicer. Depending on the complexity of your machine, a juicer can take as few as 5 minutes or as long as 20 minutes or more to clean. Unfortunately, the juicers that are the easiest to clean are often the ones that rank lower on the scale of juice quality and yield. The quickest cleanup, for instance, comes with a centrifugal ejection juicer, which has only four parts. A hydraulic press juicer, which yields the highest-quality juice, takes the longest time to clean.

High Yield

Some methods are more efficient than others at extracting juice from your produce—and this is important. In the long run, the more juice you can extract from a carrot, for instance, the fewer carrots you'll need to buy. Also, you will get more nutrients from your produce if the juicer leaves behind a dry, sawdust-like pulp than if the pulp is juicy and wet. With regard to yield, juicers come in a wide range of efficiencies, with hydraulic presses being the top producers.

Invest in a Good-Quality Juicer

We definitely recommend making an investment in a premium juicer that ranks high in all the important criteria, if that's within your means. You can easily discover whether a particular brand is a good-quality machine by checking its ratings. Over the long term, a good juicer is a sound investment and the key to a lifetime of good health. A high-quality juicer can last for years, and most come with a guarantee on the parts.

A high-yielding, high-quality juicer will save you money in the long run because it requires fewer fruits and vegetables to produce a similar quantity of juice. And cheaper juicers have to be replaced more often, which can end up costing you more over time. An added bonus is that if your juicer is easy to clean, it will make your job that much simpler and help you stick to your habit. It's definitely true that you get what you pay for, and this is absolutely true when it comes to buying a juicer.

If cost is an issue, base your choice of juicer on the qualities that are most important to you. Keep in mind that there is no perfect juicer, so it is best to choose one based on your specific needs and budget and the types of juices you'll be making.

Our Advice

For Daily Juicing, we recommend a machine such as a vertical-auger "slow" juicer, which ranks high in all categories, has a midline price range, and takes an average of 10 minutes to clean from top to bottom.

Types of Juicers

Masticating Juicers

How They Work: Masticating juicers resemble grinders. They are built horizontally rather than vertically, so they are long and low on the counter. This type of juicer is designed to first grate and then masticate—in other words, chew—the produce to break it down into pulp. The machine then mechanically squeezes the pulp to extract the juice.

Advantages: A masticating juicer does a good job of efficiently juicing every type of vegetable, including leafy greens. It gets high marks for versatility and extracts a good amount of juice.

Disadvantages: The downside of the masticating juicer is that it can heat the juice to higher temperatures than some other types of juicing machines. Some people believe that heat destroys nutrients and enzymes in the juice, although this claim has not been proven by any studies. Masticating juicers also cause more oxidation than other types, so your juice quality will suffer. Cleanup can also be relatively difficult, which is a deterrent to many would-be juicers.

Single-Auger ("Slow") Juicers

How They Work: Traditional single-auger juicers look much like masticating juicers but they work very differently. This type of juicer uses a single auger—a device that looks like a drill bit—which crushes the produce into the walls (or screen) of the juicer to extract juice.

Advantages: Compared to the masticating juicer, this type of juicer runs at fewer revolutions per minute (rpm), which is highly recommended, since your juice will not oxidize as quickly. These machines were originally designed to juice wheatgrass, but newer models are also capable of juicing vegetables and fruits fairly efficiently (with the exception of carrots and soft fruits), making them relatively high-yielding and versatile. They also do an excellent job of juicing leafy green veggies.

Juicer on a Budget

Good economical options exist for the budget juicer. New, well-rated juicers are available on Amazon for as low as $100. If you want a top-of-the-line juicer but aren't willing to pay the high price, try online sources such as Craigslist, eBay or a local lawn or estate sale. You'll be surprised at how many people buy new juicers with good intentions but never make juicing a habit. Often you can get a never-used or lightly used juicer at a good price—sometimes even in the original packaging. Also, think about contacting manufacturers of quality juicers to see whether they sell refurbished machines, which are like new but sold at reduced prices.

Disadvantages: A single-auger juicer is not efficient for juicing carrots (it produces a smaller yield), and often the resulting juice is pulpy. Fruits and non-leafy vegetables should be cut into small cubes for best results when using these juicers. Slow juicers also do not perform well when juicing soft fruits such as melon. For best results, alternate hard and soft produce through this juicer. Slow juicers fall somewhere in the middle in terms of cleanup time, and some people complain that the screens are difficult to scrub free of pulpy debris. Finally, the greater efficiency (compared to masticating and centrifugal juicers) of the single-auger juicer comes with a price—it takes longer for the produce to run through the machine, which means longer juicing times overall.

Vertical-Auger Juicers

How They Work: The vertical-auger or "vertical slow" juicer has a revolutionary design: it takes the single-auger style and turns it upright. This type has all the advantages and disadvantages of a traditional auger juicer, with one important difference. The vertical design means it doesn't take up so much counter space—a big plus if you don't have a large kitchen or don't like clunky machines littering your workspace. This machine is good for juicing fruits, vegetables and leafy greens, and it also does a fair job of juicing wheatgrass. The cleanup is pretty quick, once you get the hang of it.

An Excellent Starter Juicer: This is an excellent juicer for a beginner at Daily Juicing. In fact, we use this type for our own Daily Juice, even though we have more sophisticated (and pricier) juicers in our house. We find that it yields a good amount of juice from produce, works relatively quickly, has decent versatility and can be relatively easy to clean up. This juicer also creates only a small amount of oxidation when juicing.

Citrus Juicers

Not a great alternative for Daily Juicing, citrus juicers are available in both manual and electric designs. They come with a ridged cone-shaped center that extracts juice either by manual pressure or by electronically spinning against your fruit. The obvious disadvantage of this type of juicer is its limited versatility and range. That's why we do not recommend a citrus juicer for Daily Juicing. Nevertheless, these machines are relatively inexpensive. But even for citrus fruits they are less effective than other juicers, because they don't juice the white inner rind, or pith. The pith contains added nutrients; by discarding it, you'll miss out on some of the nutritional benefits of citrus fruit.

Centrifugal Juicers

How They Work: Centrifugal juicers are one of the oldest designs on the market. This type uses a grater or shredder disc and a strainer basket with straight sides to hold the pulp in the machine. The shredder disk at the bottom of the basket revolves at a high speed (approximately 3,600 rpm). You place the produce in a chute at the top of the machine and it moves down toward the shredder disc. As the produce gets shredded, juice is produced and comes out the front of the machine.

Advantages: This type of juicer works well for most fruits and vegetables. Like masticating juicers, centrifugal juicers get high marks for versatility. And because they are more commonplace, these juicers tend to be among the more affordable options. Also, they tend to process fruits and vegetables much more quickly than other juicers.

Disadvantages: The major downside of centrifugal juicers is that the pulp stays inside the machine instead of being ejected, as with other juicers. As a result, you must interrupt the process after making 1 or 2 quarts (1 to 2 L) of juice, to clean the pulp out of the machine. Oxidation is another major concern. This juicer creates the most oxidation of any machines tested, because the blade spins at a considerably higher speed than in other juicers. Also, centrifugal juicers are not as good as single-auger juicers for juicing leafy greens.

Centrifugal Ejection Juicers

This style of juicer was made popular by the Juiceman infomercials in the 1990s. It is similar in operation to a traditional centrifugal juicer. The difference is that the sides of the basket are slanted, which allows the juicer to self-clean —meaning you don't need to stop to clean out the pulp. The pulp is usually ejected into a collection bin or basket.

Advantages: These juicers are easy to use and to clean. They are good for juicing most fruits and vegetables and are usually quite cost-effective.

Disadvantages: The major downside to centrifugal ejection juicers is that they do not yield a lot of juice. In other words, the lower price tag on the juicer will be quickly offset by higher grocery bills. Also, because of the short contact time of the pulp in the basket, these juicers need to spin faster than a regular centrifugal juicer—usually around 6,300 rpm.

This leads to greater oxidation of your juice. Some people also believe that the juice gets heated, resulting in further enzyme and nutrient destruction.

Twin-Gear Juicers

How They Work: Twin-gear juicers have two gears that basically replicate the chewing process to press the juice out of the produce. These juicers are horizontal rather than vertical, so they take up a relatively significant amount of counter space.

Advantages: These juicers can be top-quality and extremely efficient. In fact, the stainless steel version of this type of juicer is one of the best on the market. The gears spin at a desirably low 90 to 110 rpm, which produces considerably less heat and oxidation. Twin-gear juicers get top marks for both juice quality and yield. These machines are excellent for juicing vegetables, since the process requires the fibrous vegetable pulp to push through the machine efficiently. They are also great for juicing wheatgrass.

Disadvantages: Twin-gear juicers aren't generally efficient at juicing fruits. Some twin-gear machines do allow for an optional attachment, however, that makes juicing fruits easier and more efficient. The cleanup process for this juicer can be somewhat slow, but the quality of juice you'll extract is excellent. The best of these juicers can also be extremely pricy.

Manual Juicers

How They Work: Manual juicers resemble grinders and can clamp onto the edge of any table or kitchen counter.

Advantages: Manual juicers were originally designed to juice wheatgrass, but they also do a fair job of juicing carrots and leafy greens. They are a fun way to introduce children to juicing because they are easy to use. Kids love seeing (and drinking) the immediate results of their efforts. We prefer to use one to whip up a quick wheatgrass shot. Also, these juicers travel well, so they are a great option for keeping the juicing habit alive during a vacation or trip. The price for these machines is modest.

Disadvantages: As everyday juicers, these machines have very low yield and versatility. A considerable amount of work and effort are required to make a glass of juice with this type of juicer. We do not recommend them for typical Daily Juicing.

Check the Warranty

While most juicers have a history of lasting for years, before purchasing your machine, always check the warranty. See what it covers and what it does not cover. For example, the vertical single-auger juicer we now own has a 10-year warranty on all of its parts. But a virtually identical juicer we owned from a different manufacturer did not. You should factor this sort of information into your purchasing decision, since you might be better off paying a bit more for better coverage.

Hydraulic Press Juicers

Not surprisingly, the best juicer on the market can also be the most expensive. These machines are true appliances, built to last. They can also be quite attractive, although they are large and space-consuming.

How They Work: A hydraulic juice press employs a two-step process. First it grinds the produce and then the user wraps the pulp in a special cloth, which is placed in the press to extract the juice.

Advantages: If you will be making a large volume of juice (for a juice fast, for example, or a large number of Daily Juicers), hydraulic presses are very effective. These juicers are used by high-end juice bars to create what is referred to as "cold-pressed" juice. Refrigerated juice from these machines can last from five to seven days when stored in an airtight container—another major advantage. They are also extremely effective at extracting juice from your produce, leaving behind only a sawdust-like pulp. They run slowly to grind your produce, resulting in lower heat, less oxidation and excellent juice quality.

Disadvantages: Hydraulic presses do have some significant drawbacks. These machines are heavy, expensive and take time to learn how to use correctly. Also, the cleanup time is longer than for other juicers. Even the juicing process itself takes significantly longer, because of the two-step process. We have one of these machines ourselves, and we love to use it for juice cleanses. It's simply too time-consuming, however, for our Daily Juice habit. We find that a vertical single-auger juicer better meets our needs for Daily Juicing.

Part 3

Juice Guru Recipes and More

Chapter 7

Juice Guru's Guide to the Best Ingredients

You could have the best juicer, recipes and intentions, but a great juice really comes down to great ingredients. So make sure that you purchase the freshest fruits and veggies you can find. Choose your recipes based on your tastes, of course, but favor produce that is in season. Shop locally as often as possible, such as at farmers' markets and in supermarket produce sections labeled "local." Produce not identified as local may have been chilled and shipped long distances (including internationally) before it appeared on your grocer's shelf. This results in significant nutrient (and flavor) loss, well before you've even taken it home to juice.

Select fruits and vegetables that are firm and ripe. Ideally, most produce, including green leafy vegetables and herbs, should be stored in your refrigerator for no longer than two to three days, so their nutrients can remain intact. Some can last longer; apples, celery, carrots and beets, for instance, can stay ripe and crisp in your refrigerator for a week or more.

As we've said before, every fruit and vegetable has unique benefits for your body and mind. So, as well as selecting recipes that appeal to your taste buds, you might want to think about choosing recipes that provide nutrients that are especially beneficial for your well-being, whether you have a particular health condition or just want to have more energy or glowing skin. In this chapter we'll give you information about the nutrients in the most used ingredients in our Juice Guru recipes, with a particular emphasis on the template recipes. We also include other tips and important information on how to select produce so you'll get the most out of your Daily Juice habit.

Look for the Seal

If you want to make sure you are eating organic, look for the Quality Assurance Internat onal seal. Producers of these fruits and vegetables have gone through extra steps to certify their farms as organic.

The Power of Organic

We strongly recommend using organic ingredients rather than so-called conventional produce. Simply put, organic foods are better for your body because they are grown without using harmful pesticides, herbicides or fungicides. When you are juicing large quantities of fruits and vegetables every day, those substances and their harmful effects can really add up. Organic produce is also more nutritious.

Reduced Chemical Exposure

Consider the following: pentachlorobenzene, oxydemeton-methyl, fentin acetate, sodium dimethyldithiocarbamate. These substances sound like something you might use to remove paint from your car, but in actuality they are names of farm pesticides. More than 100,000 chemicals are approved for farm use in the United States alone. And these hard-to-pronounce substances don't just sound scary—they *are* scary.

According to the United States Environmental Protection Agency (EPA), 60% of the chemicals used to control weeds, 90% of those used to inhibit mold growth, and 30% of those used to stop insects may cause cancer. Additionally, many of these chemicals are linked to Alzheimer's disease and other horrific illnesses, and almost all are linked to birth defects. Recently a study by scientists from the University of Montreal and Harvard University found that exposure to pesticide residues on vegetables and fruit may double a child's risk of attention deficit hyperactivity disorder (ADHD), a condition that can cause inattention, hyperactivity and impulsivity in both children and adults.

Organophosphates, a particularly concerning group of chemicals, are a class of 50 pesticides that were initially designed as chemical warfare agents—directed at people. Exposure to organophosphate pesticides can cause dizziness, confusion, vomiting, convulsions, numbness in the limbs and even death. They have also been linked to developmental delays, reduced IQ and behavioral problems in exposed children. Despite this, the US government still allows their use on food crops.

Organic fruits and vegetables are certified to be grown free from these substances. Instead of using harmful chemicals, organic farmers use natural techniques such as composting, introducing beneficial insects, and using plants with pungent smells to deter pests. But while chemicals have been avoided during their production, organic produce does, sadly, contain some residues from environmental cross-contamination. However, this contamination is significantly less than for conventionally grown produce (see above), and a considerable amount of that residue can be removed with proper cleaning techniques (see page 81).

More Nutrition

As more and more studies are being done that compare organic to conventionally grown produce, it is becoming clear that organic foods are more nutritious. A recent review of

Sourcing Organic Produce

Local farmers' markets are the best sources for organic produce, and often they enable you to experience different varieties of a food. For instance, your nearest large-chain grocery store may carry only one variety of cucumber, while the farmers' market may have four or five different varieties. This allows you to introduce more subtle flavors into your juices.

343 different studies, by a group of scientists mostly based in Europe, concluded that organic fruits and vegetables deliver between 20% and 40% more antioxidants than conventional produce. And in a study out of the University of Missouri, chemists were shocked to discover that the smaller organically grown oranges delivered 30% more vitamin C than the large conventionally grown ones. Other studies have reported similar findings.

Better Taste and Benefits for the Planet

Food grown using organic methods tastes better than food grown with chemicals. For instance, in blind taste tests conducted at Washington State University, people consistently found that organic berries tasted sweeter than those grown using conventional techniques.

Organic farming practices also benefit the environment and the planet. Conventional practices take a costly toll, washing away precious topsoil to the tune of $40 billion per year in the United States alone. Topsoil is where plants get their nutrients. Organic practices nurture the topsoil so it can be reused and continue to yield healthier, more nutritious fruits and vegetables.

Do Your Best

Sometimes you won't be able to find organic produce for one or more ingredients of your juice. Other times your budget may not allow for the extra expense. In that case, just do your best. It's better to juice imperfectly every day than not to juice at all. And the cleaning methods and tools we've highlighted (see page 81) will often remove much of the chemical residue clinging to conventional produce.

When choosing fruits and vegetables to juice, pay close attention to the Environmental Working Group's "Shopper's Guide to Pesticides in Produce." The "Dirty Dozen Plus" list includes those fruits and vegetables that are the most heavily treated with chemicals, while the "Clean Fifteen" lists those that contain the least pesticide residue when grown conventionally. Both lists contain produce that isn't suitable

Papayas Are Special

Although papayas make the "Clean Fifteen" list, we recommend buying organic papayas, because most conventionally grown papayas have been genetically modified.

Juice Guru Philosophy: *A Temperate Balance*

Our advice is to buy organic whenever you can and limit as much as possible the number of ingredients that are not organic. Stay away from the Dirty Dozen. Scrub and soak your ingredients well, as we outlined earlier in this book. In a nutshell, just do your best.

---

for juicing, such as potatoes and snap peas (Dirty Dozen Plus) and eggplant, avocados, cauliflower, onions, sweet corn and frozen sweet peas (Clean Fifteen). We've therefore drawn from those lists to make the following recommendations for the healthiest juicing.

Buy Organic

....

apples	celery	chile peppers
peaches	spinach	cherry tomatoes
nectarines	sweet bell	kale and collard
strawberries	peppers	greens
grapes	cucumbers	

Comfortable with Conventional

....

pineapples	mangos	grapefruit
cabbage	kiwifruit	cantaloupes

Core Ingredients for Daily Juice

You can probably find ingredients for your juice that start with every letter of the alphabet, and each one would provide unique and myriad benefits for your body, mind and soul. But while you might one day choose to juice a rambutan (a fruit native to the Malay archipelago that looks hairy on the outside but tastes sweet like a grape), chances are—at least for now—that you'll stick to the fruits and vegetables most commonly juiced. These are the core ingredients we use in our recipes, particularly in the Juice Guru Template Recipes.

One template recipe, Juice Guru Daily Classic (page 108), has a cucumber and celery base and can serve as your core juice for building a strong body and keeping it healthy. The other, Juice Guru Cleansing Juice (page 109), has an apple base. Because fruits have a detoxifying effect on the human body, this recipe can serve as your basic cleansing juice. There is plenty of additional information about the health benefits of both these juices in the recipe pages.

Apples

Incredibly, the little old apple—the fruit your mom almost always included with your school lunch—is actually a powerhouse of nutrition. It's also a staple in juicing. Apples often serve as the

The Dirty Dozen list, while a good starting point, provides only limited protection against ingesting pesticides and other harmful chemicals. The organization that prepares the list, the Environmental Working Group (EWG), fails to consider that some toxins are more harmful than others, even in small doses. Instead the EWG ranks all toxins equally in determining which produce ends up on its lists. As a result, some fruits and vegetables that are not on the list may contain small amounts of very harmful toxins. Nor does the list consider whether a fruit or vegetable is genetically modified (GMO). This is why it's always best to buy organic whenever possible.

base for a juice, and one or two added to any juice can sweeten it up and add more flavor. Apples are brimming with antioxidants, which significantly boost your immune system. These include polyphenols, which have proven anti-asthma benefits.

If you are feeling sluggish, drinking a glass of apple juice can be a great fix, because apples can help to regulate your blood-sugar level. Their skins contain phlorizin, which, studies show, inhibits glucose intake by 52%. And according to a 2004 article in *Nutrition Journal*, a number of studies have linked apples with a significant reduction in your risk of cancer, particularly lung cancer. Regularly consuming apples—just one a day—also helps to reduce total cholesterol and LDL ("bad") cholesterol.

Using Apples in Juice

We recommend Fuji apples if you prefer a sweet-tasting juice or one that appeals to children. Green apples, such as Granny Smiths, have a mellower flavor and work well in green juices. Combining them with more potent ingredients such as bitter dandelion greens will give your juice just the right amount of balance. Try Nothin' But the Greens (page 119) for a mellow green apple–inspired juice, or Green Giant (page 113) for a sweet complement to bitter dandelion greens.

Selecting Apples

When choosing apples, look for ones that have tight, blemish-free skin and that snap back when you press your finger into them. They are in season from August through spring, depending on the variety.

Beets

Beets are the perfect ingredient to include in your juice. They are full of unique phytonutrients, such as betalain and vulgaxanthin, that aren't commonly found in fruits and vegetables. These nutrients, as well as others provided by beets, have antioxidant and anti-inflammatory effects. The more we learn about inflammation, the more concerning it becomes. For instance, recent studies, as reported in *Clinical Cardiology: New Frontiers*, suggest that atherosclerosis (hardening of the arteries), which plays a major role in heart disease, "is largely a result of inflammation."

Other research suggests that inflammation plays a role in the development of type 2 diabetes, so it is believed that the anti-inflammatory effects of beets may help in the treatment of this condition as well. Beyond their anti-inflammatory effects, these little red gems help to reduce the risk of heart disease in other ways. They are packed full of nitrates that help burst open blood vessels so oxygen can flow better, which has been proven to regulate your blood pressure. Beets are also superb at keeping your kidneys strong and healthy, because they support the body's detoxification process.

Using Beets in Juice

Beet juice is a great pick-me-up throughout the day. In fact, long-distance runners often use it to increase stamina. Beets have a strong flavor, so you may prefer to offset the taste with apples and lemon—try a Redhead Supreme (page 146). Be prepared for a red tinge in your urine after you drink a strong beet juice. Don't worry, this is normal.

Selecting Beets

Choose beets with firm roots, smooth skin and a deep color. Avoid those with obvious blemishes or wet spots that indicate spoilage. Beets are available all year long but are best between June and October.

Carrots

Carrots are loaded with health-promoting beta-carotene. This antioxidant, which is responsible for their bright orange color, converts to vitamin A in your body. Vitamin A is essential for healthy skin and a well-functioning immune system. It is also the reason why carrots are known to promote good vision, especially night vision. A diet rich in carrots has also been found to decrease the risk of coronary heart disease (CHD). A 2011 study published in the *British Journal of Nutrition*, for instance, found that consumption of yellow-orange vegetables—particularly carrots—resulted in a significantly lower risk of CHD.

The rich carotenoid content of carrots helps to combat health-damaging free-radical activity and prevent premature aging. While most research on carrots has focused on carotenoids and their incredible antioxidant benefits, recent studies have identified another category of phytonutrients in carrots, known as polyacetylenes. These compounds can help inhibit the growth of colon cancer cells.

Using Carrots in Juice

Carrot roots (the part we usually eat) have a crunchy texture and a sweet, minty taste. The greens, which are becoming popular, are fresh-tasting and slightly bitter. Carrots can help to sweeten any juice and add a good dose of nutrition. Try a Carrot Beet Ginger Lemon Mantra (page 161) and see for yourself. We recommend including the greens in your carrot juice for an added boost of nutrients and chlorophyll. Since they are bitter, try using only one or two leaves to start with; work your way up if you're drawn to the taste.

Sugar Surge
Today's carrots are hybridized—they have been bred to be sweeter and thus contain more sugar than even a decade ago. If you are looking to lower your sugar intake, purchase heirloom carrots. They are easy to identify, as they come in vibrant colors such as purple, yellow and red. And because they have been around since farmers began raising crops, they are significantly lower in sugar.

Selecting Carrots

Carrots are available in markets throughout the year. Locally grown carrots are in season in the summer and fall, when they are the freshest and most flavorful. We recommend using heirloom varieties, as they tend to be less hybridized than traditional carrots; that means they contain less sugar and have even more nutritional value. You'll notice that heirloom varieties come in various colors, including purple, white, yellow and dark orange.

If you purchase carrot roots with attached green tops, the tops should be cut off before storing in the refrigerator. Otherwise they will cause the carrots to wilt prematurely, as they pull moisture from the roots. Since you may want to juice the green tops along with the carrots, we recommend storing them separately. Carrots are hardy vegetables that will last longer than most others (about two weeks) if stored properly.

Celery

If you've been thinking that celery is just a crunchy but not very important addition to your Chinese food or veggie party platter, think again. Celery contains more than a dozen key antioxidants and phytonutrients that your body craves. It has nutrients that support a healthy digestive system, including protection from ulcers and other stomach disease.

Celery is also a powerful anti-inflammatory, particularly in the cardiovascular system. It's known to help relax the muscles surrounding your blood vessels, which increases blood flow and consequently decreases blood pressure. In addition, celery contains organic sodium. Unlike the salt found in the shaker on your table, organic sodium encourages the body to use other nutrients more efficiently.

Using Celery in Juice

Celery's salty flavor comes through in juice, and it can be enhanced with lemon or complemented by ingredients such as tomatoes and basil. Try the Juice Guru Daily Classic template recipe (page 108), substituting cilantro or basil and tomato for the ginger.

Selecting Celery

Choose celery that looks crisp and snaps easily when pulled apart. The leaves should be pale to bright green, not yellow or brown. Celery is available in most supermarkets year-round, but it is in season in the fall through the spring.

Cilantro

Cilantro is rich in an array of healing phytonutrients and antioxidants. It provides vitamins A, C and K, calcium, iron, manganese, potassium and trace amounts of B vitamins. Cilantro is an excellent blood-builder and can help prevent anemia. When juiced on a regular basis, cilantro can help reduce the amount of damaged fats (lipid peroxides) in the cell membranes.

Using Cilantro in Juice

We love the flavor cilantro brings to our green juices. Milder than parsley, this herb offers a delicious boost to juice. Try a Beauty Builder (page 117) to experience the delicious flavor and health-promoting effects of cilantro.

Selecting Cilantro

When purchasing cilantro, look for bright green color and a clean, fresh scent. Avoid brown spots and moldy or wilted leaves. You'll want to juice cilantro within one to two days of your purchase. Wash it right before you use it. To keep cilantro fresh, refrigerate in a plastic bag filled with air and closed securely.

Cucumbers

Cucumbers belong to the same botanical family as melons (including watermelon and cantaloupe) and squash (including summer squash, winter squash, zucchini and pumpkin). Recent studies indicate that cucumbers have more health-promoting value than previously thought. They feature phytonutrients that are connected with reduced risk of cardiovascular disease as well as several types of cancer, including breast, uterine, ovarian and prostate cancers. Also, cucumbers have recently been shown to feature both antioxidant and anti-inflammatory properties.

Using Cucumbers in Juice

Cucumbers have a mellow flavor and produce a lot of liquid, making them perfect as a base for many juices. Try a Celery Cucumber Carrot (page 164) to experience the refreshing addition that cucumbers bring to any juice.

Selecting Cucumbers

Since cucumbers are sensitive to heat, we recommend choosing varieties that are displayed in refrigerated cases in the market. They should have a bright to medium dark green color and be firm to the touch and rounded at the edges. Cucumbers should be stored in the refrigerator, where they will keep for several days. For best quality, juice your cucumbers within one to two days of purchase.

Give or Take

The yield from our juice recipes depends on the type of juicer you use and the size of the produce. If you come up short in any recipe, just add cucumber. Its juice has a neutral, refreshing flavor that complements any recipe. Cucumber is also a high-yielding vegetable—a little goes a long way.

Dandelion Greens

Dandelion greens are not the most common ingredient in juicing, but based on their nutritional value, they should be. Drinking a tall glass of green juice featuring dandelion greens is a great way to feed your body with important nutrients, such as vitamin K, that it needs. Dandelion greens provide more than 500 micrograms of this valuable nutrient per cup (250 mL). With daily intake, vitamin K has been connected with a decrease in bone fractures and the risk of some cancers, according to a study published in 2008 in *PLOS Medicine*.

Dandelion greens are also a great source of calcium. Just 1 cup (250 mL) contains 103 milligrams of calcium (10% of the recommended daily value). And they are packed with iron, which helps keep oxygen flowing freely throughout your body. When your body has enough iron, your brain works faster, so you can thrive at work or ace that big exam.

Using Dandelion Greens in Juice

The drawback to dandelion greens is their bitter taste, so make sure you combine them with a sweeter option such as apples. Try a Green Giant (page 113), which balances the bitter greens with sweet Fuji apples and flavorful cilantro and mint leaves.

Selecting Dandelion Greens

Choose dandelion greens that have not yet blossomed and do not have yellow buds. They are seasonal in the springtime.

Ginger

There is nothing quite like the effect you get from adding ginger to your juice. This is a natural way to keep away nausea during pregnancy or to ward off motion sickness of any kind. Ginger is full of antioxidant and immune-boosting power. It not only makes you feel warm on a cold day but can actually help your body to sweat out flu and colds. Ginger is also an extremely effective anti-inflammatory, helping rid the body of symptoms such as the pain and swelling associated with both rheumatoid arthritis and osteoarthritis. Finally, gingerroot has been shown to be a potent defender against the development of colon and ovarian cancers.

Using Ginger in Juice

We recommend the medicinal use of ginger to aid in alleviating nausea or for ongoing management of arthritis. Also, ginger adds a delicious zing to most juices and will keep you warm on a cold day. We highly recommend Ginger Citrus Spice (page 132) to deliciously warm you up from the inside out.

Selecting Ginger

When purchasing fresh ginger root, make sure it is firm, smooth and free of mold. You can find it year-round in your local grocery store.

Kale

This cruciferous vegetable boasts fantastic health benefits and should be a staple in your Daily Juice routine two or three times per week. Kale adds an earthy flavor to your juice and contains more nutritional value for fewer calories than almost any other food available today. Along with its cholesterol-lowering benefits, recent studies indicate that kale boasts risk-lowering benefits for at least five different types of cancer. This leafy green also provides comprehensive support for the body's detoxification system.

Using Kale in Juice

We recommend using curly kale in your juices, as we've found that dinosaur kale (also known as Tuscan or black kale) can be somewhat bitter. Curly kale has a pleasing taste that works well even in kid-friendly juices. Try whipping up a Kale Is Fun (page 190) for you and your little ones. Except for the green color, they'll never know the kale is in there ... but their bodies will.

Selecting Kale

Three types of kale are available in markets. Curly kale has ruffled leaves and a thick stalk and is usually deep green in color; it offers a lively flavor. Ornamental kale is a newer species that is also known as "salad savoy." It has green, white or purple leaves, a mellower flavor and a more tender texture. "Dinosaur kale" is the common name for the variety also known as lacinato, black or Tuscan kale. It has dark blue-green leaves with an embossed texture and is the most bitter of the kale varieties.

When shopping, look for kale with firm, deeply colored leaves and moist, hardy stems. The kale should be displayed in a cool environment, since warm temperatures will cause it to wilt and negatively affect its flavor.

Lemons and Limes

Lemons are another great fruit for juicing. Juicing a lemon into a glass of water is the perfect way to break your fast in the morning, as the juice will help kick-start your digestive tract. It's also believed to aid in rapid weight loss, as lemons help the body eliminate waste.

Like other citrus fruits, lemons and limes are particularly high in vitamin C, one of the most important antioxidants in nature. Vitamin C fights free radicals, which are known

---

Kale Alert

Kale is one of the most nutrient-dense foods on the planet. There is no dispute about that. Although the jury is still out on this, juicing excessive amounts of kale may concentrate certain compounds that may disrupt the production of thyroid hormones. If you have a pre-existing thyroid condition or at risk, it may be prudent to carefully watch and limit the amount of kale (and other cruciferous vegetables) you juice. That is why our recipes call for no more than 2 cups (500 mL) of kale.

to speed up aging. Aside from keeping your cells young, the antioxidant power of vitamin C in lemons and limes is known to combat inflammation from arthritis and help slow the progression of heart disease. Compounds in lemons and limes, called limonoids, have been shown to help fight cancers of the mouth, skin, lung, breast, stomach and colon.

Using Lemons and Limes in Juice

Be sure to remove only the outer layer of the peel. One benefit of juicing is that you can use the inner pith (the white part) of lemons and limes, which contains additional nutrients. But perhaps the best part about including these fruits in your juice is that they are natural flavor enhancers. Juices come alive when you add one or two to the mix. Try a Kickin' Green Machine (page 125) to experience the flavor-enhancing quality of lemon juice.

Selecting Lemons and Limes

Choose lemons that are heavy for their size; this indicates that they have thinner peel and are therefore juicier. They should be fully yellow in color. Limes should also be firm and heavy for their size, and they should have a glossy skin that is deep green in color. Lemons and limes are available all year, although limes are more plentiful from mid-spring through mid-fall.

Melons

You can juice any melon, but the most commonly juiced are watermelon, cantaloupe and honeydew. These melons (especially watermelon) produce a significant amount of juice, so even a relatively small one will go a long way. Melons provide a quick and easy way to get your Daily Juice while giving your body terrific health benefits, including an ample dose of antioxidant and anti-inflammatory support. New studies indicate that watermelon in particular may provide cardiovascular benefits. Melons are extremely detoxifying and a great way to cleanse your body and blood of built-up toxins. They also serve as an excellent diuretic and help keep you hydrated.

Using Melons in Juice

You might think that the fleshy part in the center of a melon is the only nutrient-rich area, far more so than the lighter-colored flesh near the rind. It is time to discard that idea. Recent studies indicate that the inner rind of melons (often discarded when we eat them) can prove extremely beneficial. You'll find a myriad of vitamins and antioxidants there, which is why we recommend including the rind whenever you are juicing melons. Try Watermelon Mint (page 131) for a refreshing treat on a hot summer day.

Hold the Melon?

Melons (such as cantaloupe and watermelon) are among the few fruits that do not have a low glycemic index (GI), the measure for how much a food raises blood glucose. Considering their medium GI, and despite their high nutritional value, we do not recommend melon juice for anyone with diabetes or a prediabetic condition, or for anyone who is looking to lose a significant amount of weight.

Selecting Melons

When choosing a melon, there are several features you'll want to evaluate. First is the weight—a fully ripe melon will feel heavy for its size. Also, some ripe melons, such as cantaloupes, will smell sweet at the stem end and bottom. Uncut melons are best stored at room temperature. They don't ripen on the countertop, so keep that in mind when you make your choice. Most melons will last only two to three days, so be sure to juice your fruit soon after purchase.

Parsley

Often used as a garnish, parsley is actually a powerhouse of nutrients. It provides a large amount of vitamins K and C and also good amounts of vitamin A, folate and iron. Parsley contains volatile oils that provide incredible health benefits. These oils help protect your body from various carcinogens, including smoke from cigarettes and charcoal grills. It is also a rich source of antioxidant nutrients. Regularly consuming parsley is a good way to help protect your heart and prevent rheumatoid arthritis.

Using Parsley in Juice

You can juice either the Italian flat-leaf or curly variety of parsley. However, we prefer the flat-leaf; it has a milder flavor and tends to complement juices better than the curly variety. Always choose fresh parsley for juice, as opposed to the dried form of the herb. Parsley has a strong flavor, so you'll want to balance it with sweeter or more mellow flavors. Try a Tropical Flush (page 140) for a sweet, tangy flavor that offsets the healthful parsley.

Selecting Parsley

Choose fresh parsley that looks fresh and crisp and is deep green in color. You'll want to avoid parsley that has wilted leaves or is yellowing. Fresh parsley should be washed right before you juice it, since it is very fragile.

Pears

Pears are particularly rich in phytonutrients; in fact, they are the number-two fruit in terms of flavanol content. Flavanol and other phytonutrients in pears have been shown to act as potent antioxidants and anti-inflammatories. As a result, regular consumption of pears has been shown to reduce the risks of type 2 diabetes and heart disease.

Cut It Up

Most juicers have a problem processing large pieces of parsley. The tough stems can wrap around the juicer blades, slowing down and eventually stopping the machine. We recommend cutting your parsley into ½-inch (1 cm) segments before juicing. Your machine will thank you.

Using Pears in Juice

While we suggest that you might like to strain your juice before consumption, this is definitely not the case when it comes to juicing pears. Recent studies show that with their pulp removed, pear juices lose up to 40% of their total phytonutrients and their antioxidant capacity is significantly reduced. You'll want to consume all the pulp from your pear juice to make sure you reap its many benefits. "Cloudy" pear juice is definitely the way to go. For this same reason, make sure to juice the skins of your pears as well—they contain at least three to four times as many phytonutrients as the flesh. Try Dragon Juice (page 188) for you or your kids; it combines apples and pears with a hint of mint.

Selecting Pears

Choose pears that are firm but not too hard. They should have a smooth skin without bruises or mold. Good-quality pears do not need to be uniform in color, and there can even be some brown speckled patches on the skin. Pears are highly perishable once they are ripe; buy them unripe and allow them a few days to ripen on your countertop. Once they have ripened, you can keep them in the refrigerator for a few days.

Pineapples

Making a glass of fresh pineapple juice is not only easy but incredibly healthy. Many skin blemishes, such as eczema and acne, are a result of swelling in the body. The great news is that drinking pineapple juice reduces swelling naturally. The bromelain in pineapples has been shown to help people with arthritis move more easily and helps with indigestion. Amazingly, this same nutrient helps in treating coughs and colds and naturally boosts your immunity.

Using Pineapples in Juice

Pineapples are great by themselves or in combination with other fruits and vegetables, because they produce a considerable amount of juice. One of our favorite juices of all time is Lemon Drop (page 136). It features no lemon at all, but its sweet and tangy flavor is reminiscent of the old-fashioned hard candy.

Selecting Pineapples

Choose pineapples that are large in size (and therefore have more flesh to juice) and free from dark spots and blemishes. Also, make sure they have a sweet, rather than fermented or musty, smell at the stem end. Pineapples are generally available

---

Pass on the Pineapple

Like melons, pineapples are brimming with nutrients that help to keep you youthful and healthy. But, just like melons, they are among the few fruits that do not have a low glycemic index (they have a medium GI). If, like us, you don't have issues with sugar, we highly recommend treating yourself to pineapple juice at least once a week, to enjoy its delicious taste and for a pleasant boost. Otherwise, pass on the pineapple.

year-round. Peak season for Hawaiian pineapples is April and May; for Caribbean pineapples it is December through February, and again from August through September.

Romaine Lettuce

Romaine lettuce stands out from other varieties of lettuce because of its high nutritional value. The vitamins, minerals and phytonutrients found in romaine are especially good for preventing or alleviating many common health issues. It provides a good amount of vitamins A and K, folate and molybdenum. Minerals found in romaine include manganese, potassium, copper and iron, along with vitamins B_1 and C and biotin.

Using Romaine in Juice

Because of its mellow flavor, romaine is the easiest leafy green vegetable to add to your Daily Juice. Get your greens deliciously with Pineapple Turmeric Gold (page 133).

Selecting Romaine Lettuces

When choosing romaine, be sure the lettuce is crisp-looking, with firm leaves that are free from dark or slimy spots. Romaine lettuce will keep for five to seven days in the refrigerator. You can wash and dry it before storing in the refrigerator; just be sure to remove all excess moisture—your salad spinner is highly recommended for this task. The lettuce can be stored either in a plastic bag or wrapped in a damp cloth in the refrigerator crisper.

Spinach

Generally when you think of spinach, you think of its rich iron content; it's the iron in spinach that gives you healthy blood and energy. But spinach has emerged as a potent cancer fighter too, particularly for cancers of the stomach, skin and breast, as well as aggressive prostate cancer. Drinking spinach juice is a great way to enjoy the health benefits of two C's: chlorophyll and carotene. Together these nutrients have been shown to pack a powerful punch against cancer by preventing the cells from dividing. Spinach is also extremely high in vitamin K, which leads to healthy bones. This leafy green is rich in antioxidants and contributes to healthy eyes.

Using Spinach in Juice

Spinach is a mild-tasting leafy green veggie, which makes it a perfect addition to many juices. For a quick, low-cost, delicious juice, try Apple Spinach Juice (page 206).

Easy as 1-2-3
Want to save some time prepping your veggies for juicing? Many farms sell tubs of triple-washed spinach and other dark greens. If you're in a time crunch, have some on hand to juice quickly with a base of apples, celery or cucumber.

Selecting Spinach

Your spinach should look fresh and tender and have deep green leaves and stems with no signs of yellowing. It is readily available in markets year-round, but the freshest spinach is available in the spring.

Tomatoes

Tomatoes are excellent for reducing your risk of heart disease. They do so in two ways. First, they are rich in antioxidants—including vitamins E and C—which provide critical support to your cardiovascular system in circulating oxygen through your bloodstream. Second, tomatoes have been shown to lower both total and "bad" (LDL) cholesterol in your body. But that's not all they can do. Usually when thinking about building strong bones, you don't ask, "Got tomatoes?" But you should. Tomatoes have been linked to good bone health, and researchers believe this is because of the abundance of antioxidants found in these delicious fruits. Finally, the beautiful red color of tomatoes comes from lycopene, a nutrient that helps to prevent cancer, including prostate cancer.

Using Tomatoes in Juice

Tomatoes are not a staple in most juices, but they can be a fantastic addition to a savory green juice to make it taste more like a meal. Try the Juice Guru Daily Classic template recipe (page 108) and substitute tomatoes and basil for the ginger.

Selecting Tomatoes

Choose tomatoes that have a rich color: deep reds are a great choice, but so are vibrant oranges, yellows and purples. They should be smooth-skinned, with no wrinkles, cracks, bruises or soft spots. The most flavorful ones available are heirloom tomatoes, which are varieties that are still open-pollinated and have never been hybridized or tampered with. They can look different from traditional tomatoes and may appear misshapen, mottled or spotted. Don't be fooled—adding an heirloom tomato to your juice will create a taste sensation like no other. They are most abundantly available in the summer and early fall.

Juice Guru Template Recipes

The Juice Guru Template Recipes are designed to make your juices as nutritious as they can be and to help you incorporate Daily Juicing into your lifestyle as easily as possible.

Readily Available Ingredients

The Juice Guru Template Recipes enable you to shop weekly for core recipe ingredients that are usually readily available year-round. This means they will always be on hand, ready to juice. But they also contain enough diversity to serve as go-to juices for your daily dose of nutrients and energy. Variety in your nutritious fruits and vegetables is the key to a lifetime of good health.

Flexible Templates

Most of the ingredients in the Juice Guru Template Recipes—including apples, cucumbers, lemons, greens and ginger—are basic to a wide variety of juices. If you get bored with the same juices, the templates (pages 108 and 109) include a number of variations that allow you to easily swap ingredients for a completely different flavor profile.

Less Waste

The templates allow for flexibility but revolve around the same three to five core ingredients, depending upon the recipe you choose. This allows you to use up your produce more efficiently and helps to reduce waste. If you were to switch from a beet-based to an apple-based to a cucumber-based juice three days in a row, some of your produce would likely go bad before you got around to juicing it. These recipes will help you avoid that problem. The templates also reduce "time waste" by allowing you to have your core ingredients ways on hand and ready to juice.

Juice Guru Daily Classic

1	stalk celery, chopped	1
2 cups	packed chopped kale leaves	500 mL
3	cucumbers, quartered (see Tips, left)	3
1	lemon, peeled and halved (see Tips, left)	1
1	½-inch (1 cm) piece peeled gingerroot (see Tips, left)	1

Makes about 3 cups (750 mL)

This recipe is truly a template, and the ingredients listed are merely suggestions to get you started with Daily Juicing. The combinations are limited only by your imagination (see Variations, below). Use whichever leafy green is in season. Once you become comfortable with the core ingredients in this blend, we invite you to experiment with your favorite ingredients.

Tips

Several varieties of cucumber are available in supermarkets, from field (slicing) to pickling to English cucumbers. We find that field and English cucumbers yield the most juice.

When peeling lemons for juicing, be sure to leave behind as much white pith as possible. The pith of the lemon contains high concentrations of bioflavonoids such as limonene, which is believed to have anticancer properties.

To peel gingerroot quickly and easily, simply use the edge of a teaspoon. Scrape it back and forth along the root to remove the skin and reveal the yellow flesh underneath.

1. Using a juicer, process half each of the celery, kale, cucumber and lemon, plus the ginger. Following the same order, repeat with the remaining celery, kale, cucumber and lemon. Whisk well and serve immediately.

Variations

You can adjust the ingredients in this juice according to the vegetables you have on hand. Experiment to see what you like best. The following are some suggestions:

- For a boost of herbal freshness, add 10 sprigs fresh mint or fresh basil.

- Add 1 red bell pepper.

- Add 1 tomato.

- Substitute 1 cup (250 mL) packed chopped Swiss chard or dandelion greens for the kale.

- Substitute 2 cups (500 mL) packed chopped spinach or romaine lettuce for the kale.

- Substitute 1 lime, peeled and halved, for the lemon. For a more complex citrus flavor, use both lemon and lime.

- For a sweeter green juice flavor, substitute 2 Granny Smith apples, cored and sliced, for 2½ of the cucumbers.

Juice Guru Cleansing Juice

Jay Kordich, now a 92-year-old juice man, drank this juice under the guidance of Dr. Max Gerson to cure himself of a tumor when he was in his early twenties. Dr. Gerson, along with many other naturopathic doctors in clinics across Europe, had recommended this blend for decades. We have found it to be cleansing during our own juice fast programs. The taste is wonderfully sweet, with just the right kick from the ginger.

Tips

Carrots come in a variety of sizes. Our recipes are based on medium to large carrots.

There are so many varieties of apples to choose from. Fuji, Red Delicious and Granny Smith are most commonly used for juicing, but any type will produce a delicious result. We recommend using whatever is local and in season. Simply changing the variety of apple you use is an easy way to combat boredom with a particular juice blend.

6	carrots (see Tips, left)	6
4	red apples, cored and sliced (see Tips, left)	4
1	½-inch (1 cm) piece peeled gingerroot (see Tips, page 108)	1

1. Using a juicer, process half each of the carrots and apples, plus the ginger. Following the same order, repeat with the remaining carrots and apples. Whisk well and serve immediately.

Variations

You can adjust the ingredients in this juice according to the produce you have on hand. Experiment to see what you like best. The following are some suggestions:

- For a boost of herbal freshness, add 6 sprigs fresh parsley or ¼ cup (60 mL) loosely packed basil or cilantro leaves.
- Substitute 2 pears for the apples.
- Substitute a ½-inch (1 cm) piece peeled turmeric root for the ginger.

Juice Guru's Tip

Get creative with this juice by adding or omitting ingredients. Trust your intuition. Your instincts and preferences will guide you to create juices you'll love. Be sure to write down your favorite combinations in your journal so you can refer to them again and again.

Herbal Helper

Try whisking 1 tbsp (15 mL) ground cinnamon into finished juice—it can do your body good. Cinnamon has been shown to regulate blood sugar, reduce LDL ("bad") cholesterol levels, fight against bacteria and other pathogens, and reduce pain linked to arthritis.

Tips for Prepping and Measuring Ingredients

- No matter what type of juicer you are using, it is always a good idea to roughly chop greens such as spinach and kale and to cut longer vegetables such as celery and cucumbers into pieces before processing, so they flow through your juicer more efficiently and with less chance of clogging.
- When measuring leafy greens, pack the chopped greens tightly into the measuring cup to ensure that you achieve the correct measure for the recipes.
- When measuring chopped herbs, pack them into the measuring cup lightly to ensure that you achieve the correct measure for the recipes.

Juice Guru's Tip

Unless you are using a top-of-the-line juice press, even the best juicers will leave a fair amount of pulp in the final product. If, like us, you don't like pulp, we recommend straining your juice through a fine-mesh sieve into a 4-cup (1 L) measuring cup (for easy pouring). Straining your juice will make drinking it more enjoyable, since you won't end up with tiny fragments of pulp and skin that require occasional chewing.

Juicy Variation

Juicers can vary significantly in the volume of juice they produce, depending on the process the use and their efficiency with particular fruits and vegetables. Juice quantity will also fluctuate to reflect the produce used; a large apple or cucumber will yield considerably more juice than a small one. So while most of our recipes yield us approximately 3 cups (750 mL), be prepared to experience variations in the yield.

Chapter 8
Get Yer Power Greens

Energy Booster

Adding spinach to your juice is a great way to enjoy the health benefits of two C's: chlorophyll and carotene. According to a 2014 study in the *Journal of Cell Science*, chlorophyll, which has the potential to convert sunlight into energy, may help to increase your energy level. This juice contains a surprisingly delicious blend of greens—spinach, kale and microgreens—to deliver an abundance of these important nutrients.

1	stalk celery, chopped	1
6	sprigs fresh flat-leaf (Italian) parsley (see Caution, below)	6
½ cup	packed chopped spinach leaves	125 mL
6	green apples, cored and quartered (see Tips, page 114)	6
½ cup	packed chopped kale leaves	125 mL
¼ cup	packed microgreens (see Juice Guru's Tip, below)	60 mL
1	cucumber, quartered (see Tip, left)	1

1. Using a juicer, process half each of the celery, parsley, spinach, apples, kale, microgreens and cucumber. Following the same order, repeat with the remaining vegetables and apples. Whisk well and serve immediately.

Tip
Several varieties of cucumber are available in supermarkets, from field (slicing) to pickling to English cucumbers. We find that field and English cucumbers yield the most juice.

Herbal Helper
Want a cleansing kick that'll get your blood moving? Try whisking a pinch of cayenne pepper into your juice and adding fresh chile peppers to your dinner. Capsaicin, the alkaloid that gives chiles their heat, stimulates circulation, among other benefits. Population studies show that people who eat a lot of chile peppers are less likely to suffer from cardiovascular disease than those in countries where the food is blander.

Juice Guru's Tip
Microgreens are the tiny seedlings of vegetables and herbs, and they are considered among the healthiest and most nutrient-dense greens you can eat. They are picked 14 days after germination and, depending on the herb or vegetable, range from 1 to 3 inches (2.5 to 7.5 cm) tall before harvesting. While they are small in size, they are mighty in nutrient content. According to a 2012 study in the *Journal of Agricultural and Food Chemistry*, microgreens from plants such as red cabbage, cilantro and radish contain up to 40 times more nutrient value than their full-grown counterparts.

Caution
Certain phytonutrients in parsley—in concentrated amounts, as they are in juices—may act as a uterine stimulant and should likely be avoided during pregnancy. Because of the concentrated amount of oxalate it contains, parsley juice should also be avoided by people with kidney stones or a history of kidney stones.

Green Giant

Makes about
3 cups (750 mL)

While dandelion greens can taste very bitter, this juice uses sweet apples and tart limes to balance the bitterness. The result is an enticing juice with fresh, delectable flavors and a wide variety of nutrients, including beta-carotene, iron, magnesium and vitamins C and K, to name just a few. We find that drinking a nutrient-rich juice like this one first thing in the morning provides us with enough energy to sustain us until lunchtime.

Tip

Limes and lemons offer comparable amounts of vitamin C and folate. In juices you can interchange them depending on preference. Lemons have an acidic, tart flavor, while limes are generally sour.

Herbal Helper

Cilantro provides excellent support for liver health. This herb is not typically used in juices because of its distinctive taste, but if you love it (not everyone does), it will add a bold savory flavor to your juice. If you are not a fan of cilantro, simply omit it.

1	cucumber, quartered	1
½	head romaine lettuce, chopped	½
8	sprigs fresh flat-leaf (Italian) parsley (see Caution, page 112)	8
6	red apples, cored and sliced (see Tips, page 114)	6
6	sprigs fresh cilantro	6
1	lime, peeled and halved	1
¼ cup	lightly packed fresh mint leaves	60 mL
½ cup	packed dandelion greens, chopped (see Juice Guru's Tip, below)	125 mL

1. Using a juicer, process half each of the cucumber, romaine, parsley, apples, cilantro, lime, mint and dandelion leaves. Following the same order, repeat with the remaining vegetables, apples and herbs. Whisk well and serve immediately.

Juice Guru's Tip

Just ½ cup (125 mL) dandelion greens provides a whopping 178% of the recommended daily value of vitamin K, which is essential for blood clotting and bone health, among other benefits. Dandelion greens are also an excellent source of vitamin A through the antioxidant carotenoid, which is particularly good for the skin, mucous membranes and vision. Flavonoids called lutein and zeaxanthin protect the retina from ultraviolet radiation, helping to reduce age-related macular degeneration—the leading cause of preventable blindness in people over the age of 50—while other phytonutrients, primarily alpha- and beta-carotene, lutein and cryptoxanthin, protect the body from lung and mouth cancers.

Super Greens

Makes about 3 cups (750 mL)

This slightly sweet, sour and somewhat salty juice delivers a boost of energizing and healing nutrients such as vitamin C, quercetin and other bioflavonoids, alpha- and beta-carotene, lutein, zeaxanthin and vitamin K. You'll love the earthy taste, and your body will love the cancer-fighting properties of the leafy greens.

Tips

When peeling lemons for juicing, be sure to leave behind as much white pith as possible. The pith of the lemon contains high concentrations of bioflavonoids such as limonene, which is believed to have anticancer properties.

Never peel the skin from your apples before juicing. Apple skin contains an abundance of phytonutrient polyphenols, which help to regulate blood sugar.

There are so many varieties of apples to choose from. Fuji, Red Delicious and Granny Smith are most commonly used for juicing, but any type will produce a delicious juice. We recommend using whatever is local and in season. Simply changing the variety of apple you use is an easy way to combat boredom with a particular juice blend.

1	cucumber, quartered	1
2	stalks celery, chopped	2
1 cup	packed chopped kale leaves	250 mL
1	lemon, peeled and halved	1
1 cup	packed chopped spinach leaves	250 mL
2	green apples, cored and quartered (see Tips, left)	2

1. Using a juicer, process half each of the cucumber, celery, kale, lemon, spinach and apples. Repeat in the same order with the remaining fruit and vegetables. Whisk well and serve immediately.

Herbal Helper

Want to lower stress and give your health a boost? Stir $1/2$ tsp (2 mL) ashwagandha extract into this juice. Ashwagandha, an herb often used in Ayurvedic medicine, helps the body to withstand both mental and physical stress.

Guru's Grasses

**Makes about
3 cups (750 mL)**

This enzyme-rich green juice contains health-promoting organic wheatgrass (see box, right). If you find the taste of wheatgrass to be overwhelmingly sweet on its own, you'll find this earthy blend, containing apples and carrots, a sublime alternative.

Tip

Carrots come in a variety of sizes; our recipes are based on medium to large ones. We love to use purple heirloom carrots in our juices. They are lower in sugar than hybridized orange carrots, and studies have shown that heirloom carrots contain higher levels of anthocyanin, a powerful antioxidant, than orange and yellow varieties. But all carrot varieties are excellent. Orange carrots are also nutrient-dense, with excellent levels of beta-carotene—up to 65% of their total carotenoid content. Meanwhile, up to 50% of the total carotenoid content of yellow carrots consists of lutein.

6	carrots (see Tip, left)	6
2	red apples, cored and sliced	2
3	cubes frozen organic wheatgrass, thawed	3

1. Using a juicer, process half the carrots and half the apple. Following the same order, repeat with the remaining carrots and apple.

2. Add wheatgrass juice and whisk until completely incorporated. Serve immediately.

Wheatgrass: Fresh, Powdered or Frozen?

While we prefer using freshly juiced wheatgrass in our drinks, we realize that many commercial juicers have a hard time processing wheatgrass. We recommend frozen organic wheatgrass juice as a great alternative. The frozen juice is extracted from mature wheatgrass and has a more neutral flavor than fresh wheatgrass. While you get more nutrient value from fresh wheatgrass, we've personally experienced quite an energy jolt using frozen. To date there has not been extensive testing comparing frozen to fresh wheatgrass, so use your best judgment. If your juicer can process fresh wheatgrass, substitute 1 oz (30 g) for the frozen cubes.

Chef Babette's Carrot "Tuna" Salad

What a great way to use the pulp left over from making carrot juice! This plant-based take on tuna salad tastes great as a dip for celery sticks or tortilla chips, as a filling with corn-based taco shells or sprouted-grain bread, or as a delicious topping for a hearty salad. Be playful with this recipe and make it your own by adding your favorite spices, herbs or vegetables.

Tips

To produce 4 cups (1 L) carrot pulp, you will need to juice 8 to 10 medium carrots. When making any juice containing carrots, after juicing the carrots transfer the pulp to the refrigerator and store, tightly covered, until you have enough to make this recipe.

This salad will keep for up to 1 week in an airtight container in the refrigerator.

4 cups	carrot pulp (see Tips, left)	1 L
¼ cup	chopped green onion, white and green parts	60 mL
¼ cup	diced cored red bell pepper	60 mL
½ cup	raw apple cider vinegar	125 mL
½ cup	vegan mayonnaise	125 mL
3 tbsp	raw agave nectar	45 mL
1 tsp	sea salt	5 mL
1 tsp	celery seeds	5 mL
1 tsp	caraway seeds	5 mL

1. In a large bowl, combine carrot pulp, green onion, red pepper, vinegar, mayonnaise, agave nectar, salt, celery seeds and caraway seeds. Stir well.

Beauty Builder

**Makes about
3 cups (750 mL)**

This satisfying juice features a transcendent blend of flavors that will help bring out your inner glow. Ginger, which promotes clear skin and bright eyes, gives this juice a nice kick, while the cilantro adds a hint of herbal spice. The romaine and collard greens balance the flavors. The collard greens are rich in carotenoids, which protect the skin from UV damage, one of the main contributors to skin aging.

Tips

Rather than juicing aloe vera yourself, it's likely easier to use organic raw aloe vera juice, which you can find at your local health food store. Once opened, a bottle will keep for up to 2 weeks in your refrigerator. If you would like to juice it yourself, some health food stores and well-stocked supermarkets will special-order aloe vera leaves upon request.

To prepare an aloe vera leaf for juicing: Using a sharp knife, trim off the dried base and cut the leaf into 3-inch (7.5 cm) sections, discarding the narrow tip. Slide the knife just underneath the rind and carefully cut it away, leaving intact as much of the gel-like yellow center as possible. Turn over and repeat on the other side of the leaf. Repeat with remaining sections. Cut each section crosswise into 1/2-inch (1 cm) pieces. The aloe is now ready for juicing.

3	cucumbers, quartered (see Juice Guru's Tip, below)	3
1 cup	packed chopped collard green leaves (see Tips, page 127)	250 mL
1	lemon, peeled and halved (see Tips, page 118)	1
15	sprigs fresh cilantro (about 1/2 bunch)	15
1 cup	packed chopped romaine lettuce leaves	250 mL
1	1/2-inch (1 cm) piece peeled gingerroot	1
1/4 cup	raw aloe vera juice (see Tips, left)	60 mL

1. Using a juicer, process half each of the cucumbers, collard greens, lemon, cilantro and romaine, plus the ginger. Following the same order, repeat with the remaining cucumbers, greens, lemon and cilantro.

2. Add aloe vera juice and whisk well. Strain and serve immediately.

Juice Guru's Tip

Cucumbers are an excellent diuretic, helping to clean out your insides and promote a beautiful and glowing outside. Cucumbers are also a good source of silica, which works to strengthen connective tissue and improve overall complexion and skin health.

Herbal Helper

People either love or hate the taste of cilantro. While we love it, others have compared the taste to soap. If you are not a fan, you can replace the cilantro with an equal amount of flat-leaf (Italian) parsley.

Alkalizing Aid

**Makes about
3 cups (750 mL)**

Lemons and leafy greens are two of the most alkalizing foods you can eat, and when juiced together they will help your body return to a slightly alkaline state—especially if you've recently overdone it with highly acidic foods such as meats and dairy (for more on the benefits of alkalinity, see page 38). You'll love the zesty sweet-and-sour flavor too.

Tips

Several varieties of cucumbers are available in supermarkets, from field (slicing) to pickling to English cucumbers. We find that field and English cucumbers yield the most juice.

When peeling lemons and limes for juicing, be sure to leave behind as much white pith as possible. The pith of the fruit contains high concentrations of bioflavonoids such as limonene, which is believed to have anticancer properties.

To peel gingerroot quickly and easily, simply use the edge of a teaspoon. Scrape it back and forth along the root to remove the skin and reveal the yellow flesh underneath.

2	cucumbers, quartered	2
1	red apple, cored and quartered	1
½ cup	packed chopped spinach leaves	125 mL
1	stalk celery, chopped	1
1	lemon, peeled and halved (see Tips, left)	1
½ cup	packed chopped kale leaves	125 mL
1	lime, peeled and halved	1
1	¼-inch (0.5 cm) piece peeled gingerroot (see Tips, left)	1

1. Using a juicer, process half each of the cucumbers, apple, spinach, celery, lemon, kale and lime, plus the ginger. Following the same order, repeat with the remaining vegetables and fruit. Whisk well and serve immediately.

Balancing Acidity and Alkalinity

Eating foods such as eggs, meats, unripe fruit, cheese and pasteurized butter can result in increased levels of acidity in the body, leading to headache, irritability, sluggishness, lethargy, muscle spasms and sinus problems. Balancing our intake of acid-forming foods with alkaline-forming foods—such as watermelon, mangos, broccoli, raisins and sweet potatoes (to name but a few)—can help treat these symptoms and restore our bodies to a somewhat more alkaline state. Using Grade B pure maple syrup to sweeten your smoothies or nut milk can also help, because of both its high mineral content and alkalinity. Remember, the goal is not to be completely alkaline, since an alkaline body is no more balanced than an acidic body.

Nothin' But the Greens

Makes about 3 cups (750 mL)

Greens, greens, nothing but greens! All greens contain chlorophyll, the green pigment in plants that is responsible for photosynthesis. Chlorophyll is a good source of beta-carotene and vitamin K and provides significant antioxidant and anticancer effects. This earthy blend is loaded with some of our favorite greens and has a delightfully complex flavor.

Tip

Several varieties of cucumbers are available in supermarkets, from field (slicing) to pickling to English cucumbers. We find that field and English cucumbers yield the most juice.

Herbal Helper

Cilantro provides excellent support for liver health. This herb is not typically used in juices because of its distinctive taste, but if you love it (not everyone does), it will add a bold savory flavor to your juice. If you are not a fan of cilantro, simply omit it.

Variation

The ingredients we include in this juice can also make an incredible salad! Simply mix them together and drizzle with some raw apple cider vinegar and cold-pressed extra virgin olive oil and season with Himalayan sea salt. Toss and enjoy!

1	stalk celery, chopped	1
2	green apples, cored and sliced	2
½ cup	packed chopped romaine lettuce leaves	125 mL
1	cucumber, quartered (see Tip, left)	1
½ cup	packed chopped kale leaves	125 mL
½ cup	packed chopped spinach	125 mL
½ cup	packed chopped chard	125 mL
20	sprigs fresh cilantro (about 1 bunch)	20

1. Using a juicer, process half each of the celery, apple, romaine, cucumber, kale, spinach, chard and cilantro. Following the same order, repeat with the remaining apple and vegetables. Whisk well and serve immediately.

Juice Guru's Tip

You might not think to juice lettuce, but romaine adds an incredible boost of nutrition. It's an excellent source of vitamins A and K, folate and molybdenum. It also contains manganese, potassium, copper and iron, along with vitamins B_1 and C. Because the taste of romaine is neutral, you can add it to many different green juices without affecting the overall flavor profile.

Morning Energizer

**Makes about
3 cups (750 mL)**

We know, we know...
we have those sluggish
mornings too. Whether
it's because you stayed up
too late, had one too many
drinks with your buddies, or
are just burning the candle
at both ends, this zesty
and surprisingly satisfying
juice will help you get back
into gear. Both parsley
and carrots are extremely
energizing and known to
increase alertness.

Tip

Carrots come in a variety of
sizes; our recipes are based on
medium to large ones. We love
to use purple heirloom carrots
in our juices. They are lower in
sugar than hybridized orange
carrots, and studies have shown
that heirloom carrots contain
higher levels of anthocyanin,
a powerful antioxidant, than
common orange and yellow
varieties. But all carrot varieties
are excellent. Orange carrots
are also nutrient-dense, with
excellent levels of beta-
carotene—up to 65% of their
total carotenoid content.
Meanwhile, up to 50% of the
total carotenoid content of
yellow carrots consists of lutein.

6	carrots (see Tip, left)	6
20	sprigs fresh flat-leaf (Italian) parsley (about 1 bunch; see Caution, below)	20
3	stalks celery, chopped	3

1. Using a juicer, process half each of the carrots, parsley and celery. Following the same order, repeat with the remaining carrots, parsley and celery. Whisk well and serve immediately.

Caution
Certain phytonutrients in parsley—in concentrated amounts, as they are in juices—may act as a uterine stimulant and should likely be avoided during pregnancy. Because of the concentrated amount of oxalate it contains, parsley juice should also be avoided by people with kidney stones or a history of kidney stones.

Herbal Helper
Parsley is rich in vitamin C, flavonoids and carotenes, which may inhibit the cancer-causing properties of deep-fried foods. We always recommend combining parsley juice with other vegetables—it has a very strong taste that is more palatable when mixed with a sweeter vegetable such as carrot.

Nothin' But the Greens
(page 119)

Ginger Citrus Spice (page 132)

Pomegranate Punch (page 141)

Wheatgrass Cleanser (page 142)

Redhead Supreme (page 146)

Easy as ABC (page 156)

Holy Basil Supreme (page 170)

Tropical Turmeric (page 181)

Chef Babette's Carrot Mango Dressing

This dressing provides yet another use for carrot pulp. In addition to being high in fiber from the carrot pulp, it is delicious and nutritious—thanks in part to turmeric, which has been shown to have anti-inflammatory properties (see Herbal Helper, right). Apple cider vinegar is antibacterial and tamari is an excellent alternative to salt. Mangos are a good source of vitamin C and provide a creamy texture in this recipe, as well as giving the dressing a pleasant sweet/tart overtone. Drizzle this dressing over a fresh green salad or Chef Babette's Carrot "Tuna" Salad (page 116).

Tips

To produce 4 cups (1 L) carrot pulp, you will need to juice 8 to 10 medium carrots. When making any juice containing carrots, after juicing the carrots transfer the pulp to the refrigerator and store, tightly covered, until you have enough to make this recipe.

This dressing will last for up to 3 weeks in an airtight container in the refrigerator.

1 cup	chopped peeled mango	250 mL
2 cups	carrot pulp (see Tips, left)	500 mL
¼ cup	vegan mayonnaise	60 mL
2 cups	filtered water	500 mL
¼ cup	raw apple cider vinegar	60 mL
1 tbsp	tamari	15 mL
1 tbsp	ground turmeric	15 mL

1. In a blender, combine mango, carrot pulp, mayonnaise, water, vinegar, tamari and turmeric. Blend at high speed until smooth.

Herbal Helper

Turmeric has a warm, bitter taste and is used to treat a variety of ailments, including arthritis, heartburn, stomach pain, headache and even kidney problems. Turmeric's clout comes from a group of phytonutrients called curcuminoids. While not essential nutrients like vitamins and minerals, these compounds have been well researched for their anti-inflammatory properties in people who suffer from conditions such as inflammatory bowel disease, dementia or rheumatoid arthritis.

King Kale

**Makes about 3 cups
(750 mL)**

Kale is one of the most nutritious greens on the planet. For starters, it is brimming with antioxidants (see box, right). This juice combines two of the most common varieties of kale in a delicious, heart-healthy drink that will build your immune system and help prevent cancer too. Not only that, it has a sweet, earthy taste that you'll love!

Tips

Several varieties of cucumber are available in supermarkets, from field (slicing) to pickling to English cucumbers. We find that field and English cucumbers yield the most juice.

When peeling lemons for juicing, be sure to leave behind as much white pith as possible. The pith of the lemon contains high concentrations of bioflavonoids such as limonene, which is believed to have anticancer properties.

1	stalk celery, chopped	1
½ cup	packed chopped curly kale leaves	125 mL
2	red apples, cored and sliced	2
½ cup	packed chopped lacinato (Tuscan) kale leaves	125 mL
2	cucumbers, quartered (see Tips, left)	2
1	red bell pepper, quartered	1
1	lemon, peeled and halved (see Tips, left)	1

1. Using a juicer, process half each of the celery, curly kale, apples, lacinato kale, cucumbers, red pepper and lemon. Following the same order, repeat with the remaining fruit and vegetables. Whisk well and serve immediately.

Antioxidant Supreme

Kale's extreme anticancer and body-healing virtues are attributed to a combination of two very strong types of antioxidants known as carotenoids and flavonoids. Eating carotenoid-rich foods such as kale, which contains high levels of lutein and beta-carotene, has been shown to raise blood levels of this dynamic duo. Research has conclusively demonstrated that these antioxidants help our bodies alleviate oxidative stress and health issues associated with this stress, including cataracts, chronic obstructive pulmonary disease (COPD) and atherosclerosis. They also reduce the risk of many types of cancer, including lung, skin, breast and prostate cancers.

Flu Buster

Feel a sniffle coming on? Feeling a little down, with a slight fever kicking in? You'll want to juice up this combo two or three times a day to help fight off pending flu or even a seasonal cold. This health-promoting elixir is a delicious way to get your daily dose of garlic, cayenne, ginger and lemon, all of which have been linked with antiviral properties.

Tips

Never peel the skin from your apples before juicing. Apple skin contains an abundance of phytonutrient polyphenols, which help to regulate blood sugar.

There are so many varieties of apples to choose from. Fuji, Red Delicious and Granny Smith are most commonly used for juicing, but any type will produce a delicious juice. We recommend using whatever is local and in season. Simply changing the variety of apple you use is an easy way to combat boredom with a particular juice blend.

To peel gingerroot quickly and easily, simply use the edge of a teaspoon. Scrape it back and forth along the root to remove the skin and reveal the yellow flesh underneath.

1	cucumber, quartered	1
2	green apples, cored and sliced (see Tips, left)	2
½ cup	packed chopped kale leaves	125 mL
1	lemon, peeled and halved	1
2	cloves garlic	2
1	¼-inch (0.5 cm) piece peeled gingerroot (see Tips, left)	1
1	⅛-inch (3 mm) piece peeled turmeric root	1
⅛ tsp	cayenne pepper	0.5 mL

1. Using a juicer, process half each of the cucumber, apples, kale, lemon and garlic, plus the turmeric and ginger. Following the same order, repeat with the remaining apple, kale, lemon and garlic.

2. Add cayenne and whisk well. Serve immediately.

Herbal Helper

Are you looking to strengthen your immune system and get rid of that flu for good? We suggest adding ½ to 1¼ tsp (2 to 6 mL) organic astragalus extract to your juice. Drink this mixture three times daily for therapeutic effect (you can also mix the extract into plain water). An herb native to China, astragalus is hepatoprotective (meaning it prevents damage to the liver), antiviral and antibacterial, regulates blood sugar, and rejuvenates the immune system.

Note: Because astragalus is somewhat bitter, if adding it to this recipe you may want to use red apples to neutralize the flavor.

Blue-Green Protein Juice

Here's a juice that provides as much protein as a glass of milk, with the added benefit of lowering your cholesterol while tempering inflammation, thanks to its antioxidant properties. Its main ingredients, spirulina and chlorella, have also been shown to lower blood pressure, which may lower the risk for cardiovascular diseases (including stroke) in people with elevated blood pressure. As an added bonus, spirulina has been shown to alleviate allergy symptoms. Yes, this juice delivers all these benefits and more, thanks to its powerful ingredients. It also has a smooth, fresh, earthy flavor.

Tips

Several varieties of cucumber are available in supermarkets, from field (slicing) to pickling to English cucumbers. We find that field and English cucumbers yield the most juice.

Never peel the skin from your apples before juicing. Apple skin contains an abundance of phytonutrient polyphenols, which help to regulate blood sugar.

4	cucumbers, quartered (see Tips, left)	4
1	lime, peeled and halved	1
2	red apples, cored and sliced (see Tips, left)	2
1 tbsp	spirulina powder (see Juice Guru's Tip, below)	15 mL
1 tbsp	chlorella powder	15 mL

1. Using a juicer, process half each of the cucumbers, lime and apples. Following the same order, repeat with the remaining cucumbers, lime and apple.

2. Add spirulina and chlorella and whisk well. Serve immediately.

Juice Guru's Tip

Spirulina is a protein-rich blue-green alga that thrives in warm fresh water. Chlorella is a chlorophyll-rich green alga that contains 10 times more protein than spirulina. Both of these algae help to detoxify your body by removing heavy metals (spirulina has been shown to remove toxic mercury from the body). We recommend using organic spirulina and chlorella powders from a reputable company—one that offers independent third-party lab verification that the spirulina contains iodine, not bromine, and is both radiation- and toxin-free—to avoid the risk of contaminants, molds or heavy metals.

Kickin' Green Machine

Makes about 3 cups (750 mL)

This satisfying green juice, with its added kick of cayenne pepper, defines the old expression "get up and go." You'll love the way the cucumber mellows the flavor while the lemon and ginger provide a complementary zing. Cayenne pepper improves blood circulation, among other benefits. Both the kale and spinach provide an incredible energy boost.

Tips

Several varieties of cucumber are available in supermarkets, from field (slicing) to pickling to English cucumbers. We find that field and English cucumbers yield the most juice.

When peeling lemons for juicing, be sure to leave behind as much white pith as possible. The pith of the lemon contains high concentrations of bioflavonoids such as limonene, which is believed to have anticancer properties.

To peel gingerroot quickly and easily, simply use the edge of a teaspoon. Scrape it back and forth along the root to remove the skin and reveal the yellow flesh underneath.

3	cucumbers, quartered (see Tips, left)	3
½ cup	packed chopped kale leaves	125 mL
1	stalk celery, chopped	1
1	lemon, peeled and halved (see Tips, left)	1
15	sprigs fresh cilantro (about ½ bunch)	15
½ cup	packed chopped spinach leaves	125 mL
1	¼-inch (0.5 cm) piece peeled gingerroot (see Tips, left)	1
¼ tsp	cayenne pepper	1 mL

1. Using a juicer, process half each of the cucumbers, kale, celery, lemon, cilantro and spinach, plus the ginger. Following the same order, repeat with the remaining vegetables and lemon.

2. Add cayenne and whisk well. Serve immediately.

Juice Guru's Tip

If you enjoy a spicy drink, double the quantity of cayenne pepper.

Herbal Helper

You may already know that ginger can help alleviate some of the symptoms of motion sickness, but did you know it can also help prevent morning sickness? A 2007 study by the faculty of medicine at Thammasat University (Thailand) showed that participants who took 1 gram of ginger every day for four days reported less vomiting compared to those who took a placebo.

Green Living Lemonade

This sweet, tart and zesty juice is the perfect antidote for a hot summer day. Mom-tested and kid-approved, it's also a nourishing alternative to traditional processed lemonade, because it's loaded with living enzymes and nutrients and has no added sugars or fillers. Drink up!

Tips

There are so many varieties of apples to choose from. Fuji, Red Delicious and Granny Smith are most commonly used for juicing, but any type will produce a delicious juice. We recommend using whatever is local and in season. Simply changing the variety of apple you use is an easy way to combat boredom with a particular juice blend.

When peeling lemons for juicing, be sure to leave behind as much white pith as possible. The pith of the lemon contains high concentrations of bioflavonoids such as limonene, which is believed to have anticancer properties.

4	red apples, cored and sliced (see Tips, left)	4
½ cup	packed chopped kale leaves	125 mL
1	lemon, peeled and halved (see Tips, left)	1
3 cups	red grapes (see Tips, left)	750 mL

1. Using a juicer, process half each of the apples, kale, lemon and grapes. Following the same order, repeat with the remaining fruits and vegetables. Whisk well and serve immediately.

Juice Guru's Tip

When selecting red grapes, look for a rich crimson hue and even color. Choose grapes that are plump and hearty. A silvery white "bloom" on the skins indicates freshness. The grapes should be firmly attached to stems that are brown or beige and healthy-looking, moist and flexible.

Longevity Booster

This delicious sour-yet-sweet juice is loaded with antioxidants to help your immune system function at full capacity. Collard greens deliver a healing combination of antioxidants, anti-inflammatories and detoxification benefits. This juice is also loaded with vitamin C from the apples, vitamin A (via carotenoids) from the collard greens and kale, and manganese from the collard greens. While it doesn't contain as much as nuts and seeds, this juice will provide about 8% of the recommended daily intake of vitamin E, thanks again to the collard greens.

Tips

When choosing collard greens, pick leaves that are relatively small and firm. Avoid greens that show signs of yellowing or have holes in them. Collard greens can go limp quickly, so it is best to use them within 2 to 3 days of purchase. To store collard greens, as soon as you get them home from the store, wrap them loosely in damp paper towels, place inside a plastic bag and refrigerate.

When peeling lemons for juicing, be sure to leave behind as much white pith as possible. The pith of the lemon contains high concentrations of bioflavonoids such as limonene, which is believed to have anticancer properties.

1	cucumber, quartered	1
3	green apples, cored and quartered	3
½ cup	packed chopped collard greens (see Tips, left)	125 mL
1	lemon, peeled and halved (see Tips, left)	1
½ cup	packed chopped kale leaves	125 mL
15	sprigs fresh cilantro (about ½ bunch)	15

1. Using a juicer, process half each of the cucumber, apples, collard greens, lemon, kale and cilantro. Following the same order, repeat with the remaining fruits and vegetables. Whisk well and serve immediately.

Herbal Helper

Cilantro provides excellent support for liver health. This herb is not typically used in juices, but if you love it (not everyone does), it will add a bold savory flavor to your juice.

Tips for Prepping and Measuring Ingredients

- No matter what type of juicer you are using, it is always a good idea to roughly chop greens such as spinach and kale and to cut longer vegetables such as celery and cucumbers into pieces before processing, so they flow through your juicer more efficiently and with less chance of clogging.
- When measuring leafy greens, pack the chopped greens tightly into the measuring cup to ensure that you achieve the correct measure for the recipes.
- When measuring chopped herbs, pack them into the measuring cup lightly to ensure that you achieve the correct measure for the recipes.

Juice Guru's Tip

Unless you are using a top-of-the-line juice press, even the best juicers will leave a fair amount of pulp in the final product. If, like us, you don't like pulp, we recommend straining your juice through a fine-mesh sieve into a 4-cup (1 L) measuring cup (for easy pouring). Straining your juice will make drinking it more enjoyable, since you won't end up with tiny fragments of pulp and skin that require occasional chewing.

Juicy Variation

Juicers can vary significantly in the volume of juice they produce, depending on the process the use and their efficiency with particular fruits and vegetables. Juice quantity will also fluctuate to reflect the produce used; a large apple or cucumber will yield considerably more juice than a small one. So while most of our recipes yield us approximately 3 cups (750 mL), be prepared to experience variations in the yield.

Chapter 9
Cleansing Juices

Honeydew Kick

**Makes about
3 cups (750 mL)**

The refreshing sweet, sour and herbal combination of melon, lime and cilantro in this juice will leave you feeling as though you're in a tropical paradise. Honeydew is loaded with vitamin C and vitamin A (as carotenoids), as well as potassium and copper. Potassium is great for maintaining healthy blood pressure levels, and vitamin C and copper promote healthy skin and tissue repair.

Tips

Choose a honeydew melon that is evenly round, with a light yellow rind (if the rind is white or greenish white, it's overripe). Gently press the sides of the melon with the tips of your fingers. If it gives to that gentle pressure, it's ripe and perfect for juicing. Ripe honeydew melons also give off a discernible sweet scent. If you don't smell anything, the melon likely isn't ripe.

When shopping for limes, look for fruits that are heavy and firm for their size. Be sure they are clean and devoid of mold or signs of decay. The skin should be deep green and glossy. Keep in mind that limes become yellower as they ripen; the deep green indicates they are ready to go.

1	honeydew melon, rind removed, chopped (see Tips, left and below)	1
15	sprigs fresh cilantro (about ½ bunch)	15
1	lime, peeled and halved (see Tips, left)	1

1. Using a juicer, process half each of the melon, cilantro and lime. Following the same order, repeat with the remaining melon, cilantro and lime. Whisk well and serve immediately.

Juice Guru's Tip

Melons are among the few fruits that do not have a low glycemic index (the measure of how a food affects blood sugar). If you have blood sugar issues, you should limit your consumption of melon or consult with your doctor.

Herbal Helper

Cilantro provides excellent support for liver health. This herb is not typically used in juices, but if you love it (not everyone does) it will add a bold savory flavor to your juice.

Watermelon Mint

Makes about 3 cups (750 mL)		

**Makes about
3 cups (750 mL)**

½	watermelon, inner-rind intact, chopped (see Tips, left)	½
1	lemon, peeled and halved (see Tips, left)	1
15	sprigs mint (about ½ bunch)	15

This juice packs an extra-intense punch of flavor, thanks to the mint, which brings out the sweetness of watermelon in a most delightful way. Watermelon is, of course, loaded with water, and the inner-rind contains concentrated amounts of vitamin C and potassium.

1. Using a juicer, process half each of the watermelon, lemon and mint. Following the same order, repeat with the remaining watermelon, lemon and mint. Whisk well and serve immediately.

Tips

Look for a watermelon that is firm, symmetrical and free of major bruises or scars (minor scratches are okay). Since a watermelon is 92% water, your melon should be relatively heavy for its size; the ripest ones contain the most water. Ripe watermelons are dark green, but be sure to check the bottom for the "ground spot"— where the melon sat, soaking up the sun, as it grew. If this spot is white or greenish, your watermelon may have been picked too soon and might not be as ripe as it should be.

When peeling lemons for juicing, be sure to leave behind as much white pith as possible. The pith of the lemon contains high concentrations of bioflavonoids such as limonene, which is believed to have anticancer properties.

Herbal Helper

Mint has been used for centuries to soothe upset stomachs and improve digestion. Recent research suggests that it may also alleviate the symptoms of irritable bowel syndrome (IBS). Although these studies were based on the use of peppermint oil and not fresh mint, we believe adding mint to your juice may provide similar relief.

Ginger Citrus Spice

The effervescent sweet-and-sour blend of carrots, lemon and oranges comes alive with a bit of ginger. This refreshing juice is simple to make, complex in flavor and a favorite before or after a hard day of work. The abundant vitamin C and flavonoids in oranges provide overall energy, strengthen the immune system and support connective tissue in the body.

Tips

Look for oranges that are brightly colored, firm and heavy, with a fine-textured skin. Avoid fruits that are severely bruised, soft or puffy. Refrigerated, oranges will keep well for more than a week.

To peel gingerroot quickly and easily, simply use the edge of a teaspoon. Scrape it back and forth along the root to remove the skin and reveal the yellow flesh underneath.

3	carrots, sliced, greens intact	3
1	lemon, peeled and halved	1
3	oranges, peeled and halved (see Tips, left)	3
1	¼-inch (0.5 cm) piece peeled gingerroot (see Tips, left)	1

1. Using a juicer, process half each of the carrots, lemon and oranges, plus the ginger. Following the same order, repeat with the remaining carrot, lemon and orange. Whisk well. Serve immediately.

Herbal Helper
Ginger is one of the most widely used spices, not only for its flavor but also because it has a long history of medicinal use. It is well known as a treatment for nausea and motion sickness and as a digestion enhancer. It also has powerful anti-inflammatory properties.

Pineapple Turmeric Gold

This tropical-tasting juice will supercharge your body with a boost of healing nutrients. Pineapple is rich in bromelain, a sulfur-containing proteolytic (protein-digesting) enzyme, which is excellent for reducing inflammation and has been used experimentally as an anticancer agent. Pineapple also provides the trace mineral manganese, an essential cofactor in a number of enzymes used for energy production and antioxidant defense. You'll also love the earthy taste and the anticancer benefits that the romaine and spinach leaves provide.

Tips

Look for a plump pineapple with fresh, deep green leaves. The skin should yield slightly to the touch. To store pineapple, remove the skin, cut into chunks and place in an airtight container in the refrigerator for up to 3 days.

Pineapples are among the few fruits that do not have a low glycemic index (the measure for how a food affects blood sugar). If you have blood-sugar issues, you should consider avoiding pineapple in your juice or consult your doctor.

Several varieties of cucumber are available in supermarkets, from field (slicing) to pickling to English cucumbers. We find that field and English cucumbers yield the most juice.

1	pineapple, skin removed, cut into wedges (see Tips, left)	1
1	cucumber, quartered (see Tips, left)	1
1 cup	packed chopped romaine lettuce leaves (see Juice Guru's Tip, below)	250 mL
1 cup	packed chopped spinach leaves	250 mL
1	$\frac{1}{8}$-inch (3 mm) piece peeled turmeric root	1

1. Using a juicer, process half each of the pineapple, cucumber, romaine and spinach, plus the turmeric. Following the same order, repeat with the remaining pineapple, cucumber, romaine and spinach. Whisk well and serve immediately.

Juice Guru's Tip

You might not think to juice lettuce, but romaine adds an incredible boost of nutrition. It's an excellent source of vitamins A and K, folate and molybdenum. It also contains manganese, potassium, copper and iron, along with vitamins B_1 and C. Because the taste of romaine is neutral, you can add it to many different green juices without affecting the overall flavor profile.

Pineapple Grape Express

**Makes about
3 cups (750 mL)**

This juice tastes like fruit punch, offering just the right balance of sweet and sour flavors. It also supports the body's natural detoxification process, thanks to the grapes, which contain powerful antioxidants. Grapes also feature an abundance of flavonoids, which have been lauded for their ability to reduce the risk of atherosclerosis.

Tips

Pineapples do not continue to ripen after they are picked, so choose one that looks plump and has a sweet aroma. The leaves of the crown should also look fresh and green and should not pull out of the fruit easily.

To peel a pineapple, place it on a cutting board and, using a sharp knife, cut off the top and bottom to remove the leaves and stem and create flat surfaces. Resting the pineapple on a flat end, slide the knife under the skin and, with a downward motion, remove the skin in strips. Shave off any remaining bits of skin.

When selecting red grapes, look for those that have a rich crimson hue and even color. Choose grapes that are plump and hearty. A silvery white "bloom" on the skins indicates freshness. The grapes should be firmly attached to stems that are brown or beige and healthy-looking, moist and flexible.

½	pineapple, skin removed, cut into wedges (see Tips, left)	½
1 cup	red grapes (see Tips, left)	250 mL
1	lemon, peeled and halved	1
1 cup	packed spinach leaves	250 mL
1	cucumber, quartered (see Tips, page 133)	1
1	¼-inch (0.5 cm) piece peeled gingerroot	1

1. Using a juicer, process half each of the pineapple, grapes, lemon, spinach and cucumber, plus the ginger. Following the same order, repeat with the remaining fruits and vegetables. Whisk well and serve immediately.

Juice Guru's Tip

When it comes to bringing a glow to your skin, drinking this juice is as good as getting a facial. Cucumber is an excellent source of silica, which works to strengthen connective tissue and improve overall complexion and skin health. And the powerful array of nutrient-rich ingredients in this juice will make you healthy and beautiful on the inside too.

Morning Zinger

This sweet, tangy but spicy juice is an excellent way to find your get-up-and-go in the mornings. The capsaicin in cayenne pepper fights inflammation and stimulates circulation, as well as reducing blood cholesterol, triglyceride levels and platelet aggregation (blood clotting), all of which are risk factors for cardiovascular disease and some forms of dementia.

Tips

Never peel the skin from your apples before juicing. Apple skin contains an abundance of phytonutrient polyphenols, which help to regulate blood sugar.

There are so many varieties of apples to choose from. Fuji, Red Delicious and Granny Smith are most commonly used for juicing, but any type will produce a delicious juice. We recommend using whatever is local and in season. Simply changing the variety of apple you use is an easy way to combat boredom with a particular juice blend.

When peeling lemons for juicing, be sure to leave behind as much white pith as possible. The pith of the lemon contains high concentrations of bioflavonoids such as limonene, which is believed to have anticancer properties.

4	red apples, cored and sliced (see Tips, left)	4
1	lemon, peeled and halved (see Tips, left)	1
⅛ tsp	cayenne pepper	0.5 mL

1. Using a juicer, process half each of the apples and lemon. Following the same order, repeat with the remaining fruit.

2. Add cayenne and whisk well. Serve immediately.

Juice Guru's Tip

If you've been burning the midnight oil while working or caring for your family, or even if you were partying a little too much the night before, you'll find that this juice helps to get you going and keep moving throughout the day. While all the juices in this book will give you an energy jolt, we find the combination of cayenne, lemon and apple to be particularly effective.

Lemon Drop

This sweet, tart juice is reminiscent of lemon-drop candies, so it's a great juice for those days when you are craving something decadent. Despite its candy-like taste, it is extremely cleansing and nourishing.

Tips

To peel a pineapple, place it on a cutting board and, using a sharp knife, cut off the top and bottom to remove the leaves and stem and create flat surfaces. Resting the pineapple on a flat end, slide the knife under the skin and, with a downward motion, remove the skin in strips. Shave off any remaining bits of skin.

When selecting red grapes, look for those that have a rich crimson hue and even color. Choose grapes that are plump and hearty. A silvery white "bloom" on the skins indicates freshness. The grapes should be firmly attached to stems that are brown or beige and healthy-looking, moist and flexible.

To peel gingerroot quickly and easily, simply use the edge of a teaspoon. Scrape it back and forth along the root to remove the skin and reveal the yellow flesh underneath.

1	pineapple, skin removed, cut into wedges (see Tips, left and on page 133)	1
3 cups	red grapes (see Tips, left)	750 mL
1	½-inch (1 cm) piece peeled gingerroot (see Tips, left)	1

1. Using a juicer, process half each of the pineapple and grapes, plus the ginger. Following the same order, repeat with the remaining pineapple and grapes. Whisk well and serve immediately.

Juice Guru's Tip

Virtually any fresh juice provides excellent support for detoxification, but red grape juice is especially beneficial for both cleansing and nourishing your body. This is because of the high levels of flavonoids in grapes. Flavonoids have powerful antioxidant effects—including reducing inflammation, fighting aging and boosting circulation—which is why increasing your intake of fruits and vegetables can go a long way toward reducing your risk for chronic disease.

Grape Ape

This sweet and fruity juice tastes just like a refreshing strawberry ice pop. You'll be tempted to drink it quickly, but restrain yourself and savor each drop of this cleansing elixir. Both red and green grapes boast fantastic antioxidant value, increasing the antioxidant capacity of the blood and reducing overall oxidative damage.

Tip

When selecting grapes, look for those that have a rich even color and appear plump and hearty. A silvery white "bloom" on the skins indicates freshness. The grapes should be firmly attached to stems that are brown or beige and healthy-looking, moist and flexible.

3 cups	red grapes (see Tip, left)	750 mL
15	strawberries	15
3 cups	green grapes	750 mL

1. Using a juicer, process half each of the red grapes, strawberries and green grapes. Following the same order, repeat with the remaining fruit. Whisk well and serve immediately.

Juice Guru's Tip

It's amazing that a juice so delicious can be so beneficial to your health. Grapes are some of the most nutritious foods on the planet. They have been associated with reducing the risk for atherosclerosis, protecting against vascular disease and preventing platelets from clumping together and forming potentially serious blood clots—in essence, they are a longevity-boosting superfood. They also have a low glycemic index (GI). Unfortunately, grapes appear consistently on the Dirty Dozen list (see page 94) as containing significant pesticide residues, so be sure to purchase organic grapes whenever possible.

Apple Strawberry Fields

Our bodies often lack proper hydration and, as a result, are functioning under stress. This deliciously sweet and simple blend of apples, strawberries and coconut water is a natural de-stressor that will leave you feeling as if you've been transported to a tropical paradise.

Tips

There are so many varieties of apples to choose from. Fuji, Red Delicious and Granny Smith are most commonly used for juicing, but any type will produce a delicious juice. We recommend using whatever is local and in season. Simply changing the variety of apple you use is an easy way to combat boredom with a particular juice blend.

You can find young coconuts in Asian and Mexican markets, specialty health food stores and well-stocked supermarkets.

A cleaver is normally required to open the husk of a young coconut, but you can also find task-specific tools in kitchen supply stores. For convenience, you can purchase organic raw coconut water in bottles at health food stores and well-stocked supermarkets.

4	apples, cored and sliced (see Tips, left)	4
1 cup	strawberries (8 to 10)	250 mL
1 cup	young coconut water (see Tips, left)	250 mL

1. Using a juicer, process half each of the apples and strawberries. Following the same order, repeat with the remaining apples and strawberries.

2. Add coconut water and whisk well. Serve immediately.

Juice Guru's Tip

Coconut water contains an abundance of water and electrolytes. A study published in the *West Indian Medical Journal* in 2005 indicates that 71% of people who drank coconut water instead of regular water for a period of two weeks significantly lowered their blood pressure compared to the control group, which drank regular water.

Young versus Mature Coconuts

In general, two different types of coconuts are available: young and mature. Young coconuts have either a green shell or white husk. Mature coconuts are brown and covered with hair-like fibers. We recommend young coconuts for your juices. They contain more water and a gel-like "meat" that contains more of the fruit's nutrients.

We typically use only the water of young coconuts in our juices; the gel should be reserved for smoothies. As a coconut begins to age, the water begins to seep into its meat and the remaining liquid becomes less nutritious. Older mature coconuts are best used for making coconut oil and other coconut products.

Blueberry Hill

You'll find your thrill in this delicious blend of fruity goodness. The sweet and flavorful combination of apples, grapes and blueberries tastes sinful, but don't be fooled—it's so good for you! The blueberries alone are antioxidant all-stars, supporting cardiovascular and cognitive function and eye health.

Tips

Never peel the skin from your apples before juicing. Apple skin contains an abundance of phytonutrient polyphenols, which help to regulate blood sugar.

When selecting red grapes, look for those that have a rich crimson hue and even color. Choose grapes that are plump and hearty. A silvery white "bloom" on the skins indicates freshness. The grapes should be firmly attached to stems that are brown or beige and healthy-looking, moist and flexible.

Look for blueberries that are smooth and firm to the touch. The berries should be a vibrant, even blue with a whitish film (which indicates freshness). Shake the container gently to ensure that they can move around freely; if not, they may be soft, damaged or even moldy. To store blueberries, cover loosely with plastic wrap and refrigerate. Wash just before use, removing any crushed or moldy ones first.

3	apples, cored and sliced (see Tips, left)	3
2 cups	red grapes (see Tips, left)	500 mL
1 cup	blueberries (see Tips, left)	250 mL

1. Using a juicer, process half each of the apples, grapes and blueberries. Following the same order, repeat with the remaining fruit. Whisk well and serve immediately.

Juice Guru's Tip

While we recommend using green apples in our veggie juice combos, because we prefer their slightly tart flavor (Granny Smiths are our favorite), feel free to use red apples if you have a sweet tooth or are new to juicing—Fuji and Red Delicious apples are excellent. You really can't go wrong if you use whatever variety of apple is in season and local to your area—all apples are rich in nutrients.

Tropical Flush

Makes about 3 cups (750 mL)

Tangy pineapple is complemented by sweet pears and fresh greens in this cleansing and nutrient-dense juice. Pear juice is loaded with antioxidants and anti-inflammatory nutrients, such as vitamin C, and polyphenols such as catechins and epicatechins, similar to those found in green tea.

Tips

Never peel pears before juicing. The skin is an important source of many phenolic phytonutrients, which include anticancer agents, anti-inflammatory flavonoids and antioxidants.

Pineapples do not continue to ripen after they are picked, so choose one that looks plump and has a sweet aroma. The leaves in the crown should look fresh and green and should not pull out of the fruit easily.

To peel a pineapple, place it on a cutting board and, using a sharp knife, cut off the top and bottom to remove the leaves and stem and create flat surfaces. Resting the pineapple on a flat end, slide the knife under the skin and, with a downward motion, remove the skin in strips. Shave off any remaining bits of skin.

Several varieties of cucumber are available in supermarkets, from field (slicing) to pickling to English cucumbers. We find that field and English cucumbers yield the most juice.

½	pineapple, skin removed, cut into wedges (see Tips, left and on page 133)	½
1	stalk celery, chopped	1
½ cup	packed chopped kale leaves	125 mL
1	cucumber, quartered	1
½ cup	packed chopped romaine lettuce leaves	125 mL
2	pears, quartered (see Tips, left)	2
10	sprigs fresh flat-leaf (Italian) parsley (see Caution, below)	10

1. Using a juicer, process half each of the pineapple, celery, kale, cucumber, romaine, pears and parsley. Following the same order, repeat with the remaining fruits and vegetables. Whisk well and serve immediately.

Juice Guru's Tip

While we typically suggest that you strain your juice before consumption, this is not the case when it comes to pears. Recent studies have shown that with their pulp removed, pear juices lose up to 40% of their total phytonutrients and their antioxidant capacity is significantly reduced. You'll want to consume all the pulp to make sure you reap its many benefits—"cloudy" pear juice is definitely the way to go.

Caution
Certain phytonutrients in parsley—in concentrated amounts, as they are in juices—may act as a uterine stimulant and should likely be avoided during pregnancy. Because of the concentrated amount of oxalate it contains, parsley juice should also be avoided by people with kidney stones or a history of kidney stones.

Pomegranate Punch

This velvety juice features a delightful contrast of sweet and tangy, thanks to the addition of pomegranate and lime. Pomegranates are loaded with antioxidants such as punicalagin. High in vitamin K and potassium, the whole fruit also provides the minerals manganese, phosphorus, magnesium, calcium, zinc and iron, as well as vitamin C. Pomegranate juice can help to regenerate skin cells (slowing aging), eliminate dry skin, fight free radicals, protect your heart and ward off cancer, and it may increase bone quality. That's an incredible health punch!

Tips

When selecting red grapes, look for those that have a rich crimson hue and even color. Choose grapes that are plump and hearty. A silvery white "bloom" on the skins indicates freshness. The grapes should be firmly attached to stems that are brown or beige and healthy-looking, moist and flexible.

To juice a pomegranate, start by cutting it in half as you would a grapefruit. Use a spoon to gently remove the seeds from the membrane of the fruit. Keep in mind that pomegranate juice can stain, so exercise appropriate caution by wearing a kitchen apron. Process the pomegranate seeds like the other fruits in the recipe.

3	apples, cored and sliced	3
3 cups	red grapes (see Tips, left)	750 mL
1	lime, peeled and halved	1
	Seeds from 1 pomegranate (see Tips, left)	

1. Using a juicer, process half each of the apples, grapes, lime and pomegranate seeds. Following the same order, repeat with the remaining fruits. Whisk well and serve immediately.

Juice Guru's Tip

While we recommend using green apples in our veggie juice combos, because we prefer their slightly tart flavor (Granny Smiths are our favorite), feel free to use red apples if you have a sweet tooth or are new to juicing—Fuji and Red Delicious apples are excellent. You really can't go wrong if you use whatever variety of apple is in season and local to your area—all apples are rich in nutrients.

Wheatgrass Cleanser

Makes about 1 cup (250 mL)

Sweet and salty, with a slight kick from the ginger, this is a beautifully balanced juice. According to the late Steve "Sproutman" Meyerowitz, wheatgrass juice can be termed "the nectar of rejuvenation, the plasma of youth and the blood of all life." Wheatgrass juice is loaded with chlorophyll and provides a wide range of nutrients. It does, however, pack quite a punch, so you'll want to introduce this highly nutritious juice into your diet slowly, as we do in this recipe. We include celery and gingerroot to balance the taste. One of the healthiest juices you can drink, wheatgrass is a highly recommended component of successful Daily Juicing.

Tips

To peel gingerroot quickly and easily, simply use the edge of a teaspoon. Scrape it back and forth along the root to remove the skin and reveal the yellow flesh underneath.

While we recommend using fresh wheatgrass juice in this recipe, you'll also get great results with store-bought frozen organic wheatgrass shots (available in the freezer section of most health food stores). If you are juicing wheatgrass yourself, be sure to do it before juicing the celery and ginger, so it's ready to whisk in immediately.

1	stalk celery, chopped	1
1	1/8-inch (3 mm) piece peeled gingerroot (see Tips, left)	1
2 oz	wheatgrass juice (see Tips, left)	60 mL

1. Using a juicer, process celery and ginger.

2. Add wheatgrass juice and whisk well. Serve immediately.

Juice Guru's Tips

We recommend drinking only 1 cup (250 mL) of this juice per day because of wheatgrass's incredible vitamin and mineral content. A little is all you need.

Some people find the taste of wheatgrass too sweet, and it can even elicit a gag reflex. If this happens to you, just take it slowly. Once you start consuming wheatgrass on a regular basis (two to three times a week), you will build up a tolerance—as will your taste buds.

Get the Glow

**Makes about
3 cups (750 mL)**

This juice has a savory yet bright flavor. It is designed to improve blood circulation and leave the skin with a luminous glow, thanks to purple cabbage, which is rich in phytochemicals. These nutrients increase antioxidant defense and improve the body's ability to detoxify and remove harmful chemicals and hormones.

Tip

If you enjoy a bit of heat, add more jalapeño pepper to taste. However, we recommend adding only about a pinch at a time. If you overdo it, there is no turning back.

2	green apples, cored and sliced	2
1	cucumber, quartered	1
1	red bell pepper, quartered	1
1	lemon, peeled and halved	1
1	stalk celery, chopped	1
½ cup	packed chopped purple cabbage	125 mL
15	sprigs fresh flat-leaf (Italian) parsley (about ½ bunch; see Caution, below)	15
1	¹⁄₁₆-inch (2 mm) piece jalapeño pepper (see Tip, left)	1

1. Using a juicer, process half each of the apples, cucumber, red pepper, lemon, celery, cabbage, parsley and jalapeño. Following the same order, repeat with the remaining fruits and vegetables. Whisk well and serve immediately.

> **Caution**
> Certain phytonutrients in parsley—in concentrated amounts, as they are in juices—may act as a uterine stimulant and should likely be avoided during pregnancy. Because of the concentrated amount of oxalate it contains, parsley juice should also be avoided by people with kidney stones or a history of kidney stones.

Tips for Prepping and Measuring Ingredients

- No matter what type of juicer you are using, it is always a good idea to roughly chop greens such as spinach and kale and to cut longer vegetables such as celery and cucumbers into pieces before processing, so they flow through your juicer more efficiently and with less chance of clogging.
- When measuring leafy greens, pack the chopped greens tightly into the measuring cup to ensure that you achieve the correct measure for the recipes.
- When measuring chopped herbs, pack them into the measuring cup lightly to ensure that you achieve the correct measure for the recipes.

Juice Guru's Tip

Unless you are using a top-of-the-line juice press, even the best juicers will leave a fair amount of pulp in the final product. If, like us, you don't like pulp, we recommend straining your juice through a fine-mesh sieve into a 4-cup (1 L) measuring cup (for easy pouring). Straining your juice will make drinking it more enjoyable, since you won't end up with tiny fragments of pulp and skin that require occasional chewing.

Juicy Variation

Juicers can vary significantly in the volume of juice they produce, depending on the process the use and their efficiency with particular fruits and vegetables. Juice quantity will also fluctuate to reflect the produce used; a large apple or cucumber will yield considerably more juice than a small one. So while most of our recipes yield us approximately 3 cups (750 mL), be prepared to experience variations in the yield.

Chapter 10
Root and Veggie Juices

Redhead Supreme

This juice is a great choice for beginners. It's easy to make and, best of all, tastes just like old-fashioned fruit punch–flavored candy. In addition, beets are extremely beneficial, providing ample amounts of potassium and also vitamin C, calcium, magnesium and iron. Betacyanin (the purple pigment in beets) has been shown to have possible anticancer effects against breast and prostate cancer. Apples are brimming with antioxidants, which, aside from greatly boosting your immune system, can lower your risk of asthma and lung cancer.

Tips

There are so many varieties of apples to choose from. Fuji, Red Delicious and Granny Smith are most commonly used for juicing, but any type will produce a delicious juice. We recommend using whatever is local and in season. Simply changing the variety of apple you use is an easy way to combat boredom with a particular juice blend.

Choose small or medium beets with firm roots, smooth skins and deep color. Avoid beets that have spots, bruises or soft, wet areas, all of which indicate spoilage. Shriveled or spongy beets should also be avoided, as these are signs that the beets are old, tough and fibrous.

6	red apples, cored and sliced (see Tips, left)	6
1	beet, quartered (see Tips, left)	1
1	lemon, peeled and halved	1
1	½-inch (1 cm) piece peeled gingerroot	1

1. Using a juicer, process half each of the apples, beet and lemon, plus the ginger. Following the same order, repeat with the remaining apples, beet and lemon. Whisk well and serve immediately.

Herbal Helper

Want to boost your immune system? Add 2 to 5 drops of the medicinal herb *Echinacea angustifolia* to your juice and stir well. Drink three times a day. Echinacea is an easily tolerated and effective combatant against infections, viruses and inflammation.

Chef Babette's Barbecue Beet Burgers

Makes about
6 burgers

Beets are extremely nutritious and great in juices. But what about all that pulp? I dreamed up this burger as a way to salvage the valuable fiber-rich pulp left over from juicing, and in the process created one of the best veggie burgers in Los Angeles. Think a veggie burger can't be amazing? You have to try this one. Serve on a sprouted wheat bun or your favorite bread, or simply on a bed of lettuce.

Tips

No-salt seasonings usually contain a combination of dried onion and garlic, black pepper, red bell pepper, parsley, lemon peel, mustard seed, cumin, marjoram, coriander, cayenne pepper and rosemary. You can find them in health food stores and well-stocked supermarkets.

To produce $1\frac{1}{2}$ cups (375 mL) beet pulp, you will need to juice about 6 medium beets.

Uncooked patties will last for up to 1 week in an airtight container in the refrigerator. Use parchment paper to separate your patties. For the best-tasting results, do not freeze them.

$\frac{1}{2}$ cup	walnut halves	125 mL
$\frac{1}{4}$ cup	chopped red onion	60 mL
$1\frac{1}{2}$ tsp	no-salt seasoning (see Tips, left)	7 mL
$1\frac{1}{2}$ tsp	smoked sweet paprika	7 mL
$\frac{1}{2}$	package (9 oz/300 g) tempeh	$\frac{1}{2}$
$1\frac{1}{2}$ cups	beet pulp	375 mL
$1\frac{1}{2}$ tsp	red miso paste	7 mL
$1\frac{1}{2}$ tsp	tamari	7 mL
$1\frac{1}{2}$ tsp	sesame oil	7 mL
$1\frac{1}{2}$ cups	cooled cooked wild rice (recipe on page 148)	375 mL
	Beet Barbecue Sauce (page 149)	

1. Using a food processor fitted with the metal blade, process walnuts, onion, no-salt seasoning, paprika and tempeh until sticky and dough-like.

2. Add beet pulp, miso, tamari and sesame oil. Process just until smooth.

3. Transfer pulp mixture to a large bowl. Add cooked wild rice and stir to combine. With your hands, form 6 patties, using about $\frac{1}{4}$ cup (60 mL) each.

4. Heat a large skillet over low heat. Lightly spray with cooking oil. Working in batches so as not to crowd the pan, cook patties for 1 to 2 minutes per side, just until lightly browned.

5. Before serving, brush on barbecue sauce to taste.

Wild Rice

We prefer wild rice—technically not a grain but rather the seed of an aquatic grass—over white rice, which is refined and can cause inflammation. Wild rice has appreciable amounts of vitamins B_3 (niacin), B_5 (pantothenic acid), B_6 (pyridoxine) and folate and the minerals magnesium, phosphorus, potassium and zinc.

| 3½ cups | water | 875 mL |
| 1½ cups | wild rice | 375 mL |

1. In a large saucepan, combine water and rice and bring to a boil. Reduce heat and simmer for 40 to 45 minutes, until rice is tender. Drain and set aside to cool completely.

Chef Babette's Beet Barbecue Sauce

Makes 5 cups (1.25 L)

With its deep ruby-red color, this barbecue sauce is the prettiest we've ever seen. Combine that with a tangy sweet-and-sour flavor and you have an exciting and delicious alternative to regular barbecue sauce. It's a great way to use beet juice in a nourishing recipe.

Tips

To yield 3 cups (750 mL) fresh beet juice for this sauce, you'll need to juice 3 large beets.

When using beet pulp in a recipe, juice the beets first. Set the beet pulp aside, then cover and refrigerate until you have the required quantity.

Arrowroot powder is a natural starch derived from the root of the tropical South American plant *Maranta arundinacea*. It is used as a thickener. You'll find it in the baking section of most health food stores and well-stocked supermarkets.

This sauce will keep for up to 2 weeks in an airtight container in the refrigerator.

3 cups	fresh beet juice (see Tips, left)	750 mL
1 tbsp	beet pulp	15 mL
2 tbsp	arrowroot powder (see Tips, left)	30 mL
¼ cup	raw agave nectar	60 mL
3 tbsp	raw apple cider vinegar	45 mL
2 tbsp	tamari	30 mL
1 tbsp	sweet smoked paprika	15 mL

1. In a small saucepan over low heat, whisk together beet juice, beet pulp and arrowroot powder until well combined. Add agave nectar, vinegar, tamari and paprika and whisk well. Bring to a simmer and cook, whisking often, for about 5 minutes, until sauce has thickened. Serve cold, warm or at room temperature.

Fresh-Eight

**Makes about
3 cups (750 mL)**

Why purchase sodium-filled vegetable juice when it's so easy to make your own? Our version tastes better and is loaded with eight fresh enzyme-rich, longevity-boosting vegetables. The colorful combination creates an addictive juice that is both sweet and salty—it's so good! Many health-care providers agree that eating a variety of vegetables and fruit is necessary to obtain the high levels of essential vitamins, minerals and phytonutrients needed for optimum health. Drinking them via a fresh juice allows these nutrients to be absorbed more quickly.

Tip
Carrots come in a variety of sizes. Our recipes are based on medium to large carrots.

8	carrots (see Tip, left)	8
½	head romaine lettuce, chopped	½
1	stalk celery, halved	1
8	sprigs watercress (see Juice Guru's Tip, below)	8
2	tomatoes, quartered	2
¼	beet, quartered	¼
2 cups	packed chopped spinach leaves	500 mL
8	sprigs fresh flat-leaf (Italian) parsley (see Caution, below)	8

1. Using a juicer, process half each of the carrots, romaine, celery, watercress, tomatoes, beet, spinach and parsley. Following the same order, repeat with the remaining vegetables. Whisk well and serve immediately.

Juice Guru's Tip

Watercress—an aquatic plant found near springs and slow-moving streams—is an often overlooked leafy green. A close cousin of mustard greens, cabbage and arugula, it contains phytonutrients (such as isothiocyanates) and antioxidants with a plethora of disease-preventive properties.

Caution
Certain phytonutrients in parsley—in concentrated amounts, as they are in juices—may act as a uterine stimulant and should likely be avoided during pregnancy.

Chef Babette's Carrot Cakes

Makes 6 mini Bundt cakes

When I gave up dairy, I needed to rethink how I would make one of my favorite desserts—carrot cake. With this recipe, which takes advantage of leftover carrot pulp and carrot juice, I can confidently say we nailed it. People line up outside my restaurant every time I make it.

Tips

To yield enough carrot juice for this recipe (both cake and frosting), you need to juice about 9 carrots. You will be left with more than enough carrot pulp for this recipe. Use the extra to make Carrot "Tuna" Salad (page 116).

Serve cakes within 24 hours for the best taste and consistency. Refrigerate any leftovers in an airtight container for up to 3 days.

- **Preheat oven to 350°F (180°C)**
- **6-cup (1.5 L) mini Bundt cake pan, lightly greased**

Cakes

1 cup	buckwheat flour	250 mL
½ tsp	baking powder	2 mL
½ tsp	sea salt	2 mL
½ tsp	alcohol-free organic vanilla extract	2 mL
½ tsp	ground cinnamon	2 mL
1¼ cups	carrot juice (see Tips, left)	300 mL
½ cup	raw agave nectar	125 mL
6 tbsp	coconut oil, melted	90 mL
¼ cup	carrot pulp	60 mL
¼ cup	diced pineapple	60 mL
¼ cup	raisins	60 mL
¼ cup	walnuts, chopped (optional)	60 mL

Frosting

½ cup	pineapple chunks	125 mL
2 tbsp	carrot juice	30 mL
½ cup	soaked and rinsed cashews	125 mL
1½ tbsp	carrot pulp	22 mL
½ cup	raw agave nectar	125 mL
½ tsp	sea salt	2 mL
½ tsp	alcohol-free organic vanilla extract	2 mL

1. *Cakes:* In a large bowl, whisk together flour, baking powder, salt, vanilla and cinnamon. Add carrot juice, agave nectar, coconut oil and carrot pulp; stir until just combined. Fold in pineapple, raisins and walnuts (if using).

2. Fill each compartment of prepared pan three-quarters full (so cakes have room to rise). Bake in preheated oven for 30 minutes or until a toothpick inserted in the middle of a cake comes out clean.

3. Remove from oven and let cool completely in pan.

4. *Frosting:* Meanwhile, in a blender, combine pineapple, carrot juice, soaked cashews, carrot pulp, agave nectar, salt and vanilla. Blend at high speed until smooth. Cover and refrigerate for 30 minutes before frosting cooled cakes.

Carrot Kicker

This juice features a nice balance of sweet, salty and spicy flavors—it's incredibly delicious. Cayenne pepper, which provides a little kick of heat, has been proven to improve blood circulation.

Herbal Helper

Want a cleansing kick that'll get your blood moving? Try whisking a pinch of cayenne pepper into your juice and adding fresh chile peppers to your dinner. Capsaicin, the alkaloid that gives chiles their heat, stimulates circulation, among other benefits. Population studies show that people who eat a lot of chile peppers are less likely to suffer from cardiovascular disease than those in countries where the food is blander.

6	carrots (see Juice Guru's Tip, below)	6
1	stalk celery, chopped	1
1	beet, quartered	1
1/8 tsp	cayenne pepper	0.5 mL

1. Using a juicer, process half each of the carrots, celery and beet. Following the same order, repeat with remaining carrots, celery and beet.

2. Add cayenne and whisk well. Serve immediately.

Juice Guru's Tip

If desired, you can juice the leafy green tops of carrots for additional nutrients. However, we recommend limiting the amount of greens to only one or two carrots' worth. Although they are a rich source of beneficial compounds, once absorbed into the body, those compounds can react with sunlight to produce a severe sunburn or rash.

Traditional versus Heirloom Carrots

Carrots can be traced back as far as 5,000 years ago, to Central Asia, the Middle East and Europe. It's believed they were first grown as medicine, not food, to treat a variety of ailments such as flatulence, chronic coughs, windy colic and chronic renal disease. Originally carrots were widely available in a variety of colors, including red, yellow, purple and orange. As farmers propagated sweeter varieties, carrots were hybridized to become the orange variety we have become so accustomed to. These orange carrots contain much more sugar than the original varieties. For this reason—when in season and based on availability—we recommend using heirloom carrots. Look for them in health food stores and farmers' markets.

Root for Me!

This is the perfect juice for introducing friends and family to the complex and wonderful tastes of freshly pressed juice. Carrots, cilantro, beet and cucumber combine to make a deliciously sweet and savory blend that is antioxidant-rich and immune-boosting.

Tips

Several varieties of cucumber are available in supermarkets, from field (slicing) to pickling to English cucumbers. We find that field and English cucumbers yield the most juice.

To peel gingerroot quickly and easily, simply use the edge of a teaspoon. Scrape it back and forth along the root to remove the skin and reveal the yellow flesh underneath.

Herbal Helper

Ginger is excellent for stimulating digestion, relieving gas (when not taken in excess) and helping to detoxify the liver. It also has strong antioxidant properties and has been shown to reduce serum cholesterol. Ginger is well studied and very beneficial.

6	carrots	6
15	sprigs cilantro (about ½ bunch)	15
¼	beet, halved	¼
1	cucumber, quartered (see Tips, left)	1
1	1½-inch (4 cm) piece peeled gingerroot (see Tips, left)	1

1. Using a juicer, process half each of the carrots, cilantro, beet and cucumber, plus the ginger. Following the same order, repeat with the remaining carrots, cilantro, beet and cucumber. Whisk well and serve immediately.

Juice Guru's Tip

For added nutrients, juice the beet greens. While this makes the juice taste a bit earthier, the levels of vitamins and minerals go through the roof. Beet greens are an excellent source of potassium, vitamin K and the carotenoids lutein and beta-carotene, plus smaller amounts of iron, calcium and magnesium. (Please note that the greens can be somewhat bitter, so go easy. Add just a small amount at a time and taste to be sure you don't overdo it.)

Juicing Beets: A Little Goes a Long Way

You'll notice that our recipes call for only small quantities of beets. This is for two reasons: First, their juice is extremely sweet, with an earthy flavor that for some people is an acquired taste; it can easily overwhelm your juice if you add too much. Second, the purple pigment in beets may present itself when you go to the bathroom (a condition known as beeturia). For these reasons, we recommend using beets in moderation. But don't let this deter you from making them part of your juicing habit—they are extremely beneficial. Beets are excellent detoxifiers and naturally support liver health.

Chef Babette's Carrot Loaf

**Makes 1 loaf
(6 to 8 slices)**

This dish is a great alternative to turkey for Thanksgiving or Christmas dinner. You'll be shocked to find out how well these ingredients bind together to form a traditional loaf that will remind you of childhood holiday dinners, but served up in a healthier way. This dish is so good we prepare it year-round, especially when we're craving comfort food. We love serving it with traditional holiday side dishes such as mashed potatoes, roasted Brussels sprouts and cranberry sauce.

Tips

To produce 2 cups (500 mL) packed carrot pulp, you will need to juice about 9 medium carrots. You can get much of the carrot pulp you need when you make the Carrot Mushroom Gravy (page 155). For the remainder, when making a juice that contains carrots, juice the carrots first, and set the pulp aside. If not using immediately, cover and refrigerate.

- 16-cup (4 L) casserole dish, lightly greased
- Preheat oven to 350°F (180°C)

2 cups	carrot pulp (see Tip, left)	500 mL
2 cups	raw walnuts	500 mL
1 cup	chopped cremini mushrooms	250 mL
1	package (18 oz/600 g) tempeh	1
1	package (10 oz/300 g) vegan Cheddar cheese, cubed	1
1	zucchini, chopped	1
1 tsp	tamari	5 mL
1 tbsp	no-salt seasoning (see Tips, page 149)	15 mL
½ cup	filtered water	125 mL
	Carrot Mushroom Gravy (recipe opposite)	

1. In a food processor fitted with the metal blade, combine carrot pulp, walnuts, mushrooms, tempeh, cheese, zucchini, tamari, no-salt seasoning and water. Process until smooth.

2. Transfer mixture to prepared baking dish. Bake in preheated oven for 30 minutes, until golden brown.

3. Remove from oven and let cool to room temperature before slicing.

4. Divide among serving plates and spoon gravy overtop, to taste. Serve.

Carrot Mushroom Gravy

Makes 8 to 10 cups
(2 to 2.5 L)

If you've never tasted sweet gravy before, wait until you try this one! Just a touch of sweetness from the carrot juice transforms this version into something amazing. In fact, the sweeter the carrot, the better the gravy. The carrot pulp adds to the overall consistency and thickness. Trust us, you'll love it.

• • • • • • • • • • • • • • • • • •

Tip

To produce 2 cups (500 mL) carrot juice, you will need to juice about 12 medium carrots.

¼ cup	coconut oil	60 mL
1 cup	chopped red onion	250 mL
1 cup	sliced mushrooms	250 mL
1½ cups	all-purpose flour	375 mL
2½ tbsp	tamari	37 mL
2 cups	carrot juice (see Tip, left)	500 mL
2 tbsp	carrot pulp	30 mL
2½ cups	filtered water (approx.)	625 mL

1. In a saucepan over medium-high heat, heat oil. Add onion and mushrooms and sauté for 1 to 2 minutes, until soft.

2. Stir in flour and tamari and bring to a simmer, stirring occasionally.

3. Whisk in carrot juice, carrot pulp and just enough water to reach desired consistency. Bring to a boil, then reduce heat and simmer for about 5 minutes, until heated through and slightly thickened. Serve.

Easy as ABC

Whip up this easy three-ingredient juice on mornings when you need to get out the door fast. Carrots, apples and beet combine to make an energizing antioxidant blend that will leave you feeling ready to conquer your day. It tastes earthy and smooth, and it's a perfect starter juice for those new to juicing. A study published in the *Journal of the Academy of Nutrition and Dietetics* in 2012 indicated that beet juice can increase your physical stamina and performance, so try drinking this before your workout.

Tips

Never peel the skin from your apples before juicing. Apple skin contains an abundance of phytonutrient polyphenols, which help to regulate blood sugar.

There are so many varieties of apples to choose from. Fuji, Red Delicious and Granny Smith are most commonly used for juicing, but any type will produce a delicious juice. We recommend using whatever is local and in season. Simply changing the variety of apple you use is an easy way to combat boredom with a particular juice blend.

4	carrots	4
3	apples, cored and sliced (see Tips, left)	3
¼	beet, halved	¼

1. Using a juicer, process half each of the carrots, apples and beet. Following the same order, repeat with the remaining carrots, apples and beet. Whisk well and serve immediately.

Juice Guru's Tip

We mentioned earlier that you may want to juice the greens your beets, with good reason—they are loaded with nutrients. But they also contain measurable amounts of oxalates. While both the beetroot and beet greens contain oxalates, it has been shown that the greens contain substantially more. If you are trying to limit the amount of naturally occurring oxalates you consume, we recommend juicing just the beet, not the greens. Oxalates are compounds found in certain foods such as chocolate, tea, beets, spinach and rhubarb. They are also a natural waste product of metabolism that is excreted in the urine. Most people do not need to limit these compounds, but if you have a history of oxalate-based kidney stones, it's best to minimize your intake of dietary oxalate.

Pretty in Pink

This sweet and zesty strawberry and pineapple juice blend will awaken your taste buds, thanks to a surprising zing of ginger. Ginger is known to soothe tummy issues such as nausea, motion sickness and gastrointestinal distress. And the strawberries in this juice really boost its levels of vitamin C and potassium. Strawberries protect your heart, increase HDL ("good") cholesterol, lower your blood pressure and guard against cancer, as part of a healthy diet that is rich in plant foods.

Tips

Pineapples do not continue to ripen after they are picked, so choose one that looks plump and has a sweet aroma. The leaves in the crown should look fresh and green and should not pull out of the fruit easily.

To peel a pineapple, place it on a cutting board and, using a sharp knife, cut off the top and bottom to remove the leaves and stem and create flat surfaces. Resting the pineapple on a flat end, slide the knife under the skin and, with a downward motion, remove the skin in strips. Shave off any remaining bits of skin.

To peel gingerroot quickly and easily, simply use the edge of a teaspoon. Scrape it back and forth along the root to remove the skin and reveal the yellow flesh underneath.

1	pineapple, skin removed, cut into wedges (see Tips, left and page 133)	1
1/4	beet, halved	1/4
16	strawberries (see Juice Guru's Tip, below)	16
1	1/4-inch (0.5 cm) piece peeled gingerroot (see Tips, left)	1

1. Using a juicer, process half each of the pineapple, beet, and strawberries, plus the ginger. Following the same order, repeat with the remaining pineapple, beet and strawberries. Whisk well and serve immediately.

Juice Guru's Tip

Strawberries are an excellent source of ellagic acid, which is known to have strong anticancer and antioxidant properties. A study published in *Critical Reviews in Food Science and Nutrition* in 2004 indicated that strawberries topped the list of eight foods linked to lower rates of cancer death among a sample of 1,271 elderly people in New Jersey. The study found that those who ate the most strawberries were three times less likely to develop cancer than those who consumed few or no strawberries.

Sage Root

This juice is pure decadence. Zesty citrus is balanced by sweet carrots and beets; ginger and sage add pleasing earthy texture. Sage contains flavonoids, volatile oils and phenolic acids, which have anti-inflammatory properties. As part of a diet containing plenty of plant foods, sage may help to temper the inflammation associated with rheumatoid arthritis, bronchial asthma and even atherosclerosis. Sage also contains antioxidant enzymes and works to improve brain function.

Tips

When peeling lemons for juicing, be sure to leave behind as much white pith as possible. The pith of the lemon contains high concentrations of bioflavonoids such as limonene, which is believed to have anticancer properties.

When shopping for fresh sage, look for sprigs that are vibrant in color and rich in aroma. Be sure the leaves are free from dark spots or yellowing. Store your sage wrapped in a damp paper towel and sealed in an eco-friendly plastic bag in the refrigerator for up to 4 days.

To peel gingerroot quickly and easily, simply use the edge of a teaspoon. Scrape it back and forth along the root to remove the skin and reveal the yellow flesh underneath.

4	carrots	4
1	lemon, peeled and halved (see Tips, left)	1
¼	beet, halved	¼
1	orange, peeled and halved	1
¼ cup	lightly packed fresh sage leaves (see Tips, left)	60 mL
1	¼-inch (0.5 cm) piece peeled gingerroot (see Tips, left)	1

1. Using a juicer, process half each of the carrots, lemon, beet, orange and sage, plus the ginger. Following the same order, repeat with the remaining carrots, lemon, beet, orange and sage. Whisk well and serve immediately.

Herbal Helper
Sage is an excellent herbal booster that has been linked to improving digestive tract disorders, swollen airways, throat spasms, high blood pressure and liver disorders. Sage is also reported to improve memory.

Beetade

A delicious take on a favorite, this sweet yet sour and earthy juice is an incredible stamina builder. Research indicates that beet juice improves blood flow and supports improved bowel function and elimination. It has also been reported to be a great source of energy and to aid in lowering blood pressure (results were based on the consumption of 1 cup/250 mL of beet juice a day for a total of four weeks).

Tip
Several varieties of cucumber are available in supermarkets, from field (slicing) to pickling to English cucumbers. We find that field and English cucumbers yield the most juice.

Herbal Helper
Want to improve overall memory? Add 2 to 5 drops of ginkgo biloba to this juice. Ginkgo biloba oxygenates the body and promotes circulation to the brain. It is an amazing mental stimulant.

¼	beet, halved	¼
1	lime, peeled and halved	1
2	cucumbers, quartered (see Tip, left)	2
1 cup	young coconut water (see Juice Guru's Tip, below)	250 mL

1. Using a juicer, process half each of the beet, lime and cucumber. Following the same order, repeat with the remaining beet, lime and cucumber.

2. Add coconut water and whisk well. Serve immediately.

Juice Guru's Tip
This is a great juice to drink on a hot day or after a workout. Not only is it refreshing, the coconut water will restore needed electrolytes.

Turmeric Sunshine

This earthy, sweet and comforting juice is loaded with superior antioxidants (curcuminoids in this case), thanks to turmeric. The polyphenols in turmeric protect your body against toxins by supporting the liver's natural detoxification process. They also prevent LDL ("bad") cholesterol from oxidizing, its pivotal first step in damaging arteries, leading to plaque and blood clot formation. Turmeric lends a terrific flavor that is akin to orange and ginger.

Tips

Never peel the skin from your apples before juicing. Apple skin contains an abundance of phytonutrient polyphenols, which help to regulate blood sugar.

There are so many varieties of apples to choose from. Fuji, Red Delicious and Granny Smith are most commonly used for juicing, but any type will produce a delicious juice. We recommend using whatever is local and in season. Simply changing the variety of apple you use is an easy way to combat boredom with a particular juice blend.

1	¼-inch (0.5 cm) piece turmeric root, peeled and sliced (see Juice Guru's Tip, below)	1
6	red apples, cored and quartered (see Tips, left)	6

1. Using a juicer, process turmeric and apples. Whisk well and serve immediately.

Juice Guru's Tip

Slice your turmeric into pieces that your juicer can manage. Turmeric has a deep color that can actually stain the juicer, so be sure to juice it first; then the ingredients that follow can flush out the juicer. We also recommend washing stained parts of your juicer with soap and water right after juicing, to avoid long-lasting discoloration.

Big Blue (page 194)

Magic Mango Juice (page 192)

Watermelon Straight Up (page 200)

Carrots Alive (page 202)

Pineapple Express
(page 208)

Pear Me Down (page 209)

Classic Green Smoothie
(page 214)

Strawberry Açai (page 217)

Carrot Beet Ginger Lemon Mantra

Makes about 3 cups (750 mL)

You'll find this mixture soothing even on the most hectic of days. Tangy lemon nicely offsets the sweet carrots and beets, and ginger provides just the right amount of oomph. Ginger is a strong antioxidant and provides a digestive enzyme called protease, which helps to fight inflammation. *Namaste.*

Tips

When peeling lemons for juicing, be sure to leave behind as much white pith as possible. The pith of the lemon contains high concentrations of bioflavonoids such as limonene, which is believed to have anticancer properties.

To peel gingerroot quickly and easily, simply use the edge of a teaspoon. Scrape it back and forth along the root to remove the skin and reveal the yellow flesh underneath.

6	carrots (see Juice Guru's Tip, below)	6
¼	beet, halved	¼
1	lemon, peeled and halved (see Tips, left)	1
1	¼-inch (0.5 cm) piece peeled gingerroot (see Tips, left)	1

1. Using a juicer, process half each of the carrots, beet and lemon, plus the ginger. Following the same order, repeat with the remaining carrots, beet and lemon. Whisk well and serve immediately.

Juice Guru's Tip

If desired, you can juice the leafy green tops of carrots for additional nutrients. However, we recommend limiting the amount of greens to only one or two carrots' worth. Although they are a rich source of beneficial compounds, once absorbed into the body, those compounds can react with sunlight to produce a severe sunburn or rash.

Beet Green Machine

**Makes about
3 cups (750 mL)**

This juice has an earthy flavor that is nicely balanced by just a hint of sweetness, thanks to the beets. It's also nourishing and a healing source of phytonutrients and antioxidant, anti-inflammatory and detoxification support. Celery alone contains more than a dozen key antioxidants and phytonutrients that your body craves. Spinach provides both anti-inflammatory and anticancer benefits, primarily because of its abundance of phytonutrients, including flavonoids and carotenoids. Meanwhile, red cabbage delivers plenty of vitamins C and K and potassium.

Tip

Several varieties of cucumber are available in supermarkets, from field (slicing) to pickling to English cucumbers. We find that field and English cucumbers yield the most juice.

2	green apples, cored and quartered	2
1	stalk celery, chopped (see Juice Guru's Tip, below)	1
1 cup	packed chopped spinach leaves	250 mL
¼	beet, with greens, halved	¼
1	cucumber, quartered (see Tip, left)	1
½ cup	packed chopped red cabbage	125 mL

1. Using a juicer, process half each of the apples, celery, spinach, beet, beet greens, cucumber and cabbage. Following the same order, repeat with the remaining apple and vegetables. Whisk well and serve immediately.

Juice Guru's Tip

As with the beet in this recipe, you can juice every part of your celery, from stalk to leaves. That way you'll access every bit of its rich supply of potassium.

Chef Babette's Spicy Purple Cabbage Pâté

Makes about 3 cups (750 mL)

This recipe makes great use of any purple cabbage pulp you may have on hand from making our Get the Glow juice (page 143) or Beet Green Machine (page 162). The flavor of the cabbage is brightened by the addition of chipotle powder, and agave nectar adds just the right amount of sweetness. This is the perfect snack or party appetizer. Serve with brown rice crackers or sticks of celery, carrot or red bell pepper for dipping.

Tips

To soak the cashews, place in a bowl and cover with 2 cups (500 mL) water. Cover and set aside for 6 hours. Drain, discarding liquid.

To yield enough cabbage pulp to make this recipe, you need to juice ½ cup (125 mL) packed chopped cabbage.

For a spicier flavor, substitute ¼ tsp (1 mL) cayenne pepper for the chipotle chile powder.

1 cup	raw cashews, soaked (see Tips, left)	250 mL
¼ cup	diced red onion	60 mL
¼ cup	purple cabbage pulp (see Tips, left)	60 mL
¼ cup	distilled water	60 mL
1 tbsp	raw agave nectar	15 mL
1 tbsp	no-salt seasoning (see Tips, page 147)	15 mL
1 tsp	tamari	5 mL
½ tsp	chipotle chile powder (see Tips, left)	2 mL

1. Using a food processor fitted with the metal blade, combine soaked cashews, onion, cabbage pulp, water, agave nectar, no-salt seasoning, tamari and chile powder. Process until it reaches a slightly grainy consistency.

2. Transfer to a serving bowl.

Celery Cucumber Carrot

Makes about 3 cups (750 mL)

The mildly sweet and salty flavor of this juice really hits the spot and will quench your thirst on even the most active day. Carrots are an excellent source of antioxidant compounds such as alpha- and beta-carotene and falcarinol, which may reduce the risk for cardiovascular disease and cancer while promoting good vision (especially night vision).

Tip

Several varieties of cucumber are available in supermarkets, from field (slicing) to pickling to English cucumbers. We find that field and English cucumbers yield the most juice.

2	stalks celery, chopped	2
4	carrots	4
2	cucumbers, quartered (see Tip, left)	2

1. Using a juicer, process half each of the celery, carrots and cucumbers. Following the same order, repeat with the remaining celery, carrots and cucumber. Whisk well and serve immediately.

Juice Guru's Tip

Despite appearances, cucumbers are nutritional powerhouses. They are extremely hydrating and packed with vitamin K and potassium.

Veggie Goddess

**Makes about
3 cups (750 mL)**

Apples, kale, beet and ginger come together so deliciously in this sweet, spicy and earthy juice. We praise this juice blend for the incredible dose of nutrients it provides. Kale delivers high levels of vitamins B and C, beta-carotene, calcium, phosphorus, folate and magnesium. Beets help to build a strong immune system, support cardiovascular health and help to flush toxins from your system by supporting liver function.

Tip

To peel gingerroot quickly and easily, simply use the edge of a teaspoon. Scrape it back and forth along the root to remove the skin and reveal the yellow flesh underneath.

4	green apples, cored and sliced	4
1	cucumber, quartered	1
1 cup	packed chopped kale leaves	250 mL
¼	beet, halved	¼
1	¼-inch (0.5 cm) piece peeled gingerroot (see Tip, left)	1

1. Using a juicer, process half each of the apples, cucumber, kale and beet, plus the ginger. Following the same order, repeat with the remaining apples, kale and beet. Whisk well and serve immediately.

Antioxidant Supreme

Kale's extreme anticancer and body-healing virtues are attributed to a combination of two very strong types of antioxidants known as carotenoids and flavonoids. Eating carotenoid-rich foods such as kale, which contains high levels of lutein and beta-carotene, has been shown to raise blood levels of this dynamic duo. Research has conclusively demonstrated that these antioxidants help our bodies alleviate oxidative stress and hea th issues associated with this stress, including cataracts, chronic obstructive pu monary disease (COPD) and atherosclerosis. They also reduce the ris< of many types of cancer, including lung, skin, breast and prostate cancers.

Roots and Veggies

This juice is a superb balance of sweet, salty and spicy goodness. This special blend is full of heart-healthy antioxidants, thanks to the beet, and is incredibly thirst-quenching, thanks to the apple, celery and carrots. It's great to drink following an intense workout.

Tip

To peel gingerroot quickly and easily, simply use the edge of a teaspoon. Scrape it back and forth along the root to remove the skin and reveal the yellow flesh underneath.

2	green apples, cored and sliced	1
$\frac{1}{2}$	beet, halved	$\frac{1}{2}$
1	lime, peeled and halved	1
2	carrots	2
1	stalk celery, chopped	1
1	$\frac{1}{8}$-inch (3 mm) piece peeled gingerroot (see Tip, left)	1

1. Using a juicer, process half each of the apple, beet, lime, carrots and celery, plus the ginger. Following the same order, repeat with the remaining apple, beet, lime, carrot and celery. Whisk well and serve immediately.

Juice Guru's Tip

Will you be drinking this juice after exercise, as recommended? Add $\frac{1}{2}$ cup (125 mL) coconut water to the mix. When paired with coconut water, celery can help to replenish some of your lost sodium.

Hangover Helper

**Makes about
3 cups (750 mL)**

This vibrant fruit and veggie juice blend is designed to alleviate the hangover blues. Coconut water, celery and spinach provide potassium, which may help to relieve the headache that comes with hangovers and the juice is extremely hydrating. This combination has a slightly tropical flavor that is sure to please.

Tip

Never peel the skin from your apples before juicing. Apple skin contains an abundance of phytonutrient polyphenols, which help to regulate blood sugar.

3	green apples, cored and sliced (see Tip, left)	3
2	stalks celery, chopped	2
2 cups	packed chopped spinach leaves	500 mL
1	carrot, halved	1
¼ cup	coconut water	60 mL

1. Using a juicer, process half each of the apples, celery, spinach and carrot. Following the same order, repeat with the remaining apples, celery, spinach and carrot.

2. Add coconut water and whisk well. Serve immediately.

Juice Guru's Tip

While we recommend using green apples in our veggie juice combos, because we prefer their slightly tart flavor (Granny Smiths are our favorite), feel free to use red apples if you have a sweet tooth or are new to juicing—Fuji and Red Delicious apples are excellent. You really can't go wrong if you use whatever variety of apple is in season and local to your area—all apples are rich in nutrients.

Tips for Prepping and Measuring Ingredients

- No matter what type of juicer you are using, it is always a good idea to roughly chop greens such as spinach and kale and to cut longer vegetables such as celery and cucumbers into pieces before processing, so they flow through your juicer more efficiently and with less chance of clogging.
- When measuring leafy greens, pack the chopped greens tightly into the measuring cup to ensure that you achieve the correct measure for the recipes.
- When measuring chopped herbs, pack them into the measuring cup lightly to ensure that you achieve the correct measure for the recipes.

Juice Guru's Tip

Unless you are using a top-of-the-line juice press, even the best juicers will leave a fair amount of pulp in the final product. If, like us, you don't like pulp, we recommend straining your juice through a fine-mesh sieve into a 4-cup (1 L) measuring cup (for easy pouring). Straining your juice will make drinking it more enjoyable, since you won't end up with tiny fragments of pulp and skin that require occasional chewing.

Juicy Variation

Juicers can vary significantly in the volume of juice they produce, depending on the process the use and their efficiency with particular fruits and vegetables. Juice quantity will also fluctuate to reflect the produce used; a large apple or cucumber will yield considerably more juice than a small one. So while most of our recipes yield us approximately 3 cups (750 mL), be prepared to experience variations in the yield.

Chapter 11

Superfood Tonics and Elixirs

Holy Basil Supreme

Makes about 3 cups (750 mL)

This juice tastes similar to a bowl of warm tomato basil soup on a cold winter day. The tried-and-true flavors will remind you of home. Tomato provides a rich, creamy flavor, apples bring a touch of sweetness, celery adds a tinge of saltiness, and fragrant basil complements it all perfectly. Tomatoes provide potassium and the carotenoids alpha- and beta-carotene and lycopene. The lycopene in tomatoes has been shown to reduce the risk for heart disease, cataracts and macular degeneration.

Tip

Never peel the skin from your apples before juicing. Apple skin contains an abundance of phytonutrient polyphenols, which help to regulate blood sugar.

Herbal Helper

Holy basil (also known as tulsi) extract helps minimize the effects of stress and promotes mental clarity. Try replacing your morning cup of tea or coffee with this mixture: 1½ cups (375 mL) water, 4 drops holy basil extract and the juice of half a lemon.

3	red apples, cored and sliced (see Tip, left)	3
1	celery stalk, chopped	1
15	sprigs fresh parsley (about ½ bunch; see Caution, below)	15
1	tomato, quartered	1
20 drops	organic holy basil extract	20 drops

1. Using a juicer, process half each of the apples, celery, parsley and tomato. Following the same order, repeat with the remaining apples, celery, parsley and tomato.

2. Add holy basil extract and whisk. Serve immediately.

> **Caution**
> Certain phytonutrients in parsley—in concentrated amounts, as they are in juices—may act as a uterine stimulant and should likely be avoided during pregnancy. Because of the concentrated amount of oxalate it contains, parsley juice should also be avoided by people with kidney stones or a history of kidney stones.

Detox Juice

**Makes about
3 cups (750 mL)**

This quick and easy juice is cleansing and energizing. It features an earthy combination of flavors balanced by just the right kick of spice. Lemons are particularly high in vitamin C, one of the most important antioxidants in nature. Vitamin C fights free radicals, which are known to speed up aging. Cayenne pepper helps promote good blood circulation.

Tips

There are so many varieties of apples to choose from. Fuji, Red Delicious and Granny Smith are most commonly used for juicing, but any type will produce a delicious juice. We recommend using whatever is local and in season. Simply changing the variety of apple you use is an easy way to combat boredom with a particular juice blend.

When peeling lemons for juicing, be sure to leave behind as much white pith as possible. The pith of the lemon contains high concentrations of bioflavonoids such as limonene, which is believed to have anticancer properties.

1	⅛-inch (3 mm) piece burdock root (see Juice Guru's Tip, below)	1
4	red apples, cored and sliced (see Tips, left)	4
1	lemon, peeled and halved (see Tips, left)	1
Pinch	cayenne pepper	Pinch

1. Using a juicer, process the burdock root and half each of the apples and lemon. Following the same order, repeat with the remaining apples and lemon.

2. Add cayenne pepper and whisk well. Serve immediately.

Juice Guru's Tip

Burdock root has been used in traditional Chinese medicine and Western folk medicine for thousands of years, primarily for its skin-healing and blood-cleansing properties. Studies of its effects on rats reveal that it has the ability to regenerate liver cells damaged by artificially induced alcohol poisoning— evidence that supports its traditional use.

Lavender Elixir

You'll love the slightly floral, sweet and earthy taste of this soothing juice, and enjoy its health benefits. Lavender is extremely calming. Cucumbers contain phytonutrients known as lignans—lariciresinol, pinoresinol and secoisolariciresinol—which have been connected with reduced risk of cardiovascular disease and also several types of cancer, including breast, uterine, ovarian and prostate cancers. Apples are brimming with antioxidants that, aside from greatly boosting your immune system, can lower your risk of asthma and lung cancer.

Tips

Several varieties of cucumber are available in supermarkets, from field (slicing) to pickling to English cucumbers. We find that field and English cucumbers yield the most juice.

When peeling lemons for juicing, be sure to leave behind as much white pith as possible. The pith of the lemon contains high concentrations of bioflavonoids such as limonene, which is believed to have anticancer properties.

3	cucumbers, quartered (see Tips, left)	3
1	lemon, peeled and halved (see Tips, left)	1
2	green apples, cored and sliced	2
10 drops	edible organic lavender extract	10 drops

1. Using a juicer, process half each of the cucumbers, lemon and apple. Following the same order, repeat with the remaining cucumber, lemon and apple.

2. Add lavender extract and whisk well. Serve immediately.

Juice Guru's Tip

Lavender is well known for its abilities to ease stress and promote sleep. Lavender essential oil may be useful in alleviating insomnia, anxiety, stress and postoperative pain. The essential oil is also being studied for its possible antibacterial and antiviral benefits.

Coconut Shiitake

**Makes about
3 cups (750 mL)**

This juice is loaded with nutrients and features a sweet tropical flavor that is quite soothing. Coconut water is extremely hydrating, wheatgrass juice helps to restore your body's enzymes, vitamins and hormone levels, and shiitake extract can provide an excellent boost for your immune system.

3 cups	young coconut water	750 mL
3 tbsp	wheatgrass juice	45 mL
5 drops	organic shiitake extract (see Juice Guru's Tip, below)	5 drops

1. In a pitcher, combine coconut water, wheatgrass juice and shiitake extract. Whisk well and serve immediately.

Juice Guru's Tip

Shiitake mushrooms contain an abundance of antioxidants that have been shown to improve immunity and protect against cancer. They also contain a potent polysaccharide, lentinan, which is largely responsible for their anticancer effect.

Cinnamon Blast

**Makes about
3 cups (750 mL)**

This juice tastes like homemade apple pie— sweet, tangy and slightly warming. Apples can help reduce total cholesterol and LDL ("bad") cholesterol. Lemons contain vitamin C and are rich in bioflavonoids, phytonutrients that help to combat inflammation and may help slow the progression of heart disease. Cinnamon has been shown to regulate blood sugar, reduce LDL cholesterol levels, fight against bacteria and other pathogens, and reduce pain linked to arthritis.

5	red apples, cored and sliced (see Tips, page 171)	5
1	lemon, peeled and halved (see Tips, page 172)	1
1 tbsp	ground cinnamon	15 mL

1. Using a juicer, process half each of the apples and lemon. Following the same order, repeat with the remaining apples and lemon.

2. Add cinnamon and whisk well. Serve immediately.

Goji Power

Makes about 3 cups (750 mL)

This incredibly healthy and delicious juice highlights the sweet, slightly bitter flavor of goji berries, which are often identified as a superfood. You'll find the taste positively addicting. Cucumber provides small amounts of phytonutrients, such as beta-carotene, that are connected with a reduced risk of cardiovascular disease as well as several types of cancers, including breast, uterine, ovarian and prostate cancers.

Tips

Several varieties of cucumber are available in supermarkets, from field (slicing) to pickling to English cucumbers. We find that field and English cucumbers yield the most juice.

When peeling lemons for juicing, be sure to leave behind as much white pith as possible. The pith of the lemon contains high concentrations of bioflavonoids such as limonene, which is believed to have anticancer properties.

To peel gingerroot quickly and easily, simply use the edge of a teaspoon. Scrape it back and forth along the root to remove the skin and reveal the yellow flesh underneath.

1	cucumber, quartered (see Tips, left)	1
2	lemons, peeled and halved (see Tips, left)	2
2	red apples, cored and sliced	2
1	1-inch (2.5 cm) piece peeled gingerroot (see Tips, left)	1
20 drops	organic goji berry extract (see Juice Guru's Tip and Caution, below)	20 drops
$\frac{1}{8}$ tsp	cayenne pepper	0.5 mL

1. Using a juicer, process half each of the cucumber, lemons and apples, plus the ginger. Following the same order, repeat with the remaining cucumber, lemon and apple.

2. Add goji berry extract and cayenne and whisk well. Serve immediately.

Juice Guru's Tip

Preliminary studies published in the *Journal of Alternative and Complementary Medicine* in 2008 indicated that goji berry juice can induce feelings of well-being and calmness, increase athletic performance and improve quality of sleep and weight loss.

Caution

Goji berries may interact with warfarin (a blood thinner), diabetes drugs, and blood pressure medications. Consult with your doctor if you have concerns.

Happy Hemp Juice

This juice is a complex and glorious blend of flavors—at once nutty, sweet and minty—and well worth the effort to make. Carrots deliver antioxidants such as carotenoids and phytonutrients such as polyacetylenes, and pears have been shown to decrease the risk of type 2 diabetes, heart disease and cancer. Mint not only soothes your stomach, it is being studied for its potential as an anticancer agent.

Tip

Pears change color as they ripen. Bosc pears turn brown, Anjou and Bartlett pears turn yellow and Comice pears turn green. If you can't remember the colors, go by feel: fresh pears yield slightly to gentle pressure, similar to an avocado.

3	carrots	3
3	pears, quartered (see Tip, left)	3
10	sprigs fresh mint	10
2 tsp	organic lucuma powder (see Juice Guru's Tips, below)	10 mL
2 tbsp	cold-pressed hempseed oil (see Juice Guru's Tips, below)	30 mL

1. Using a juicer, process half each of the carrots, pears and mint. Following the same order, repeat with the remaining carrots, pear and mint.

2. Add lucuma powder and hempseed oil and whisk well. Serve immediately.

Juice Guru's Tips

Hempseed oil contains all of the essential amino acids, is rich in essential fatty acids and also contains antioxidants such as vitamin E as well as minerals, including phosphorus, potassium, sodium, magnesium, sulfur, calcium, iron and zinc. It also has the ideal balance of omega-3 and omega-6 fatty acids, which is great for glowing skin and nails.

Lucuma is a fruit native to Peru. While it can be used as a sweetener, lucuma provides a rich supply of beta-carotene, vitamin B_3, iron, zinc, calcium, magnesium and other vitamins and minerals. Preliminary studies published in the *Journal of Medicinal Foods* in 2009 indicate that the fruit can aid in the management of diabetes and high blood pressure. Manufacturers claim that lucuma powder has similar healing effects. You can find the powder in well-stocked health food stores.

Maca Magic

Ready for a seemingly magical energy boost? Turn to this powerful blend of sweet, earthy flavors that features maca, which is known for its energizing properties, as well as apples, cucumber and pears. The latter are rich in polyphenols, potent antioxidants that, as part of a diet rich in fruits and vegetables, are associated with a lower risk for cardiovascular disease and cancer in general. This tasty trio also provides potassium, which helps to maintain healthy blood pressure.

Tips

Several varieties of cucumber are available in supermarkets, from field (slicing) to pickling to English cucumbers. We find that field and English cucumbers yield the most juice.

Never peel pears before juicing. The skin is an important source of many phenolic phytonutrients, which include anticancer agents, anti-inflammatory flavonoids and antioxidants.

2	red apples, cored and sliced	2
1	cucumber, halved (see Tips, left)	1
2	pears, quartered (see Tips, left)	2
1 tsp	organic maca powder (see Juice Guru's Tip, below)	5 mL

1. Using a juicer, process half each of the apples, cucumber and pears. Following the same order, repeat with the remaining apple, cucumber and pear.

2. Add maca powder and whisk well. Serve immediately.

Juice Guru's Tip

Grown in the Andes Mountains of Peru, maca root, also known as Peruvian ginseng, is a tuber that contains minerals such as calcium, magnesium, manganese, potassium and iron. Studies support its traditional use as an adaptogen, a compound that helps the body respond to stress, including improved exercise performance, as well as having a positive impact on hormone levels.

Cold Cure

Makes about 3 cups (750 mL)

This cold-busting blend of tart elderberry, sweet strawberry and tangy orange works wonderfully to combat cold symptoms, and it can also provide immune-building support, thanks to the echinacea. Oranges provide a strong dose of vitamin C, which aids in supporting your immune system.

Tip

When peeling lemons for juicing, be sure to leave behind as much white pith as possible. The pith of the lemon contains high concentrations of bioflavonoids such as limonene, which is believed to have anticancer properties.

3	oranges, peeled and halved	3
8	strawberries	8
1	lemon, peeled and halved (see Tip, left)	1
20 drops	organic echinacea extract (see Juice Guru's Tips, below)	20 drops
20 drops	organic elderberry extract (see Juice Guru's Tips, below)	20 drops

1. Using a juicer, process half each of the oranges, strawberries and lemon. Following the same order, repeat with the remaining oranges, strawberries and lemon.

2. Add echinacea and elderberry extracts and whisk well. Serve immediately.

Juice Guru's Tips

Echinacea is an herb that is believed to strengthen the immune system and help prevent seasonal flus and colds. You can find echinacea extract in health food stores and well-stocked supermarkets.

Elderberries are nutritional powerhouses, abundant in antioxidants known as flavonoids, which stimulate the immune system. They also contain compounds known as anthocyanins, which are proven to have anti-inflammatory effects and may be the reason for reports that they also help alleviate aches, pain and fever. A 2002 study in the *Journal of Alternative and Complementary Medicine* showed pronounced improvement in flu symptoms after participants consumed doses of elderberry extract for three days. The researchers hypothesized that this may have been due to the antioxidant flavonoids in the extract; they concluded that elderberry extract can be an efficient and safe treatment for flu symptoms.

Memory Enhancer

Makes about 3 cups (750 mL)

Are you looking to improve your memory and sharpen your thinking skills? The gingko biloba and ginseng in this blend may assist with that. Gingko has been shown to be effective in treating memory loss and difficulty concentrating, and Siberian ginseng is often used to help people cope with stress.

Tip

There are so many varieties of apples to choose from. Fuji, Red Delicious and Granny Smith are most commonly used for juicing, but any type will produce a delicious juice. We recommend using whatever is local and in season. Simply changing the variety of apple you use is an easy way to combat boredom with a particular juice blend.

2	red apples, cored and sliced (see Tip, left)	2
2	carrots	2
2	oranges, peeled and halved	2
20 drops	organic gingko biloba extract (see Juice Guru's Tips, below)	20 drops
20 drops	organic Siberian ginseng extract (see Juice Guru's Tips, below)	20 drops

1. Using a juicer, process half each of the apples, carrots and oranges. Following the same order, repeat with the remaining apple, carrot and orange.

2. Strain the juice. Add gingko biloba and Siberian ginseng extracts and whisk well. Serve immediately.

Juice Guru's Tips

Gingko biloba is derived from one of the oldest living tree species. It is an antioxidant that has been shown to improve circulation by opening up blood vessels and making the blood less sticky. Some studies show that gingko helps to improve memory in people with dementia.

Siberian ginseng has been used for centuries in countries such as Russia and China. It contains an active ingredient called eleutheroside, which may stimulate the immune system. Preliminary studies indicate that Siberian ginseng can improve memory, and some studies have reported other benefits, including increased energy, vitality and longevity.

Fountain of Youth

This citrusy yet earthy juice boasts anti-aging benefits. Celery supports a healthy digestive system and is also a powerful anti-inflammatory agent that can lower cholesterol levels and may extend your lifespan. Limes and lemons are loaded with vitamin C, which fights the free radicals known to speed up aging. Apples lower cholesterol and reduce oxidative damage that contributes to hardening of the arteries. Ginger boosts your immune system and acts as an anti-inflammatory.

Tips

When peeling lemons for juicing, be sure to leave behind as much white pith as possible. The pith of the lemon contains high concentrations of bioflavonoids such as limonene, which is believed to have anticancer properties.

To peel gingerroot quickly and easily, simply use the edge of a teaspoon. Scrape it back and forth along the root to remove the skin and reveal the yellow flesh underneath.

2	red apples, cored and sliced	2
1	lime, peeled and halved	1
3	stalks celery, chopped	3
1	lemon, peeled and halved (see Tips, left)	1
1	1-inch (2.5 cm) piece peeled gingerroot (see Tips, left)	1
20 drops	organic reishi extract (see Juice Guru's Tip, below)	20 drops

1. Using a juicer, process half each of the apples, lime, celery and lemon, plus the ginger. Following the same order, repeat with the remaining apple, lime, celery and lemon.

2. Add reishi extract and whisk well. Serve immediately.

Juice Guru's Tip

Reishi is a fungus (mushroom) with a woodsy, bitter taste. There is some evidence to demonstrate that it can boost the immune system, ward off viral infections such as flu, lower blood pressure, and even reduce symptoms of chronic fatigue syndrome. You can find reishi extract in well-stocked natural food stores.

Endless Energy Drink

**Makes about
3 cups (750 mL)**

3 cups	young coconut water (see Tip, left)	750 mL
	Juice of 1 lime	
20 drops	organic ashwagandha extract (see Juice Guru's Tip, below)	20 drops

Drinking a glass of this tropical-tasting juice is the perfect way to combat stress, fatigue, lack of energy or difficulty concentrating, thanks to the inclusion of ashwagandha extract. Coconut water is hydrating and an excellent source of electrolytes such as magnesium and potassium, which help to regulate body fluids. Limes contain compounds known as limonoids, which have been shown to be effective in the fight against cancers of the mouth, skin, lung, breast, stomach and colon.

1. In a pitcher, combine coconut water and lime juice. Add ashwagandha extract and whisk well. Serve immediately.

Tip

Drinking coconut water instead of plain water or sports drinks laden with artificial dyes and refined sugars is an excellent way to stay hydrated.

Juice Guru's Tip

Ashwagandha extract is derived from the root and leaves of the ashwagandha plant (*Withania somnifera*), which is native to India. It has long been used in Ayurvedic medicine to increase energy, combat insomnia, improve cognitive skills and prevent the effects of aging.

Tropical Turmeric

**Makes about
3 cups (750 mL)**

This juice is based on an ancient recipe that originated in India more than 5,000 years ago and was used by Rishis and Brahmans as a preparation for worship. It is tangy and slightly sour, with a pungent, satisfying bite. It's also intensely purifying, in part because of the inclusion of turmeric root. Mangos are loaded with more than 20 different vitamins and minerals, including an abundance of provitamin A, beta- and alpha-carotene, and vitamin C. Carotenoids work synergistically with vitamin A to protect your eyes from oxidative damage while protecting your vision.

Tips

To prepare a mango for juicing, cut a small slice from the top and bottom of the fruit to make flat ends. Stand mango upright on a cutting board. Using a sharp knife, cut off on all four sides the flesh surrounding the large seed in the middle. Slide a tablespoon between the skin and meat of the mango to remove the flesh. Cut each slice into halves for juicing.

When peeling lemons for juicing, be sure to leave behind as much white pith as possible. The pith of the lemon contains high concentrations of bioflavonoids such as limonene, which is believed to have anticancer properties.

1	1-inch (2.5 cm) piece turmeric root, peeled and sliced (see Juice Guru's Tip, below)	1
3	mangos, quartered, pitted and peeled (see Tips, left)	3
1	1-inch (2.5 cm) piece peeled gingerroot (see Tips, page 182)	1
2	lemons, peeled and sliced (see Tips, left)	2
12	sprigs fresh mint (about ½ bunch)	12
2 cups	young coconut water	500 mL

1. Using a juicer, process tumeric, then half each of the mangos, ginger, lemons and mint. Following the same order, repeat with the remaining mangos, ginger, lemon and mint.

2. Add coconut water and whisk well. Serve immediately.

Juice Guru's Tip

Slice your turmeric into pieces that your juicer can manage. Turmeric has a deep color that can actually stain the juicer, so be sure to juice it first; then the ingredients that follow can flush out the juicer. We also recommend washing stained parts of your juicer with soap and water right after juicing, to avoid long-lasting discoloration.

Mangosteen Powerhouse

Makes about 3 cups (750 mL)

Mangosteen, a tropical fruit grown in Southeast Asia, is an incredible superfood that contains powerful phytonutrient antioxidants, including catechins and xanthones. These and other phytonutrients neutralize harmful free radicals and help the body fight infections. The taste of mangosteen is difficult to describe; some say it tastes a bit like melon and banana, but we just say it's delicious. The red grapes in this juice, while adding sweetness, also provide anticancer benefits as well as helping to regulate blood sugar.

Tips

When selecting red grapes, look for those that have a rich crimson hue and even color. Choose grapes that are plump and hearty. A silvery white "bloom" on the skins indicates freshness. The grapes should be firmly attached to stems that are brown or beige and healthy-looking, moist and flexible.

To peel gingerroot quickly and easily, simply use the edge of a teaspoon. Scrape it back and forth along the root to remove the skin and reveal the yellow flesh underneath.

3	red apples, cored and sliced	3
1 cup	red grapes (see Tips, left)	250 mL
¼	beet, halved	¼
1 cup	packed chopped kale leaves (see Juice Guru's Tip, below)	250 mL
1	1-inch (2.5 cm) piece peeled gingerroot (see Tips, left)	1
2 tbsp	organic mangosteen powder	30 mL

1. Using a juicer, process half each of the apples, grapes, beet and kale, plus the ginger. Following the same order, repeat with the remaining apple, grapes, beet and kale.

2. Add mangosteen powder and whisk to combine. Serve immediately.

Juice Guru's Tip

As part of a diet that includes cruciferous vegetables (broccoli, cauliflower and Brussels sprouts, for example), kale can help to lower cholesterol as well as the risk for various types of cancer. Kale also provides support for the body's detoxification system through the presence of biologically active compounds such as indoles, nitriles, thiocyanates and isothiocyanates—all heavy hitters in the anticancer nutrition world.

Apple Cider Vinegar Elixir

This sweet-and-sour juice blend is extremely healing. Apple cider vinegar has potent antiviral properties, and its pungent flavor nicely offsets the sweetness of the apples and pears. Apples are excellent anti-inflammatory agents, while the pears help to protect against cancer.

Tip

Never peel pears before juicing. The skin is an important source of many phenolic phytonutrients, which include anticancer agents, anti-inflammatory flavonoids and antioxidants.

Herbal Helper

Stevia rebaudiana is a South American herb that adds a very sweet taste to food yet doesn't contain any sugar. Some early studies indicate that it may help the function of the pancreas.

2	red apples, cored and sliced	2
2	pears, quartered (see Tip, left)	2
1 cup	raw apple cider vinegar (see Juice Guru's Tip, below)	250 mL
20 drops	organic stevia extract	20 drops

1. Using a juicer, process half each of the apples and pears. Following the same order, repeat with the remaining apple and pear.

2. Add apple cider vinegar and stevia extract and whisk well. Serve immediately.

Juice Guru's Tip

Apple cider vinegar is incredibly antibacterial, antiviral and antifungal, which means it can soothe your sore throat, heal heartburn, reduce cholesterol and protect from a variety of ailments. Plus it's loaded with vitamins, minerals, fiber, enzymes and pectin. When purchasing, be sure to choose raw, unpasteurized apple cider vinegar.

Tips for Prepping and Measuring Ingredients

- No matter what type of juicer you are using, it is always a good idea to roughly chop greens such as spinach and kale and to cut longer vegetables such as celery and cucumbers into pieces before processing, so they flow through your juicer more efficiently and with less chance of clogging.
- When measuring leafy greens, pack the chopped greens tightly into the measuring cup to ensure that you achieve the correct measure for the recipes.
- When measuring chopped herbs, pack them into the measuring cup lightly to ensure that you achieve the correct measure for the recipes.

Serving Sizes for Kids

You'll notice in this chapter that our recipes yield 2 cups (500 mL) of juice rather than the usual 3 cups (750 mL). The reason is that growing bodies will benefit from smaller quantities of juice. Younger children (ages 5 to 10) will do well with 1 cup (250 mL) of fresh juice a day. For older children (ages 6 to 18), 2 cups (500 mL) of fresh juice a day is plenty. Just remember that juice quantity will vary, depending on the juicer and ingredients you use.

Juice Guru's Tip

Unless you are using a top-of-the-line juice press, even the best juicers will leave a fair amount of pulp in the final product. If, like us, you don't like pulp, we recommend straining your juice through a fine-mesh sieve into a 4-cup (1 L) measuring cup (for easy pouring). Straining your juice will make drinking it more enjoyable, since you won't end up with tiny fragments of pulp and skin that require occasional chewing.

Chapter 12
Juices Kids Love

Mighty Mighty Apple Juice

**Makes about
2 cups (500 mL)**

Your kids won't taste the
spinach in this fresh apple
juice, but they will benefit
from its full serving of this
bone-building, mineral-rich
vegetable. And they'll love
the taste too, which strikes
just the right balance
between sweet and earthy
for young palates.

Tips

Never peel the skin from your
apples before juicing. Apple
skin contains an abundance
of phytonutrient polyphenols,
which help to regulate
blood sugar.

There are so many varieties of
apples to choose from. Fuji,
Red Delicious and Granny
Smith are most commonly
used for juicing, but any
type will produce a delicious
juice. We recommend using
whatever is local and in season.
Simply changing the variety of
apple you use is an easy way
to combat boredom with a
particular juice blend.

| 4 | red apples, cored and quartered (see Tips, left) | 4 |
| 1 cup | packed chopped spinach leaves (see Juice Guru's Tip, below) | 250 mL |

1. Using a juicer, process half each of the apples and
spinach. Following the same order, repeat with the
remaining apples and spinach. Whisk well and serve
immediately.

Juice Guru's Tip

If your child is finicky or if you are just introducing him
or her to leafy greens, you may want to start slowly.
During the first week, juice just the apples. Then start
adding small amounts of spinach (two to three leaves),
increasing the amount slowly over the course of the
next two weeks. The taste won't change significantly,
and by the time your child notices the change in color,
he or she will already be hooked.

Real Fruit Punch

Kids are crazy for those store-bought overprocessed boxed fruit drinks. Serve your children this delicious take on fruit punch instead. It has the added benefit of living enzymes and an abundance of the essential vitamins and minerals that come in 100% fresh juice, such as vitamin C, potassium and numerous phytonutrients.

Tips

Never peel the skin from your apples before juicing. Apple skin contains an abundance of phytonutrient polyphenols, which help to regulate blood sugar.

Never peel pears before juicing. The skin is an important source of many phenolic phytonutrients, which include anticancer agents, anti-inflammatory flavonoids and antioxidants.

While we typically suggest that you strain your juice before consumption, this is not the case when it comes to pears. Recent studies show that with the pulp removed, pear juices lose up to 40% of their total phytonutrients and their antioxidant capacity is significantly reduced. You'll want to consume all of the pulp from your pear juice to make sure you reap its many benefits. "Cloudy" pear juice is definitely the way to go.

2	red apples, cored and sliced (see Tips, left)	2
2	pears, quartered (see Tips, left)	2
2 cups	red grapes	500 mL
1	orange, peeled and quartered	1
1 cup	strawberries	250 mL

1. Using a juicer, process half each of the apples, pears, grapes, orange and strawberries. Following the same order, repeat with the remaining fruit. Whisk well and serve immediately.

Juice Guru's Tip

The familiar fruity taste of this juice makes it perfect for children's birthday parties or sleepovers. Serve it in fun glasses with crazy straws, or dress it up with a fancy drink umbrella.

Fresh Juice Is Alive

Fresh juice is considered a live food, while store-bought pasteurized juice is not. The reason lies in enzymes. Enzymes are a type of protein that work to speed up chemical reactions in your body. Without enzymes, our cells would not be alive. But enzymes are extremely sensitive to heat and so are destroyed by cooking and pasteurization. Juicing fresh fruit retains the fruit's nutrients and enzymes—just another reason why daily juicing is the way to go!

Dragon Juice

Go ahead and ask your little ones if they dare to drink dragon juice. They'll love the challenge, and the taste of this sweet and minty kid-friendly juice. Best of all, the apples and pears are loaded with antioxidants that will help boost your kiddies' immune systems. Mint also contains antioxidants and provides vitamin C, manganese and copper.

Tips

Pears change color as they ripen. Bosc pears turn brown, Anjou and Bartlett pears turn yellow and Comice pears turn green. If you can't remember the colors, go by feel: fresh pears yield slightly to gentle pressure, similar to an avocado.

While we typically suggest that you strain your juice before consumption, this is not the case when it comes to pears. Recent studies show that with the pulp removed, pear juices lose up to 40% of their total phytonutrients and their antioxidant capacity is significantly reduced. You'll want to consume all of the pulp from your pear juice to make sure you reap its many benefits. "Cloudy" pear juice is definitely the way to go.

3	red apples, cored and sliced (see Caution, below)	3
4	sprigs fresh mint	4
3	pears, quartered (see Tips, left)	3

1. Using a juicer, process half each of the apples, mint and pears. Following the same order, repeat with the remaining apples, mint and pears. Whisk well and serve immediately.

Caution
In most cases you can juice every part of fruits and vegetables, from skin to seeds. Just be careful to avoid the seeds when juicing apples, because apple seeds contain a small amount of arsenic, which can be toxic. (Please note that there is no record of arsenic poisoning from juicing apple seeds, but we like to err on the side of caution.) We suggest investing in an apple corer and composting or tossing out the entire core.

Sweet Dreams

Makes about
2 cups (500 mL)

This juice has a deliciously sweet taste that kids love, and it's great after a long day at school. The apples provide an abundance of antioxidants; the carrots contain beta-carotene, which promotes good vision and combats health-damaging free-radical activity; and pears protect against diabetes, as well as heart disease and cancer.

3	red apples, cored and sliced	3
2	carrots	2
1	pear, quartered (see Juice Guru's Tips, below)	1

1. Using a juicer, process half each of the apples, carrots and pear. Following the same order, repeat with the remaining apples, carrot and pear. Whisk well and serve immediately.

Juice Guru's Tips

Pears come in many varieties, and some are juicier than others. For example, green Anjou pears are better for juicing than Bosc pears.

Buy your pears when they are green and leave them on the counter to ripen.

Bunny Love

**Makes about
2 cups (500 mL)**

What's up, doc? Just a juice rich in provitamin A and beta-carotene, full of vitamins and minerals, and with an earthy and sweet taste that kids will love. The apple juice perfectly balances the richness of the carrot juice. Apples are an excellent source of vitamin C, and the polyphenols in the fruit have been shown to help balance blood sugar while providing antioxidant and cardiovascular benefits. Carrots contain vitamin K, biotin and potassium.

| 2 | red apples, cored and quartered (see Tips, page 187) | 2 |
| 3 | carrots | 3 |

1. Using a juicer, process half each of the apples and carrots. Following the same order, repeat with the remaining carrots and apple. Whisk well and serve immediately.

Juice Guru's Tip

Store-bought apple juices can be high in sugar, and much of the vitamins and minerals have been lost in the processing. This fresh juice is brimming with nutrients that have anti-asthma, anticancer and other important benefits for your babies.

Kale Is Fun

By now you are probably well aware that kale is a superfood, and you've likely even wondered how in the world you can get your child to eat it. This juice is the answer. Thanks to this perfectly sweet blend with pears and apples, our son, Eli, drinks kale like a pro. And he's got so used to the idea that now he eats it too, both fresh and cooked, in his favorite meals. Loaded with vitamins K and C, manganese and copper, kale provides increased cancer protection and support for the body's detoxification system.

Tip

There are so many varieties of apples to choose from. Fuji, Red Delicious and Granny Smith are most commonly used for juicing, but any type will produce a delicious juice. We recommend using whatever is local and in season. Simply changing the variety of apple you use is an easy way to combat boredom with a particular juice blend.

2	apples, cored and quartered	2
1 cup	packed chopped kale leaves	250 mL
2	pears, quartered	2

1. Using a juicer, process half each of the apples, kale and pears. Following the same order, repeat with the remaining apple, kale and pear. Whisk well and serve immediately.

Juice Guru's Tip

We love to get kids involved in juicing. Ask your kids to help out by washing the fruits and veggies (it's fun to dry leafy greens in the salad spinner). If you have a slow juicer, you can supervise while your child pushes through the veggies and fruit—just be sure they understand that hands always stay out of the entry chute.

Antioxidant Supreme

Kale's extreme anticancer and body-healing virtues are attributed to a combination of two very strong types of antioxidants known as carotenoids and flavonoids. Eating carotenoid-rich foods such as kale, which contains high levels of lutein and beta-carotene, has been shown to raise blood levels of this dynamic duo. Research has conclusively demonstrated that these antioxidants help our bodies alleviate oxidative stress and health issues associated with this stress, including cataracts, chronic obstructive pulmonary disease (COPD) and atherosclerosis. They also reduce the risk of many types of cancer, including lung, skin, breast and prostate cancers.

Superhero Secret Weapon

**Makes about
2 cups (500 mL)**

This juice contains the perfect combination of sweet and tart and tastes just like candy—kids love it. We like to tell children that it will fuel super-powers too, by increasing strength and focus and improving vision. Apples are loaded with vitamin C, an incredible antioxidant. Beets are extremely rich in nutrients such as folate and manganese and provide antioxidant benefits as well.

3	apples, cored and sliced	3
1/4	beet, halved	1/4
1	lime, peeled and halved (see Tip, below)	1
3	carrots	3

1. Using a juicer, process half each of the apples, beet, lime and carrots. Following the same order, repeat with the remaining fruit and vegetables. Whisk well and serve immediately.

Tip
When shopping for limes, look for fruits that are firm and heavy for their size. Be sure they are clean and devoid of mold or signs of decay. The skin should be deep green and glossy. Keep in mind that limes turn more yellow as they ripen, so a deep green indicates they are ready to use.

Frosty Ice Pops

**Makes about
6 ice pops**

These ice pops taste incredibly sweet without any added sugar, and they have a delightful citrus punch. Loaded with fruit, they are nutrient-rich—the strawberries alone have good amounts of vitamin C, manganese, folate and potassium. These pops make a great after-school snack any time of the year.

Tip
If you have difficulty removing the ice pops from the molds, try running water over the tips of the molds for about 5 seconds to loosen them.

3	apples, cored and quartered	3
1	pear, quartered	1
20	strawberries	20
1/4	lemon, peeled and halved	1/4

1. Using a juicer, process half each of the apples, pear, strawberries and lemon. Following the same order, repeat with the remaining fruit. Whisk well and pour into ice-pop molds.

2. Freeze until firm, about 6 hours or overnight. Serve (see Tip, left).

Magic Mango Juice

Kids adore this delicious blend of sweet and tangy fruit with a slight kick from fresh ginger. Mangos are loaded with more than 20 different vitamins and minerals, including an abundance of provitamin A, carotenoids such as beta- and alpha-carotene, and vitamin C. Oranges are also an excellent source of vitamin C, and are great for bolstering children's immune systems while providing antioxidant protection. Pears provide copper and vitamins C and K.

Tip

To prepare a mango for juicing, cut a small slice from the top and bottom of the fruit to make flat ends. Stand mango upright on a cutting board. Using a sharp knife, cut off on all four sides the flesh surrounding the large seed in the middle. Slide a tablespoon between the skin and meat of the mango to remove the flesh. Cut into halves for juicing.

4	oranges, peeled and quartered	4
1	mango, peeled, quartered and pitted (see Tips, left)	1
1	pear, quartered	1
1	1-inch (2.5 cm) piece peeled gingerroot (see Tip, page 193 and Juice Guru's Tip, below)	1

1. Using a juicer, process half each of the oranges, mango and pear, plus the ginger. Following the same order, repeat with the remaining oranges, mango and pear. Whisk well and serve immediately.

Juice Guru's Tip

While some kids love the taste of ginger, others may find it too intense. When introducing ginger to your child, it's a good idea to start slowly, beginning with about a ¼-inch (0.5 cm) piece. As he or she gets used to the taste, you can increase the quantity.

Chicka-Chicka Juice-Juice

This delicious juice features just the right mix of sweet and tangy, and it's an incredibly health-giving juice for kids because it is packed with nutrients. Both apples and oranges offer a great boost of vitamin C. Carrots are an excellent source of alpha- and beta-carotene and vitamin K, while cucumber delivers vitamin K, potassium and copper. Spinach provides vitamin K, manganese and iron, and its beta- and alpha-carotene are converted into vitamin A.

Tip

To peel gingerroot quickly and easily, simply use the edge of a teaspoon. Scrape it back and forth along the root to remove the skin and reveal the yellow flesh underneath.

2	apples, cored and sliced	2
2	oranges, peeled and quartered	2
½	cucumber, halved	½
3	carrots	3
½ cup	packed chopped spinach leaves	125 mL
1	¼-inch (0.5 cm) piece peeled gingerroot (see Tip, left)	1

1. Using a juicer, process half each of the apples, oranges, cucumber, carrots and spinach, plus the ginger. Following the same order, repeat with the remaining apple, orange, cucumber, carrots and spinach. Whisk well and serve immediately.

Juice Guru's Tip

Even though all the juices in this book are brimming with vitamins, minerals and other nutrients, there is never any risk of toxic overload. Fresh juices are easily assimilated into the body.

Wizard's Juice

We have it from a reliable source that wizards love this sweet and salty strength- and stamina-building brew. Celery provides excellent digestive and cardiovascular support while delivering vitamin K and potassium. Apples are loaded with vitamin C, while carrots provide vitamin K.

3	apples, cored and sliced	3
3	carrots	3
1	stalk celery, chopped	1

1. Using a juicer, process half each of the apples, carrots and celery. Following the same order, repeat with the remaining apples, carrots and celery. Whisk well and serve immediately.

Juice Guru's Tip

We love to combine art with our juicing habit. Why not get out some construction paper and have your child draw the fruits and veggies you are juicing? You could even make veggie cartoons together. It's a great way to spend some one-on-one time with your child while helping to develop a lifelong juicing habit.

Big Blue

Your kids will love the color of this blue juice and its sweet taste—they're out of this world (not to mention nutritious)! The berries combine with the apples and beet to create a sweet, tangy and vibrant flavor experience. Blueberries provide vitamins C and K, as well as manganese, and have been shown to benefit cognition and support cardiovascular health. Beets contain folate, potassium, copper and iron.

3	red apples, cored and sliced	3
¼	beet, halved	¼
1 cup	blueberries	250 mL

1. Using a juicer, process half each of the apples, beet and blueberries. Following the same order, repeat with the remaining fruit. Whisk well and serve immediately.

Juice Guru's Tip

We like to have fun with kids when preparing juice. One way is by making funny faces out of the fruit and veggies before juicing them. In this case, you can create eyes from the blueberries, a large nose out of the beet, and a big smile with an apple wedge. Get creative and have fun!

The Hydrator

**Makes about
2 cups (500 mL)**

Dyes found in processed foods and drinks have been linked to behavioral difficulties in children. Sports drinks and other "enhanced" waters are loaded with these dyes. This juice, which includes natural electrolytes from the coconut water and natural color and flavor from the fruits, is a fantastic alternative. It is deliciously sweet, kid-friendly and mom-approved. It's also a great juice to serve to kids after a sports activity or trip to the playground, or just a long day at school.

Tips

Never peel the skin from your apples before juicing. Apple skin contains an abundance of phytonutrient polyphenols, which help to regulate blood sugar.

There are so many varieties of apples to choose from. Fuji, Red Delicious and Granny Smith are most commonly used for juicing, but any type will produce a delicious juice. We recommend using whatever is local and in season. Simply changing the variety of apple you use is an easy way to combat boredom with a particular juice blend.

1	apple, cored and sliced (see Tips, left)	1
10	strawberries	10
2 cups	young coconut water (see Juice Guru's Tip, below)	500 mL

1. Using a juicer, process half each of the apple and strawberries. Following the same order, repeat with the remaining fruit.

2. Add coconut water and whisk well. Serve immediately.

Juice Guru's Tip

Offering coconut water instead of plain water or sports drinks laden with artificial dyes and refined sugars is an excellent way to keep kids hydrated and replenish electrolytes. Coconut water provides nutrients and can be enjoyed as often as your child likes.

Summer Dream Punch

This juice is just what kids need on a hot summer day. Watermelon, plums and grapes are all extremely hydrating as well as nutrient-rich. Watermelons are loaded with the antioxidant carotenoids beta-carotene and lycopene, which have been shown to reduce the risk for cancer and reduce inflammation. Plums provide antioxidant phytonutrients, while red grapes are a great source of potassium, a mineral that many people don't get enough of.

Tip

When selecting red grapes, look for those that have a rich crimson hue and even color. Choose grapes that are plump and hearty. A silvery white "bloom" on the skins indicates freshness. The grapes should be firmly attached to stems that are brown or beige and healthy-looking, moist and flexible.

2 cups	chopped watermelon, inner rind intact	500 mL
2	nectarines, halved and stoned	2
2	plums, halved and stoned	2
2 cups	red grapes (see Tip, left)	500 mL

1. Using a juicer, process half each of the watermelon, nectarines, plums and grapes. Following the same order, repeat with the remaining watermelon, nectarine, plum and grapes. Whisk well and serve immediately.

Juice Guru's Tip

Red grapes contain resveratrol, a phytonutrient found in the skins that has many health benefits. We can't think of a better way to set up our kids for success in life than by providing health-giving juices such as this one.

Root for the Home Team

This combination of apples and root vegetables, with a hit of ginger, creates a mildly sweet and spicy juice that will appeal to even the pickiest child. Parsnips contain a large amount of vitamin C, potassium and folate, and apples provide additional vitamin C. Celery contains vitamin K, as well as potassium and folate.

Tips

Never peel the skin from your apples before juicing. Apple skin contains an abundance of phytonutrient polyphenols, which help to regulate blood sugar.

To peel gingerroot quickly and easily, simply use the edge of a teaspoon. Scrape it back and forth along the root to remove the skin and reveal the yellow flesh underneath.

2	apples, cored and sliced	2
2	parsnips, quartered	2
1	stalk celery, chopped	1
3	carrots	3
1	¼-inch (0.5 cm) piece peeled gingerroot	1

1. Using a juicer, process half each of the apples, parsnips, celery and carrots, plus the ginger. Following the same order, repeat with the remaining apple, parsnip, celery and carrots. Whisk well and serve immediately.

Juice Guru's Tip

While juicing, we love to teach our little ones about the importance of compost. Purchase a small compost unit for your kitchen. If you aren't saving the pulp to make one of our scrumptious pulp recipes, show your kids how to place it in the composter. In a few weeks your children will be fascinated to see that the pulp has turned into top-notch mineral-rich soil that you can use in the garden or with houseplants, or to sprinkle around trees in your yard as fertilizer.

Tips for Prepping and Measuring Ingredients

- No matter what type of juicer you are using, it is always a good idea to roughly chop greens such as spinach and kale and to cut longer vegetables such as celery and cucumbers into pieces before processing, so they flow through your juicer more efficiently and with less chance of clogging.
- When measuring leafy greens, pack the chopped greens tightly into the measuring cup to ensure that you achieve the correct measure for the recipes.
- When measuring chopped herbs, pack them into the measuring cup lightly to ensure that you achieve the correct measure for the recipes.

Juice Guru's Tip

Unless you are using a top-of-the-line juice press, even the best juicers will leave a fair amount of pulp in the final product. If, like us, you don't like pulp, we recommend straining your juice through a fine-mesh sieve into a 4-cup (1 L) measuring cup (for easy pouring). Straining your juice will make drinking it more enjoyable, since you won't end up with tiny fragments of pulp and skin that require occasional chewing.

Juicy Variation

Juicers can vary significantly in the volume of juice they produce, depending on the process the use and their efficiency with particular fruits and vegetables. Juice quantity will also fluctuate to reflect the produce used; a large apple or cucumber will yield considerably more juice than a small one. So while most of our recipes yield us approximately 3 cups (750 mL), be prepared to experience variations in the yield.

Chapter 13
Quick and Easy Juices

Watermelon Straight Up

Watermelon juice is not only refreshingly sweet and delicious but also extremely nutritious. While the juicy red flesh of watermelon is loaded with vitamin C and the carotenoid lycopene, the white part of the rind (which we typically don't eat) contains an incredible amount of phenolic antioxidants, flavonoids and more vitamin C. Juicing both the flesh and the white rind helps us get all those nutrients we normally might toss onto the compost pile.

| 1 | watermelon, prepared for juicing (see Juice Guru's Tip, below) | 1 |

1. Using a sharp knife, cut watermelon into pieces and remove outer skin, leaving the white rind intact (see Tip, below).

2. Using a juicer, process watermelon. Whisk well and serve immediately.

Juice Guru's Tip

To prepare a whole watermelon for juicing, cut off one of the ends, creating a flat surface so you can stand the melon upright. Carefully slice it in half lengthwise through the center, then cut each half in half again. Insert the knife between the skin and the rind and cut away the green skin, leaving the inner white rind intact. There is no need to discard the seeds.

Cantaloupe Straight Up

Makes about 3 cups (750 mL)

Cantaloupe is not only sweet and delicious but a very nutritious fruit. It may protect against hardening of the arteries, thanks to the anti-inflammatory action of beta-carotene and vitamin C.

| 1 | cantaloupe (see Juice Guru's Tip, below and on page 130) | 1 |

1. Using a sharp knife, remove outer skin from cantaloupe, leaving the rind intact. Cut into slices 2 inches (5 cm) wide.

2. Using a juicer, process cantaloupe. Whisk well and serve immediately.

Juice Guru's Tip

When choosing cantaloupe, look for a smooth, shallow indentation where the stem was attached. Choose melons with veining and a corky "netting" covering the surface. Avoid those that have pronounced yellowing and soft, watery flesh—they are overripe. Also, be sure to avoid bruised melons or those that have any mold.

Apple Plus

Apples and carrots store well in the refrigerator, so it's easy to keep them on hand for making this budget-friendly and extremely healthy juice. The taste is vibrant and sweet, with a slight herbal kick from the parsley. Apples are an excellent source of vitamin C, while both carrots and parsley provide a boost of provitamin A and vitamin K.

Tip

Big-box wholesale stores often sell organic carrots and apples in bulk at extremely reasonable prices. Carrots will keep for up to 2 weeks in an airtight container in the refrigerator (to avoid wilting, remove the green leaves from the tops before refrigerating). Apples will last for up to 3 months, but they do lose some nutrients as the weeks pass, so it is better to use them while they are fresh and crisp.

3	carrots	3
5	sprigs fresh flat-leaf (Italian) parsley (see Caution, below)	5
5	red apples, cored and quartered	5

1. Using a juicer, process half each of the carrots, parsley and apples. Following the same order, repeat with the remaining carrots, parsley and apples. Whisk well and serve immediately.

Herbal Helper

Parsley is rich in vitamin C, flavonoids and carotenes, which may inhibit the cancer-causing properties of deep-fried foods. We always recommend combining parsley juice with other vegetables. It has a very strong taste that is more palatable when mixed with a sweeter vegetable such as carrot.

Caution

Certain phytonutrients in parsley—in concentrated amounts, as they are in juices—may act as a uterine stimulant and should likely be avoided during pregnancy.

Carrots Alive

**Makes about
3 cups (750 mL)**

Carrots and nothing but the carrots. Make this sweet and brightly colored juice a staple of your juicing habit. Carrots are earthy-sweet and grounding. They're also an excellent source of provitamin A (beta-carotene) and a very good source of biotin, one of the B-complex vitamins. Along with calcium and iron, carrots also contain potassium, sodium and phosphorus. These nutrients help to protect against cancer and cardiovascular disease and promote good vision (especially night vision).

| 10 | medium carrots (see Juice Guru's Tip, below) | 10 |

1. Using a juicer, process carrots. Whisk well and serve immediately.

Juice Guru's Tip

We sometimes choose to use yellow or purple heirloom carrots in our juices. They are lower in sugar than hybridized orange carrots, which is good if you are trying to limit the amount of sugar in your diet.

Carrot Celery Apple Juice

**Makes about
3 cups (750 mL)**

This quick and easy juice is loaded with vitamins and minerals and packs a tasty punch—the sweet green apples and carrots are nicely balanced by the saltiness of the celery. Carrots are loaded with beta-carotene, an antioxidant; apples are loaded with vitamin C; and celery contains vitamin K and is an excellent anti-inflammatory.

3	carrots	3
4	green apples, cored and sliced	4
1	stalk celery, chopped	1

1. Using a juicer, process half each of the carrots, apples and celery. Following the same order, repeat with the remaining carrots, apples and celery. Whisk well and serve immediately.

Juice Guru's Tip

If you like the contrast of salty and sweet, mixing celery with fruits is the way to go. Celery is loaded with approximately 35 mg of sodium per stalk. If you are salt-sensitive you can still enjoy celery in juice, but be sure to monitor your intake.

Chef Babette's Carrot Croquettes

These croquettes are a huge hit at my restaurant, and you are sure to love them too. They are extremely easy to make, good for you (baked, not deep-fried), and a great way to put carrot pulp to use after juicing. You'll be amazed just how much the sweetness from the carrot pulp complements the kale and seaweed.

Tips

To yield enough carrot pulp to make this recipe, you will need to juice 8 to 10 medium carrots. You can have carrot pulp on hand by juicing the carrots in any recipe before the other ingredients and setting the pulp aside, refrigerated if necessary. Or make a Carrots Alive Juice (page 202).

No-salt seasonings usually contain a combination of dried onion and garlic, black pepper, red bell pepper, parsley, lemon peel, mustard seed, cumin, marjoram coriander, cayenne pepper and rosemary. You can find them in health food stores and well-stocked supermarkets.

You can use any ready-to-bake cornbread mix you like.

2 cups	carrot pulp (see Tips, left)	500 mL
1/4 cup	packed chopped kale leaves	60 mL
1/4 cup	diced red onion	60 mL
1	package (0.18 oz/5 g) roasted seaweed	1
1 tbsp	no-salt seasoning (see Tips, left)	15 mL
1 tbsp	tamari	15 mL
1 cup	organic ready-to-bake cornbread mix (see Tips, left)	250 mL
1 tbsp	coconut oil	15 mL

1. In a large bowl, combine carrot pulp, kale, onion, seaweed, no-salt seasoning, tamari and cornbread mix. Stir well.

2. Using your hands, form 8 croquettes, each about 1/2 cup (125 mL).

3. In a large skillet over medium-high heat, heat oil. Working in batches so as not to crowd the pan, cook croquettes for 2 minutes per side, until browned. Serve.

Apple Lemon Kale Juice

In this yummy juice, lemon really brightens and balances the sweet and earthy flavors of the apples and kale. Lemons are an excellent source of vitamin C and contain flavonoid compounds that provide antioxidant and anticancer support. Kale contains provitamin A and vitamin K, along with phytonutrient glucosinolates, which provide antioxidant, anti-inflammation and anticancer support.

Tip

When peeling lemons for juicing, be sure to leave behind as much white pith as possible. The pith of the lemon contains high concentrations of bioflavonoids such as limonene, which is believed to have anticancer properties.

6	red apples, cored and sliced (see Caution, below)	6
1 cup	packed chopped kale leaves	250 mL
1	lemon, peeled and halved (see Tip, left)	1

1. Using a juicer, process half each of the apples, kale and lemon. Following the same order, repeat with the remaining apples, kale and lemon. Whisk well and serve immediately.

Juice Guru's Tip

Apples and lemons are high-yielding fruits. That means they contain a lot of juice and you can get your juicing done in less time.

Caution

In most cases you can juice every part of fruits and vegetables, from skin to seeds. Just be careful to avoid the seeds when juicing apples, because apple seeds contain a small amount of arsenic, which can be toxic. (Please note that there is no record of arsenic poisoning from juicing apple seeds, but we like to err on the side of caution.) We suggest investing in an apple corer and composting or tossing out the entire core.

Carrot Apple Ginger Juice

Make this juice on busy days when you're on the go. You'll love the simple and sweet blend of earthy carrots and sweet apples accented by just a slight zing of ginger. The carrots and apples juice up quickly, while the ginger gives you just what you need to fight inflammation. Apples are an excellent source of vitamin C and increase antioxidant activity in your blood. Carrots are loaded with vitamin A and help with vision while also protecting against cardiovascular disease and cancer.

Tip

To peel gingerroot quickly and easily, simply use the edge of a teaspoon. Scrape it back and forth along the root to remove the skin and reveal the yellow flesh underneath.

4	red apples, cored and sliced (see Juice Guru's Tip, below)	4
2	carrots	2
1	1-inch (2.5 cm) piece peeled gingerroot (see Tip, left)	1

1. Using a juicer, process half each of the apples and carrots, plus the ginger. Following the same order, repeat with the remaining apples and carrot. Whisk well and serve immediately.

Juice Guru's Tip

While we recommend using green apples in our veggie juice combos, because we prefer their slightly tart flavor (Granny Smiths are our favorite), feel free to use red apples if you have a sweet tooth or are new to juicing—Fuji and Red Delicious apples are excellent. You really can't go wrong if you use whatever variety of apple is in season and local to your area—all apples are rich in nutrients.

Apple Spinach Juice

Makes about 3 cups (750 mL)

This simple blend of apples and spinach is a fantastic way to (quickly) get a full day's dose of spinach goodness, and then some. Spinach provides the provitamin A carotenoids alpha- and beta-carotene, as well as vitamin K, and is an excellent antioxidant. In addition, it helps to maintain bone health. Apples are high in vitamin C and polyphenols, which are incredible antioxidants too.

| 5 | red apples, cored and sliced (see Tips, page 207) | 5 |
| 2 cups | packed chopped spinach leaves | 500 mL |

1. Using a juicer, process half each of the apples and spinach. Following the same order, repeat with the remaining apples and spinach. Whisk well and serve immediately.

Apple Pear Ginger Juice

Makes about 3 cups (750 mL)

The pears in this juice slightly mellow the sweetness of the apples, and the ginger kicks it all together to create a refreshing blend. The pears also add body to the juice. They are a great source of potassium and copper and help decrease your risk of type 2 diabetes and heart disease.

Tip
To peel gingerroot quickly and easily, simply use the edge of a teaspoon. Scrape it back and forth along the root to remove the skin and reveal the yellow flesh underneath.

3	apples, cored and sliced	3
2	pears, quartered (see Juice Guru's Tip, below)	2
1	1-inch (2.5 cm) piece peeled gingerroot (see Tip, left)	1

1. Using a juicer, process half each of the apples and pears, plus the ginger. Following the same order, repeat with the remaining apples and pear. Whisk well and serve immediately.

Juice Guru's Tip
Never peel pears before juicing. The skin is an important source of many phenolic phytonutrients, including anticancer agents, anti-inflammatory flavonoids and antioxidants.

Cucumber Celery Lemon Apple Juice

Makes about 3 cups (750 mL)

Apples, celery, lemon and cucumber—this juice delivers a perfect combination of sweet, sour and salty flavors that you'll adore. The fruits and vegetables are easy to prepare and yield a lot of juice, so this blend comes together quite quickly. These ingredients are also relatively low-cost and available all year long.

Tips

There are so many varieties of apples to choose from. Fuji, Red Delicious and Granny Smith are most commonly used for juicing, but any type will produce a delicious juice. We recommend using whatever is local and in season. Simply changing the variety of apple you use is an easy way to combat boredom with a particular juice blend.

Never peel the skin from your apples before juicing. Apple skin contains an abundance of phytonutrient polyphenols, which help to regulate blood sugar.

Several varieties of cucumber are available in supermarkets, from field (slicing) to pickling to English cucumbers. We find that field and English cucumbers yield the most juice.

2	red apples, cored and sliced (see Tips, left)	2
1	stalk celery, chopped	1
1	lemon, peeled and halved (see Tips, page 210)	1
1	cucumber, quartered (see Tips, left)	1

1. Using a juicer, process half each of the apples, celery, lemon and cucumber. Following the same order, repeat with the remaining apple, celery, lemon and cucumber. Whisk well and serve immediately.

Juice Guru's Tip

Cucumber is an excellent complexion booster, among other benefits. It is a good source of silica, which works to strengthen connective tissue and improve overall complexion and skin health. And the powerful array of nutrient-rich ingredients in this juice will make you healthy and beautiful on the inside too.

Pineapple Express

Pineapples are available year-round, so you can enjoy this delicious blend whenever the mood strikes you. Pineapples are loaded with vitamins B_1, B_6 and C and folate, as well as manganese, copper, potassium, magnesium, iron and calcium. They provide antioxidant protection, immune support, digestive aid and anti-inflammatory benefits. Apples contain vitamin C and polyphenols, which provide antioxidant and cardiovascular support.

Tips

Pineapples do not continue to ripen after they are picked, so choose one that looks plump and has a sweet aroma. The leaves in the crown should also look fresh and green and should not pull out of the fruit easily.

To peel a pineapple, place it on a cutting board and, using a sharp knife, cut off the top and bottom to remove the leaves and stem and create flat surfaces. Resting the pineapple on a flat end, slide the knife under the skin and, with a downward motion, remove the skin in strips. Shave off any remaining bits of skin.

1	pineapple, skin removed, cut into 2-inch (5 cm) wedges	1
2	red apples, cored and sliced	2

1. Using a juicer, process half each of the pineapple and apples. Following the same order, repeat with the remaining pineapple and apple. Whisk well and serve immediately.

Juice Guru's Tip

While we recommend using green apples in our veggie juice combos, because we prefer their slightly tart flavor (Granny Smiths are our favorite), feel free to use red apples if you have a sweet tooth or are new to juicing—Fuji and Red Delicious apples are excellent. You really can't go wrong if you use whatever variety of apple is in season and local to your area—all apples are rich in nutrients.

Honeydew Thrill

When picked at its peak during the summer, there is nothing more enjoyable than the sweet and mellow flavor of honeydew melon. This melon is an excellent source of vitamins C, B_1, B_3 and B_5 and folate, as well as potassium, magnesium and copper. Because it is rich in potassium, honeydew melon can help to maintain healthy blood pressure levels and healthy skin.

| 1 | honeydew melon, skin removed, roughly chopped (see Juice Guru's Tip, below) | 1 |

1. Using a juicer, process melon. Whisk well and serve immediately.

Juice Guru's Tip

When preparing the melon, be sure to cut away only the pale yellow outer skin, leaving the inner rind intact. The rind is said to include added nutrients, although this claim has not been confirmed by the USDA; we include it just in case.

Pear Me Down

Pear juice is thick and naturally sweet, with a slightly earthy quality. And there are many different varieties of pears to choose from—Anjou, Bosc, Bartlett and Comice, for example—in a variety of colors from green to brown to red to yellow. All are excellent for juicing. Pears are a great source of pectin, which helps to lower cholesterol levels, and they also provide plenty of potassium.

| 6 | pears, quartered (see Juice Guru's Tip, below) | 6 |

1. Using a juicer, process pears. Whisk well and serve immediately.

Juice Guru's Tip

While we typically suggest that you strain your juice before consumption, this is not the case when it comes to pears. Recent studies show that with the pulp removed, pear juices lose up to 40% of their total phytonutrients, and their antioxidant capacity is significantly reduced. You'll want to consume all of the pulp from your pear juice to make sure you reap its many benefits. "Cloudy" pear juice is definitely the way to go.

Real Deal Lemonade

Who needs added sugar?
Thanks to the addition of
apples, this lemonade is
both sweet and sour and
refreshes without added
empty (and unhealthy)
calories. It's perfect
for a hot summer day.
Lemons are an excellent
source of vitamin C,
potassium, flavonoids and
a phytochemical known
as limonene, which can
be used to help dissolve
gallstones. New research is
showing that lemons can
be effective in the fight
against cancer.

Tips

When peeling lemons for
juicing, be sure to leave
behind as much white pith as
possible. The pith of the lemon
contains high concentrations of
bioflavonoids such as limonene,
which is believed to have
anticancer properties.

There are so many varieties of
apples to choose from. Fuji,
Red Delicious and Granny
Smith are most commonly
used for juicing, but any
type will produce a delicious
juice. We recommend using
whatever is local and in season.
Simply changing the variety of
apple you use is an easy way
to combat boredom with a
particular juice blend.

| 2 | lemons, peeled and halved (see Tips, left and Juice Guru's Tip, below) | 2 |
| 5 | red apples, cored and sliced (see Tips, left) | 5 |

1. Using a juicer, process half each of the lemons and apples. Following the same order, repeat with the remaining lemon and apples. Whisk well and serve immediately.

Juice Guru's Tip

Want an even sweeter lemonade? Try using
Meyer lemons, which are naturally sweeter than
traditional lemons.

Cuckoo for Coconuts

. . . .

Makes about 3 cups (750 mL)

Coconut water tastes deliciously earthy, sweet and tropical. It is low in calories and fat-free and also contains an abundance of potassium—higher intake of potassium can reduce the risk for high blood pressure and cardiovascular disease. Drinking fresh coconut water is also a nutritious way to keep well hydrated and restore lost electrolytes, which makes it an excellent alternative to sugary sports drinks after a workout.

. . . .

Tip

A cleaver is normally required to open the husk of a young coconut, but you can also find task-specific tools in kitchen supply stores. For convenience, you can purchase organic raw coconut water in bottles in health food stores and well-stocked supermarkets.

| 3 | young coconuts (see Tip, left) | 3 |

1. Open coconuts and pour coconut water into a glass. Serve immediately.

Juice Guru's Tip

In general, two different types of coconuts are available: young and mature. Young coconuts have either a green shell or a white husk. Mature coconuts are brown and covered with hairlike fibers. We recommend young coconuts for your juices. Young coconuts contain more water and a gel-like "meat" that maintains more of the fruit's nutrients. We typically use only the water of young coconuts in our juices; the gel should be reserved for smoothies. As a coconut begins to age, the water begins to seep into its meat and the remaining liquid becomes less nutritious. Older mature coconuts are best used for making coconut oil and other coconut products. You can find young coconuts in Asian and Mexican markets, specialty health food stores and well-stocked supermarkets.

Chapter 13: Quick and Easy Juices   211

Smoothie Portion Sizes

Thanks to the abundance of fiber in these nutritious and delicious smoothies, we recommend consuming only 2 cups (500 mL) per day.

Chapter 14
Delicious Smoothies

Classic Green Smoothie

While we know it is important to eat lots of greens, some of us just don't like the taste. Green smoothies are an excellent way to consume leafy green vegetables, because the (sometimes bitter) taste is neutralized by the fruit. This smoothie is sweet and nutty, with just a hint of vanilla. It provides potassium, provitamin A and vitamins C, E and K (to name a few), as well as biotin. It's also extremely hydrating, restores electrolytes and is antioxidant, anticancer and anti-inflammatory.

Herbal Helper

Vanilla gives your smoothie a creamy, delicious taste, but did you know it also may help to prevent cancer? Recent evidence published in the *Journal of Agricultural and Food Chemistry* indicates that vanillin, a compound found in vanilla, has been shown to suppress cancer cell migration and metastasis, although its mechanism of action is unknown. More studies are needed, but this does sound promising.

1 cup	young coconut water	250 mL
1	frozen banana	1
½ cup	strawberries (fresh or frozen)	125 mL
2 tbsp	raw almond butter	30 mL
1 cup	packed chopped spinach leaves (see Juice Guru's Tips, below)	250 mL
¼ tsp	alcohol-free organic vanilla extract (see Juice Guru's Tips, below)	1 mL

1. In a blender, combine coconut water, banana, strawberries, almond butter, spinach and vanilla. Blend at high speed until smooth. Serve immediately.

Juice Guru's Tips

As you get accustomed to the pleasing taste of greens in your smoothie, we recommend increasing the amount of spinach to 2–3 cups (500–750 mL), which will amp up the nutritional value.

We recommend using alcohol-free extracts whenever possible, because alcohol is not part of a healthy diet. However, we do understand that only a small amount is used in extracts (to preserve the product), so choose whichever brand works best for you. We recommend using organic products to reduce your exposure to pesticides and other chemicals.

Tropical Smoothie

Makes about 2 cups (500 mL)

This sweet, tropical-tasting blend is a healthy substitute for sugary juices that are devoid of nutrients. Spinach provides vitamin K, which can strengthen your bones, as well as beta-carotene, lutein and zeaxanthin. These carotenoids can support your immune system and improve eyesight by protecting the retina, specifically the macula, which is the part of the eye responsible for central vision.

Tips

Pineapples do not continue to ripen after they are picked, so choose one that looks plump and has a sweet aroma. The leaves in the crown should also look fresh and green and should not pull out of the fruit easily.

To peel a pineapple, place it on a cutting board and, using a sharp knife, cut off the top and bottom to remove the leaves and stem and create flat surfaces. Resting the pineapple on a flat end, slide the knife under the skin and, with a downward motion, remove the skin in strips. Shave off any remaining bits of skin.

To prepare a mango for blending, cut a small slice from the top and bottom of the fruit to make flat ends. Stand the fruit upright on a cutting board. Using a sharp knife, cut off on all four sides the flesh surrounding the large seed in the middle. Slide a tablespoon between the skin and meat of the mango to remove the flesh. Cut into halves.

½ cup	chopped fresh pineapple (see Tips, left)	125 mL
	Juice of 2 lemons, freshly squeezed	
½ cup	chopped pitted, peeled mango (see Tips, left)	125 mL
4	pitted dates	4
1 cup	packed chopped spinach leaves	250 mL

1. In a blender, combine pineapple, lemon juice, mango, dates and spinach. Blend at high speed until smooth. Serve immediately.

Variation

If you love mangos, omit the pineapple and increase the amount of mango to 1 cup (250 mL).

Razzmatazz Smoothie

1 cup	fresh apple juice (see Tips, left)	250 mL
1	cucumber, coarsely chopped	1
3 cups	raspberries (fresh or frozen)	750 mL
15	sprigs fresh cilantro (about ½ bunch)	15

Makes about 2 cups (500 mL)

This deliciously tart raspberry smoothie is nicely balanced by sweet apple juice and the bold flavor of cilantro. Raspberries are a fantastic source of vitamin C, fiber, manganese and flavonoids called anthocyanidins, which act as an antioxidant. They also contain ellagic acid, which is a cancer-fighting compound.

Tips

You will need to juice 3 to 4 apples to yield 1 cup (250 mL) juice, depending on the output of your juicer.

If you are not a fan of cilantro, you can substitute ½ cup (125 mL) spinach for a milder flavor.

1. In a blender, combine apple juice, cucumber, raspberries and cilantro. Blend at high speed until smooth. Serve immediately.

Herbal Helper

Cilantro provides excellent support for liver health. This herb is not typically used in juices and smoothies because of its distinctive taste, but if you love it (not everyone does), it will add a bold savory flavor to your smoothie. If you are not a fan of cilantro, simply omit it.

Strawberry Açai

Sweet strawberries and tart orange perfectly balance the mild-tasting Swiss chard in this yummy smoothie, and açai raises its nutritional value to a new level (see Juice Guru's Tip, right). Swiss chard delivers an abundance of provitamins A and K, potassium, and decent amounts of vitamin C, magnesium and manganese. This smoothie will help to regulate blood sugar, promote good bone health and provide antioxidant support.

1½ cups	strawberries (fresh or frozen)	375 mL
3	oranges, peeled and quartered	3
3	stalks celery	3
3 cups	firmly packed chopped Swiss chard leaves	750 mL
2 tbsp	organic açai berry powder	30 mL

1. In a blender, combine strawberries, oranges, celery, Swiss chard and açai powder. Blend at high speed until smooth. Serve immediately.

Juice Guru's Tip

Açai berries contain an extraordinary amount of antioxidants that protect the tissues and cells of the body, as well as a wide array of phytonutrients, which makes it one of the most popular superfoods among health enthusiasts. Phytonutrients are natural chemicals found in all plant foods. Unlike vitamins and minerals, these phytochemicals don't necessarily help keep us alive, but they may help prevent disease and keep the body working properly.

Berry Blast

Pineapple Bana

**Makes about
2 cups (500 mL)**

Almond milk forms the basis of this creamy mixed-berry smoothie. It has a sweet yet tart flavor complemented by a touch of earthy vanilla. Almonds are a good source of protein, calcium, potassium, magnesium, zinc, iron and vitamin E; they are helpful for fighting heart disease and lowering cholesterol. The berries have an abundance of vitamins C and K, manganese, copper and fiber. This smoothie provides cardiovascular, cognitive and anticancer support and also helps to balance blood sugar.

1½ cups	almond milk	375 mL
½ cup	raspberries (fresh or frozen)	125 mL
½ cup	blackberries (fresh or frozen)	125 mL
½ cup	blueberries (fresh or frozen)	125 mL
5	pitted dates	5
2 cups	packed chopped trimmed kale leaves	500 mL
¼ tsp	alcohol-free organic vanilla extract	1 mL

1. In a blender, combine almond milk, raspberries, blackberries, blueberries, dates, kale and vanilla. Blend at high speed until smooth. Serve immediately.

Variation

For an incredibly tasty and nutritious smoothie, substitute 2 packets (200 g) frozen açai berries for the other berries. Açai is loaded with antioxidants that protect the tissues and cells of the body, as well as a wide variety of phytonutrients.

Pineapple Banana Smoothie

Makes about 2 cups (500 mL)

The baby spinach in this sweet and tropical-tasting smoothie provides extra calcium, iron and other essential vitamins and minerals. Spinach is an excellent source of vitamin K, which can help strengthen bones.

Tips

Pineapples do not continue to ripen after they are picked, so choose one that looks plump and has a sweet aroma. The leaves in the crown should also look fresh and green and should not pull out of the fruit easily.

To peel a pineapple, place it on a cutting board and, using a sharp knife, cut off the top and bottom to remove the leaves and stem and create flat surfaces. Resting the pineapple on a flat end, slide the knife under the skin and, with a downward motion, remove the skin in strips. Shave off any remaining bits of skin.

1	banana (fresh or frozen)	1
½ cup	fresh or frozen pineapple chunks (see Tips, left)	125 mL
2 cups	packed baby spinach leaves	500 mL
¼ tsp	alcohol-free organic vanilla extract	1 mL
½ cup	young coconut water	125 mL

1. In a blender, combine banana, pineapple, spinach, vanilla and coconut water. Blend at high speed until smooth. Serve immediately.

Variation

Instead of using coconut water, you can simply use ½ cup (125 mL) filtered water. For a sweeter result, substitute ½ cup (125 mL) fresh apple juice (the juice of 2 to 3 apples).

Minty Watermelon Smoothie

This tasty smoothie quenches your thirst, thanks to the hydrating watermelon, which is also an excellent source of vitamin C, potassium and fiber. Fresh mint really brings out the sweet flavors of the melon and berries.

2 cups	chopped seedless watermelon	500 mL
2 cups	strawberries (fresh or frozen)	500 mL
1	banana (fresh or frozen)	1
5	sprigs fresh mint	5
1 cup	filtered water	250 mL

1. In a blender, combine watermelon, strawberries, banana, mint and water. Blend at high speed until smooth. Serve immediately.

Variation

For a tropical take on this smoothie, substitute an equal amount of cantaloupe or honeydew melon for the watermelon. Cantaloupe provides an excellent mix of provitamins A and C, as well as potassium and copper; like watermelon, it also provides antioxidant and anti-inflammatory support.

Goji Chia Smoothie

This smoothie is the perfect afternoon snack—it's filling and the chia and hemp seeds provide a good source of protein and nutrients. Chia seeds deliver protein, fiber, omega fatty acids, calcium and antioxidants, with minimal calories. Hemp seeds provide protein, fiber, potassium, phosphorus, magnesium and iron. This smoothie will also help to protect your heart and immune system. Goji berries are high in vitamin C and fiber and offer high levels of antioxidants, including zeaxanthin, which helps to protect your cells.

Tip

To soak the goji berries, chia seeds and hemp seeds, place them all together in a bowl and add 1 cup (250 mL) warm water. Cover and set aside for 5 minutes. Drain, discarding soaking liquid.

15	strawberries (fresh or frozen)	15
½ cup	raspberries (fresh or frozen)	125 mL
½ cup	blueberries (fresh or frozen)	125 mL
2 tbsp	dried goji berries, soaked (see Tip, left)	30 mL
1 tbsp	chia seeds, soaked (see Tip, left)	15 mL
1 tbsp	hulled hemp seeds, soaked (see Tip, left)	15 mL
2 cups	packed chopped romaine lettuce leaves	500 mL

1. In a blender, combine strawberries, raspberries, blueberries, soaked goji berries, chia seeds, hemp seeds and romaine. Blend at high speed until smooth. Serve immediately.

Juice Guru's Tip

Strawberries are an excellent source of ellagic acid, which is known to have strong anticancer and antioxidant properties. A study published in *Critical Reviews in Food Science and Nutrition* in 2004 indicated that strawberries topped the list of eight foods linked to lower rates of cancer death among a sample of 1,271 elderly people in New Jersey. The study found that those who ate the most strawberries were three times less likely to develop cancer than those who consumed few or no strawberries.

Chocolate Almond Butter Smoothie

Makes about 2 cups (500 mL)

This decadent smoothie will satisfy your chocolate cravings while providing an abundance of nutrients. Cacao is an excellent source of flavonoid antioxidants, which are important for protecting arteries. It can also prevent blood clots and reduce the risk of heart disease and stroke. This smoothie makes a great dessert replacement any time of the day.

Herbal Helper

One of the best sources of flavanols, cacao has been found to lower serum levels and blood pressure, according to a 2011 study done by the Indonesian Department of Clinical Nutrition. Another 2011 study, published by the department of pharmacology at the National Autonomous University of Mexico, indicates that cacao extracts may help to control arterial blood pressure. The cardiovascular benefits of cacao are attributed in part to its antioxidant and anti-inflammatory properties.

1	banana (fresh or frozen)	1
½ cup	young coconut water	125 mL
1 tbsp	raw almond butter	15 mL
1 tbsp	raw cacao powder (see Juice Guru's Tip, below)	15 mL
1 cup	packed chopped romaine lettuce leaves	250 mL
½ tsp	alcohol-free organic vanilla extract	2 mL

1. In a blender, combine banana, coconut water, almond butter, cacao powder, romaine and vanilla. Blend at high speed until smooth. Serve immediately.

Juice Guru's Tip

Cacao contains more than 300 healthy compounds, including protein, fat, carbohydrates, fiber, iron, zinc, copper, calcium and magnesium. It also contains caffeine, so keep that in mind if you also consume caffeinated coffee and tea. You might want to limit drinking this smoothie to once a week.

Avocado Smoothie

**Makes about
2 cups (500 mL)**

Avocados are a fantastic source of monounsaturated fatty acids, potassium, vitamin E, vitamin B and fiber. They also contain oleic and linoleic acids, which are helpful in lowering cholesterol levels.

¾ cup	young coconut water or filtered water	175 mL
½	avocado, pitted and peeled (see Juice Guru's Tip, below)	½
1	mango, peeled and pitted	1
1	banana (fresh or frozen)	1
2 cups	packed chopped kale leaves	500 mL

1. In a blender, combine coconut water, avocado, mango, banana and kale. Blend at high speed until smooth. Serve immediately.

Juice Guru's Tip

A ripe, ready-to-blend avocado is slightly soft to the touch and should have no dark sunken spots or cracks. To ripen a firm avocado, place it in a paper bag or a fruit basket and set aside at room temperature for a few days, until ready to use.

Resources

Ahuja, K.D., and Ball, M.J. "Effects of daily ingestion of chili on serum lipoprotein oxidation in adult men and women." *Br J Nutr.* August 2006.

All about Juicing. "Benefits of Chlorophyll in Greens." Available: http://www.all-about-juicing.com/chlorophyll.html.

Alleyne, T., Roache, S., Thomas, C., and Shirley, A. "The control of hypertension by use of coconut water and mauby: Two tropical food drinks." *West Indian Med J.* January 2005.

Amieva, H., Meillon, C., Helmer, C., et al. "*Ginkgo biloba* extract and long-term cognitive decline: A 20-year follow-up population-based study." *PLoS One.* January 2013.

Aruna, D., and Naidu, M.U. "Pharmacodynamic interaction studies of *Ginkgo biloba* with cilostazol and clopidogrel in healthy human subjects." *Br J Clin Pharmacol.* September 2006.

Arushanian, E.B., and Shikina, I.B. "Improvement of light and color perception in humans upon prolonged administration of eleutherococcus." *Eksp Klin Farmakol.* July–August 2004.

Ashton, A.K., Ahrens, K., Gupta, S., et al. "Antidepressant-induced sexual dysfunction and *Ginkgo biloba*." *Am J Psychiatry.* May 2000.

Australia. National Measurement Institute. "Breville Juicer/Blender Trials 2013." Report issued December 2013, reissued June 2014.

Bae, E.A., Han, M.J., and Kim, D.H. "In vitro anti–*Helicobacter pylori* activity of some flavonoids and their metabolites." *Planta medica.* June 1999.

Baranski, M., Srednicka-Tober, D., and Volakakis, N. "Higher antioxidant and lower cadmium concentrations and lower incidence of pesticide residues in organically grown crops: A systematic literature review and meta-analyses." *Br J Nutr.* September 2014.

Birks, J., and Grimley, E.J. "*Ginkgo biloba* for cognitive impairment and dementia." *Cochrane Database Syst Rev.* January 2009.

Bleakney, T.L. "Deconstructing an adaptogen: *Eleutherococcus senticosus.*" *Holist Nurs Pract.* July–August 2008.

Bouchard, M.F., Bellinger, D.C., and Wright, R.O. "Attention-deficit/hyperactivity disorder and urinary metabolites of organophosphate pesticides." *Pediatrics.* May 2010.

Boyanapalli, S.S., and Kong, T. "Curcumin, the king of spices: Epigenetic regulatory mechanisms in the prevention of cancer, neurological, and inflammatory diseases." *Curr Pharmacol Rep.* April 2015.

Boyer, J., and Hai Liu, R. "Apple phytochemicals and their health benefits." *Nutr J.* May 2004.

Boyles, S. "Peppermint oil, fiber can treat IBS: Study shows older treatments work well for irritable bowel syndrome." Available: www.webmd.com/ibs/news/20081113/peppermint-oil-fiber-can-treat-ibs.

Breinholt, V., Schimerlik, M., Dashwood, R., et al. "Mechanisms of chlorophyllin anticarcinogenesis against aflatoxin B_1: Complex formation with the carcinogen." *Chem Res Toxicol.* June 1995.

Brent, G.A. "Environmental exposures and autoimmune thyroid disease." *Thyroid.* July 2010.

Bucci, L.R. "Selected herbals and human exercise performance." *Am J Clin Nutr.* August 2000.

Cecchini, M., and LoPresti, V. "Drug residues store in the body following cessation of use." *Med Hypotheses.* August 2006.

Cermak, N.M., Gibala, M.J., and van Loon, L.J. "Nitrate supplementation's improvement of 10-km time-trial performance in trained cyclists." *Int J Sport Nutr Exerc Metab.* February 2012.

Chang, L. "Tiny microgreens packed with nutrients." *WebMD.* August 2012. Available: www.webmd.com/diet/20120831/tiny-microgreens-packed-nutrients.

Cheung, A.M., Tile, L., Lee, Y., et al. "Vitamin K supplementation in post-menopausal women with osteopenia (ECKO Trial): A randomized controlled trial." *PLOS Medicine.* October 2008.

Cheuvront, S.N., and Carter, R. "Ginkgo and memory." *JAMA.* February 2003.

Choi, W.S., Choi, C.J., Kim, K.S., et al. "To compare the efficacy and safety of nifedipine sustained release with *Ginkgo biloba* extract to treat patients with primary Raynaud's phenomenon in South Korea: Korean Raynaud study (KOARA study)." *Clin Rheumatol.* January 2009.

Cialdini, R.B. *Influence: The Psychology of Persuasion,* rev. ed. New York: HarperCollins, 2007.

Cicero, A.F., Derosa, G., Brillante, R., et al. "Effects of Siberian ginseng (*Eleutherococcus senticosus maxim*) on elderly quality of life: A randomized clinical trial." *Arch Gerontol Geriatr Suppl.* 2004.

Cieza, A., Maier, P., and Poppel, E. "Effects of *Ginkgo biloba* on mental functioning in healthy volunteers." *Arch Med Res.* September–October 2003.

Cingi, C., Conk-Dalay, M., Cakli, H., et al. "The effects of spirulina on allergic rhinitis." *Eur Arch Otorhinolaryngol.* October 2008.

Connolly, D.A., McHugh, M.P., Padilla-Zakour, O.I., et al. "Efficacy of a tart cherry juice blend in preventing the symptoms of muscle damage." *Br J Sports Med.* August 2006.

Conyers, R.A., Bais, R., and Rofe, A.M. "The relation of clinical catastrophes, endogenous oxalate production, and urolithiasis." *Clin Chem.* October 1990.

Cousens, G. "NCD zeolite review." *Pure Liquid Zeolite.* Available: www.pureliquidzeolite.com/ncd-zeolite-review-by-dr-gabriel-cousens.

Curhan, G.C., Willett, W.C., Rimm, E.B., et al. "A prospective study of dietary calcium and other nutrients and the risk of symptomatic kidney stones." *N Engl J Med.* March 1993.

Dai Q., et al. "Fruit and vegetable juices and Alzheimer's disease: The *Kame* Project." *Am J Med.* September 2006.

Dai, X., Stanilka, J.M., Rowe, C.A., et al. "Consuming *Lentinula edodes* (shiitake) mushrooms daily improves human immunity: A randomized dietary intervention in healthy young adults." *J Am Coll Nutr.* April 2015.

Dal Maso, L., Bosetti, C., La Vecchia, C., et al. "Risk factors for thyroid cancer: An epidemiological review focused on nutritional factors." *CCC.* February 2009.

Dasgupta, A., Wu, S., Actor, J., et al. "Effect of Asian and Siberian ginseng on serum digoxin measurement by five digoxin immuno-assays: Significant variation in digoxin-like immuno-reactivity among commercial ginsengs." *Am J Clin Pathol.* February 2003.

Dashwood, R., Yamane, S., and Larsen, R. "Study of the forces of stabilizing complexes between chlorophylls and heterocyclic amine mutagens." *Environ Mol Mutagen.* 1996.

Davydov, M., and Krikorian, A.D. "*Eleutherococcus senticosus* (Rupr. & Maxim.) Maxim. (Araliaceae) as an adaptogen: A closer look." *J Ethnopharmacol.* October 2000.

Dean, J. *Making Habits, Breaking Habits.* Boston, MA: Da Capo Press, 2013.

DeKosky, S.T., Williamson, J.D., Fitzpatrick, A.L., et al. "*Ginkgo biloba* for prevention of dementia: A randomized controlled trial." *JAMA.* December 2008.

Delimaris, I. "Adverse effects associated with protein intake above the recommended dietary allowance for adults." *ISRN Nutrition.* June 2013.

Deng, R., and Chow, T. "Hypolipidemic, antioxidant and anti-inflammatory activities of microalgae spirulina." *Cardiovasc Ther.* August 2010.

de Souza dos Santos, M.C, Goncalves, C.F.L., Vaisman, M., et al. "Impact of flavonoids on thyroid function." *Food Chem Toxicol.* October 2011.

Deutsch, M., and Gerard, H.B. "A study of normative and informational social influences upon individual judgment." Research Center for Human Relations, New York University. 1955.

Doerge, D.R., and Chang, H.C. "Inactivation of thyroid peroxidase by soy isoflavones, in vitro and in vivo." *J Chromatogr.* September 2002.

Doss, A. "Top six alkaline foods to eat every day for vibrant health." *Natural News.* December 2012. Available: www.naturalnews.com/038274_alkaline_foods_improved_health_conscious_eating.html.

Dourado, G.K., and Cesar, T.B. "Investigation of cytokines, oxidative stress, metabolic, and inflammatory biomarkers after orange juice consumption by normal and overweight subjects." *Food Nutr Res.* October 2015.

Drew, S., and Davies, E. "Effectiveness of *Ginkgo biloba* in treating tinnitus: Double blind, placebo-controlled trial." *BMJ.* January 2001.

Drugs.com. "Parsley." 2009. Available: www.drugs.com/npc/parsley.html.

Egner, P.A., Munoz, A., and Kensler, T.W. "Chemoprevention with chlorophyllin in individuals exposed to dietary aflatoxin." *Mutat Res.* February–March 2003.

Engelsen, J., Nielsen, J.D., and Hansen, K.F. "Effect of coenzyme Q10 and *Ginkgo biloba* on warfarin dosage in patients on long-term warfarin treatment: A randomized, double-blind, placebo-controlled cross-over trial." *Ugeskr Laeger.* April 2003.

Eschbach, L.F., Webster, M.J., Boyd, J.C., et al. "The effect of Siberian ginseng (*Eleutherococcus senticosus*) on substrate utilization and performance." *Int J Sport Nutr Exerc Metab*. December 2000.

Evans, J.R. "*Ginkgo biloba* extract for age-related macular degeneration." *Cochrane Database Syst Rev*. January 2013.

Federation of American Societies for Experimental Biology (FASEB). "Eating green leafy vegetables keeps mental abilities sharp." *Science Daily*. March 2015.

Fiore, A., La Fauci, L., Cervellati, R., et al. "Antioxidant activity of pasteurized and sterilized commercial red orange juices." *Mol Nutr Food Res*. December 2005.

Florence. M.D., Asbridge, M., and Veugelers, P.J. "Diet quality and academic performance." *J Sch Health*. April 2008.

Franceschi, C., and Campisi, J. "Chronic inflammation (inflammaging) and its potential contribution to age-associated diseases." *J Gerontol A Biol Sci Med Sci*. June 2014.

Freedman, J.E., Parker, C., Li, L., et al. "Select flavonoids and whole juice from purple grapes inhibit platelet function and enhance nitric oxide release." *Circulation*. March 2001.

Fugh-Berman, A. "Herb-drug interactions." *Lancet*. January 2000.

Gabrielian, E.S., Shukarian, A.K., Goukasova, G.I., et al. "A double blind, placebo-controlled study of *Andrographis paniculata* fixed combination Kan Jang in the treatment of acute upper respiratory tract infections including sinusitis." *Phytomedicine*. November 2002.

Ghosh, S., Banerjee, S., and Sil, P.C. "The beneficial role of curcumin on inflammation, diabetes and neurodegenerative disease: A recent update." *Food Chem Toxicol*. September 2015.

Glassman, K. "Why are hemp seeds good for me?" *WebMD*. Available: www.webmd.com/food-recipes/why-are-hemp-seeds-good-for-me.

Glatthaar-Saalmuller, B., Sacher, F., and Esperester, A. "Antiviral activity of an extract derived from roots of *Eleutherococcus senticosus*." *Antiviral Res*. June 2001.

Gómez-Pinilla, F. "Brain foods: The effects of nutrients on brain function." *Nat Rev Neurosci*. July 2008.

Goulet, E.D., and Dionne, I.J. "Assessment of the effects of *Eleutherococcus senticosus* on endurance performance." *Int J Sport Nutr Exerc Metab*. February 2005.

Gruenwald, J., Brednler, T., and Jaenicke, C. *PDR for Herbal Medicines*, 4th ed. Montvale, NJ: Thomson Healthcare, 2007.

Guillén, M.D., and Uriarte, P.S. "Aldehydes contained in edible oils of a very different nature after prolonged heating at frying temperature: Presence of toxic oxygenated α,β unsaturated aldehydes." *Food Chemistry*. April 2012.

Gyllenhaal, C., Merritt, S.L., Peterson, S.D., et al. "Efficacy and safety of herbal stimulants and sedatives in sleep disorders." *Sleep Med Rev*. June 2000.

Hampl, R., Ostatnikova, D., Celec, P., et al. "Short-term effect of soy consumption on thyroid hormone levels and correlation with phytoestrogen level in healthy subjects." *Endocr Regul*. June 2008.

Harkey, M.R., Henderson, G.L., Gershwin, M.E., et al. "Variability in commercial ginseng products: An analysis of 25 preparations." *Am J Clin Nutr*. June 2001.

Hartley, D.E., Elsabagh, S., and File, S.E. "Gincosan (a combination of *Ginkgo biloba* and *Panax ginseng*): The effects on mood and cognition of 6 and 12 weeks' treatment in post-menopausal women." *Nutr Neurosci*. October–December 2004.

Hartz, A.J., Bentler, S., Noyes, R., et al., "Randomized controlled trial of Siberian ginseng for chronic fatigue." *Psychol Med*. January 2004.

Hayes, J.D., Kelleher, M.O., and Eggleston, I.M. "The cancer chemopreventive actions of phytochemicals derived from glucosinolates." *Eur J Nutr*. May 2008.

He, F.J., Nowson C.A., Lucas, M., and MacGregor, G.A. "Increased consumption of fruit and vegetables is related to a reduced risk of coronary heart disease: Meta-analysis of cohort studies." *J Hum Hypertens*. September 2007.

He, F.J., Nowson, C.A., and MacGregor, G.A. "Fruit and vegetable consumption and stroke: Meta-analysis of cohort studies." *Lancet*. January 2006.

Hilton, M., and Stuart, E. "*Ginkgo biloba* for tinnitus." *Cochrane Database Syst Rev*. 2004.

Horsch, S., and Walther, C. "Ginkgo biloba special extract EGb 761 in the treatment of peripheral arterial occlusive disease (PAOD): A review based on randomized, controlled studies." *Int. J Clin Pharmacol Ther*. February 2004.

Howatson, G., Bell, P.G., Tallent, J., et al. "Effect of tart cherry juice (*Prunus cerasus*) on melatonin levels and enhanced sleep quality." *Eur J Nutr*. December 2012.

Huang, S.Y., Jeng, C., Kao, S., et al. "Improved haemorrheological properties by *Ginkgo biloba* extract (Egb 761) in type 2 diabetes mellitus complicated with retinopathy." *Clin Nutr.* August 2004.

Huff, E. "Mangosteen fruit shown to kill breast cancer cells without causing harm." *Natural News.* July 2014. Available: www.naturalnews.com/046110_mangosteen_fruit_breast_cancer_apoptosis.html.

Hunnum, S.M. "Potential impact of strawberries on human health: A review of the science." *Crit Rev Food Sci Nutr.* 2004.

Hurst, R.D., Wells, R.W., Hurst, S.M., et al. "Blueberry fruit polyphenolics suppress oxidative stress–induced skeletal muscle cell damage in vitro." *Mol Nutr Food Res.* March 2010.

Hyson, D.A. "A comprehensive review of apples and apple components and their relationship to human health." *Adv Nutr.* September 2011.

Ihl, R. "Effects of *Ginkgo biloba* extract EGb 761 in dementia with neuropsychiatric features: Review of recently completed randomised, controlled trials." *Int J Psychiatry Clin Pract.* November 2013.

Ihl, R., Tribanek, M., Bachinskaya, N., et al. "Efficacy and tolerability of a once daily formulation of *Ginkgo biloba* extract EGb761 in Alzheimer's disease and vascular dementia: Results from a randomised controlled trial." *Pharmacopsychiatry.* March 2012.

Ismail, I., Singh R., and Sirisinghe, R.G. "Rehydration with sodium-enriched coconut water after exercise-induced dehydration." *Southeast Asian J Trop Med Public Health.* July 2007.

Jacobsen, M.T. "Phytonutrients." *WebMD.* October 2014. Available: www.webmd.com/diet/guide/phytonutrients-faq.

Johnson, S.K., Diamond, B.J., Rausch, S., et al. "The effect of *Ginkgo biloba* on functional measures in multiple sclerosis: A pilot randomized controlled trial." *Explore* (NY). January 2006.

Joseph, J.A., Shukitt-Hale, B., and Willis, L.M. "Grape juice, berries, and walnuts affect brain aging and behavior." *J Nutr.* September 2009.

Kapadia, G.J., Azuine, M.A., Rao, G.S., et al. "Cytotoxic effect of the red beetroot (*Beta vulgaris* L.) extract compared to doxorubicin (Adriamycin) in the human prostate (PC-3) and breast (MCF-7) cancer cell lines." *Anticancer Agents Med Chem.* March 2011.

Kapil, V., Khambata, R.S., Robertson, A., et al. "Dietary nitrate provides sustained blood pressure lowering in hypertensive patients: A randomized, phase 2, double-blind, placebo-controlled study." *Hypertension* (American Heart Assoc.). November 2015.

Kenney, C., Norman, M., Jacobson, M., et al. "A double-blind, placebo-controlled, modified crossover pilot study of the effects of *Ginkgo biloba* on cognitive and functional abilities in multiple sclerosis." *American Academy of Neurology 54th Annual Meeting.* April 2002.

Kent, K., Charlton, K., Roodenrys, S., et al. "Consumption of anthocyanin-rich cherry juice for 12 weeks improves memory and cognition in older adults with mild-to-moderate dementia." *Eur J Nutr.* October 2015.

Khan, A., Safdar, M., Khan, M.M., et al. "Cinnamon improves glucose and lipids in people with type 2 diabetes." *Diabetes Care.* December 2003.

Kim, S.Y., Yoon, S., Kwon, S.M., et al. "Kale juice improves coronary artery disease risk factors in hypercholesterolemic men." *Biomed Environ Sci.* April 2008.

Kohler, S., Funk, P., and Kieser, M. "Influence of a 7-day treatment with *Ginkgo biloba* special extract EGb 761 on bleeding time and coagulation: A randomized, placebo-controlled, double-blind study in healthy volunteers." *Blood Coagul Fibrinolysis.* June 2004.

Krikorian, R., Nash, T.A., Shidler, M.D., et al. "Concord grape juice supplementation improves memory function in older adults with mild cognitive impairment." *Br J Nutr.* March 2010.

Krikorian, R., Shidler, M.D., Nash, T.A., et al. "Blueberry supplementation improves memory in older adults." *J Agric Food Chem.* April 2010.

Kulichenko, L.L., Kireyeva, L.V., Malyshkina, E.N., and Wikman, G. "A randomized, controlled study of Kan Jang versus amantadine in the treatment of influenza in Volgograd." *J Herb Pharmacother.* 2003.

Lally, P., van Jaarsveld, C.H.M., Potts, H.W.W, et al. "How are habits formed: Modelling habit formation in the real world." *Eur J Soc Psychol.* October 2010.

Le Bars, P.L., Kieser, M., and Itil, K.Z. "A 26-week analysis of a double-blind, placebo-controlled trial of the *Ginkgo biloba* extract EGb761 in dementia." *Dement Geriatr Cogn Disord.* July–August 2000.

Lee, J., Durst, R.W., and Wrolstad, R.E. "Impact of juice processing on blueberry anthocyanins and polyphenolics: Comparison of two pretreatments." *Food Chem Toxicol*. June–July 2002.

Li, P., Tian, W., and Ma, X. "Alpha-mangostin inhibits intracellular fatty acid synthase and induces apoptosis in breast cancer cells." *Mol Cancer*. June 2014.

Lirdprapamongko, K., Kramb, J.P., Suthiphongchai, T., et al. "Vanillin suppresses metastatic potential of human cancer cells through PI3K inhibition and decreases angiogenesis in vivo." *J Agr Food Chem*. March 2009.

MacLellan, D., Taylor, J., and Wood, K. "Food intake and academic performance among adolescents." *Can J Diet Pract Res*. September 2008.

Madero, M., Arriaga, J.C., Jalal, D., et al. "The effect of two energy-restricted diets, a low-fructose diet versus a moderate natural fructose diet, on weight loss and metabolic syndrome parameters: A randomized controlled trial." *Metabolism*. November 2011.

Magee, E. "Mad about mangos". September 2006. *WebMD*. Available: www.webmd.com/food-recipes/mad-about-mangos.

Mantle, D., Pickering, A.T., and Perry, A.K. "Medicinal plant extracts for the treatment of dementia: A review of their pharmacology, efficacy and tolerability." *CNS Drugs*. March 2000.

Manzano, S., and Williamson, G. "Polyphenols and phenolic acids from strawberry and apple decrease glucose uptake and transport by human intestinal Caco-2 cells." *Mol Nutr Food Res*. December 2010.

Masson, M. "Bromelain in blunt injuries of the locomotor system: A study of observed applications in general practice." *Fortschr Med*. July 1995.

Matejkova, J., and Petrikova, K. "Variation in content of carotenoids and vitamin C in carrots." *Not Sci Biol*. October 2010.

Mauro, V.F., Mauro, L.S., Kleshinski, J.F., et al. "Impact of ginkgo biloba on the pharmacokinetics of digoxin. *Am J Ther*. July–August 2003.

May, B.H., Lit, M., Xue, C.C., et al. "Herbal medicine for dementia: A systematic review." *Phytother Res*. December 2008.

May, B.H., Yang, A.W., Zhang, A.L., et al. "Chinese herbal medicine for mild cognitive impairment and age associated memory impairment: A review of randomised controlled trials." *Biogerontol*. April 2009.

Mazza, M., Capuano, A., Bria, P., and Mazza, S. "*Ginkgo biloba* and donepezil: A comparison in the treatment of Alzheimer's dementia in a randomized placebo-controlled double-blind study." *Eur J Neurol*. September 2006.

McCarney, R., Fisher, P., Iliffe, S., et al. "*Ginkgo biloba* for mild to moderate dementia in a community setting: A pragmatic, randomised, parallel-group, double-blind, placebo-controlled trial." *Int J Geriatr Psychiatry*. December 2008.

McCarty, M.F., DiNicolantonio, J.J., and O'Keefe, J.H. "Capsaicin may have important potential for promoting vascular and metabolic health." *Open Heart*. June 2015.

McKiernan, J. "Hempseed oil: The new healthy oil." *Natural News*. June 2012. Available: www.naturalnews.com/036039_hemp_seeds_oil_EFAs.html.

McMillan, M., "Americans living longer but obesity rising." May 2012. *WebMD*. Available: www.rochesterfirst.com/news/americans-living-longer-but-obesity-rising_20150807233259533.

Meinikovova, I., Fait, T., Kolarova, M., et al. "Effect of *Lepidium meyenii* Walp. on semen parameters and serum hormone levels in healthy adult men: A double-blind, randomized, placebo-controlled pilot study." *J Evid Based Complement Alternat Med*. September 2015.

Melchior, J., Spasov, A.A., Ostrovskij, O.V., et al. "Double-blind, placebo-controlled pilot and phase III study of activity of standardized *Andrographis paniculata* Herba Nees extract fixed combination (Kan Jang) in the treatment of uncomplicated upper-respiratory tract infection." *Phytomedicine*. October 2000.

Mercola, J. "Ignored since the 1950s: Is spirulina a new high-protein super food?" *Mercola.com*. July 2011. Available: http://articles.mercola.com/sites/articles/archive/2011/07/01/spirulina-the-amazing-super-food-youve-never-heard-of.aspx.

_____. "Nuts about coconuts: Everything you need to know about this supreme health food." *Mercola.com*. March 2004. Available: http://articles.mercola.com/sites/articles/archive/2004/03/10/coconuts.aspx.

_____. "What are mangos good for?" *Dr. Mercola Food Facts*. Available: http://foodfacts.mercola.com/mango.html.

Messina, M., and Redmond, G. "Effects of soy protein and soybean isoflavones on thyroid function in healthy adults and hypothyroid patients: A review of the relevant literature." *Thyroid*. March 2006.

Meyerowtiz, S., and Prussack, S. *Wheatgrass: Nature's Cure.* Audiobook. Fountain Valley, CA: Self-published, 2006.

Milerov, J., Cerovsk, J., Zamrazil, V., et al. "Actual levels of soy phytoestrogens in children correlate with thyroid laboratory parameters." *Clin Chem Lab Med.* February 2006.

Miller, J.A., Lang, J.E., Ley, M., et al. "Human breast tissue disposition and bioactivity of limonene in women with early-stage breast cancer." *Cancer Prev Res.* June 2013.

Miyagi, Y., Miwa, K., Inoue, H., et al., "Inhibition of human low-density lipoprotein oxidation by flavonoids in red wine and grape juice." *Am J Cardiol.* December 1997.

Mohamad, A.N., Abdullah, N., and Aminudin, N. "Anti-angiotensin converting enzyme (ACE) proteins from mycelia of *Ganoderma lucidum* (Curtis) P. Karst." *BMC Complement Altern Med.* October 2013.

Moher, D., Pham, B., Ausejo, M., et al. "Pharmacological management of intermittent claudication: A meta-analysis of randomised trials." *Drugs.* May 2000.

Moriarty, T. "Crime, commitment, and the responsive bystander: Two field experiments." *J Pers Soc Psychol.* February 1975.

Muraki, I., Imamura, F., Manson, J., et al. "Fruit consumption and risk of type 2 diabetes: Results from three prospective longitudinal cohort studies." *BMJ.* July 2013. Sample study questionnaire: www.channing.harvard.edu/nhs/questionnaires/pdfs/NHSI/2010.pdf.

Murillo, G., and Mehta, R.G. "Cruciferous vegetables and cancer prevention." *Nutr Cancer.* 2001.

Murphy, M.M., Barraj, L.M., Spungen, J.H., et al. "Global assessment of select phytonutrient intakes by level of fruit and vegetable consumption." *Br J Nutr.* September 2014.

Murray, M. "Cacao: Food of the gods." *Doctor Murray.* Available: http://doctormurray.com/sponsors/cacao.

_____. "Honeydew melons." *Doctor Murray.* Available: http://doctormurray.com/healing-facts-honeydew-melons.

_____. "Rasperries." *Doctor Murray.* Available: http://doctormurray.com/raspberries.

Murray, M.T. *The Complete Book of Juicing, Revised and Updated: Your Delicious Guide to Youthful Vitality.* New York, NY: Clarkson Potter, 2013.

Najafian, M., Jahromi, M.Z., Nowroznejhad, M.J., et al. "Phloridzin reduces blood glucose levels and improves lipids metabolism in streptozotocin-induced diabetic rats." *Mol Biol Rep.* May 2012.

Nathan, P.J., Harrison, B.J., and Bartholomeusz, C. "Ginkgo and memory." *JAMA.* February 2003.

Neal, D.T., Wood, W., Wu, M., and Kurlander, D. "The pull of the past: When do habits persist despite conflict with motives?" *Pers Soc Psychol Bull.* August 2011.

Nishino, H., Murakosh, M., et al. "Carotenoids in cancer chemoprevention." *Cancer Metastasis Rev.* February 2002.

Nishino, H., Tokuda, H., Murakoshi, M., et al. "Cancer prevention by natural carotenoids." *Biofactors.* 2000.

Oh, S.M., Chung, K.H. "Antiestrogenic activities of *Ginkgo biloba* extracts." *J Steroid Biochem Mol Biol.* August 2006.

Ong, T., Whong, W.Z., Stewart, J., et al. "Cholorophyllin: A potent antimutagen against environmental and dietary complex mixtures." *Mutat Res.* February 1987.

Organic Facts. "Health benefits of potassium." Available: www.organicfacts.net/health-benefits/minerals/health-benefits-of-potassium.html.

Oskouei, D.S., Rikhtegar, R., Hashemilar, M., et al. "The effect of *Ginkgo biloba* on functional outcome of patients with acute ischemic stroke: A double-blind, placebo-controlled, randomized clinical trial." *J Stroke Cerebrovasc Dis.* November 2013.

Oude Griep, L.M., Verschuren, W.M., et al. "Colours of fruit and vegetables and 10-year incidence of CHD." *Br J Nutr.* November 2011.

Ozgoli, G., Selselei, E.A., Mojab, F., et al. "A randomized, placebo-controlled trial of *Ginkgo biloba* L. in treatment of premenstrual syndrome." *J Altern Complement Med.* August 2009.

Panossian, A., and Wikman, G. "Evidence-based efficacy of adaptogens in fatigue, and molecular mechanisms related to their stress-protective activity." *Curr Clin Pharmacol.* September 2009.

Park, H.J., Lee, Y.J., Ryu, H.K., et al. "A randomized double-blind, placebo-controlled study to establish the effects of spirulina in elderly Koreans." *Ann Nutr Metab.* August 2008.

Payne, C. "Green smoothies: Full of health benefits or hype?" *USA Today*. August 2013. Available: www.usatoday.com/story/news/nation/2013/08/03/green-smoothies-nutrition/2518141.

Persson, J., Bringlov, E., Nilsson, L.G., and Nyberg, L. "The memory-enhancing effects of ginseng and *Ginkgo biloba* in healthy volunteers." *Psychopharmacology* (Berl). April 2004.

Petta, S., Marchesini, G., Caracausi, L., et al. "Industrial, not fruit fructose intake is associated with the severity of liver fibrosis in genotype 1 chronic hepatitis C patients." *J Hepatol*. December 2013.

Pham, L.B., and Taylor, S.E. "From thought to action: Effects of process-versus outcome-based mental simulations on performance." *Pers Soc Psychol Bull*. February 1999.

Picco, M.F., "Digestion: How long does it take?" October 2012. Available: www.mayoclinic.org/digestive-system/expert-answers/faq-20058340.

Pittler, M.H., and Ernst, E. "*Ginkgo biloba* extract for the treatment of intermittent claudication: A meta-analysis of randomized trials." *Am J Med*. March 2000.

Pongrojpaw, D., Somprasit, C., and Chanthasenanont, A. "A randomized comparison of ginger and dimenhydrinate in the treatment of nausea and vomiting in pregnancy." *J Med Assoc Thai*. September 2007.

Poolsup, N., Suthisisang, C., Prathanturarug, S., et al. "*Andrographis paniculata* in the symptomatic treatment of uncomplicated upper respiratory tract infection: Systematic review of randomized controlled trials." *J Clin Pharm Ther*. January 2004.

Quinones, M., Miguel, M., Muguerza, B., and Aleixandre, A. "Effect of a cocoa polyphenol extract in spontaneously hypertensive rats." *Food and Function*. October 2011.

Rao, P., Visweswara, G., and Siew, H. "Cinnamon: A multifaceted medicinal plant." *J Evid Based Complement Alternat Med*. April 2014.

Richter, H. *Dr. Richter's Fresh Produce Guide*. Apopka, FL: Try-Foods International Inc., 2000.

Robertson, W.G., Peacock, M., Heyburn, P.J., et al. "Should recurrent calcium oxalate stone formers become vegetarians?" *Br J Urol*. December 1979.

Roxas, M., and Jurenka, J. "Colds and influenza: A review of diagnosis and conventional, botanical, and nutritional considerations." *Altern Med Rev*. March 2007.

Sable-Amplis, R., Sicart, R., and Agid, R. "Further studies on the cholesterol-lowering effect of apple in humans: Biochemical mechanisms involved." *Nutr Res*. May 1983.

Salehi, B., Imani, R., Mohammadi, M.R., et al. "*Ginkgo biloba* for attention-deficit/hyperactivity disorder in children and adolescents: A double blind, randomized controlled trial." *Prog Neuropsychopharmacol Biol Psychiatry*. February 2010.

Schneider, L.S., DeKosky, S.T., et al. "A randomized, double-blind, placebo-controlled trial of two doses of *Ginkgo biloba* extract in dementia of the Alzheimer's type." *Curr Alzheimer Res*. December 2005.

Shan, B., Cai, Y.Z., Brooks, J.D., et al. "Antibacterial properties and major bioactive components of cinnamon stick (*Cinnamomum burmannii*) activity against foodborne pathogenic bacteria." *J Agr Food Chem*. June 2007.

Shehzad, A., Rehman, G., and Lee, Y.S. "Curcumin in inflammatory diseases." *Biofactors*. January–February 2013.

Siervo, M, Lara, J., Ogbonmwan, I., et al. "Inorganic nitrate and beetroot juice supplementation reduces blood pressure in adults: A systematic review and meta-analysis." *J Nutr*. June 2013.

Sigfúsdóttir, I.D., Kristjánsson, A.L., and Allegrante, J.P. "Health behaviour and academic achievement in Icelandic school children." *Health Educ Res*. February 2007.

Sinclair, S. "Male infertility: Nutritional and environmental considerations." *Alt Med Rev*. 2000.

Snitz, B.E, O'Meara E.S., Carlson, M.C., et al. "*Ginkgo biloba* for preventing cognitive decline in older adults: A randomized trial." *JAMA*. December 2009.

Spasov, A.A., Ostrovskij, O.V., Chernikov, M.V., et al. "Comparative controlled study of *Andrographis paniculata* fixed combination, Kan Jang and an echinacea preparation as adjuvant, in the treatment of uncomplicated respiratory disease in children." *Phytother Res*. January 2004.

Srivasta, K.C., and Mustafa, T. "Ginger (*Zingiber officinale*) and rheumatic disorders." *Med Hypotheses*. May 1989.

Statistic Brain Research Institute. "New years resolution statistics." Available: www.statisticbrain.com.

Stone, M., Ibarra, A., Roller, M., et al. "A pilot investigation into the effect of maca supplementation on physical activity and sexual desire in sportsmen." *J Ethnopharmacol*. September 2009.

Sudarma, V., Sukmaniah, S., and Siregar, P. "Effect of dark chocolate on nitric oxide serum levels and blood pressure in prehypertension subjects." *Acta Med Indones*. October 2011.

Sun, J. "D-limonene: Safety and clinical applications," *Altern Med Rev*. September 2007.

Szczurko, O., Shear, N., Taddio, A., and Boon H. "Ginkgo biloba for the treatment of vitiligo vulgaris: An open label pilot clinical trial." *BMC Complement Altern Med*. March 2011.

Tachino, N., Guo, D., Dashwood, W.M., et al. "Mechanisms of the in vitro antimutagenic action of chlorophyllin against benzo[a]pyrene: Studies of enzyme inhibition, molecular complex formation and degradation of the ultimate carcinogen." *Mutat Res*. July 1994.

Tamborini, A., and Taurelle, R. "Value of standardized *Ginkgo biloba* extract (EGb 761) in the management of congestive symptoms of premenstrual syndrome" [translated from French]. *Rev Fr Gynecol Obstet*. July–September 1993.

Taylor, E.N., Stampfer, M.J., and Curhan, G.C. "Dietary factors and the risk of incident kidney stones in men: New insights after 14 years of follow-up." *J Am Soc Nephrol*. December 2004.

Teas, J., Braverman, T.J., Kurzer, M.S., et al. "Seaweed and soy: Companion foods in Asian cuisine and their effects on thyroid function in American women." *J Med Food*. March 2007.

Thom, J.A., Morris, J.E., Bishop, A., et al. "The influence of refined carbohydrate on urinary calcium excretion." *Br J Urol*. December 1978.

Torronen, R., Kolehmainen, M., Sarkkinen, E., et al. "Berries reduce postprandial insulin responses to wheat and rye breads in healthy women." *J Nutr*. April 2013.

———. "Postprandial glucose, insulin, and free fatty acid responses to sucrose consumed with blackcurrants and lingonberries in healthy women." *Am J Clin Nutr*. September 2012.

Trick, L., Boyle, J., and Hindmarch, I. "The effects of *Ginkgo biloba* extract (LI 1370) supplementation and discontinuation on activities of daily living and mood in free living older volunteers." *Phytother Res*. July 2004.

Uchida, K. "Role of reactive aldehyde in cardiovascular diseases." *Free Radic Biol Med*. June 2000.

Uebel-von Sandersleben, H., Rothenberger, A., Albrecht, B., et al. "Ginkgo biloba extract EGb 761 in children with ADHD." *Z Kinder Jugendpsychiatr Psychother*. September 2014.

University of Maryland Medical Center. "*Ginkgo biloba*." June 2015. Available: https://umm.edu/health/medical/altmed/herb/ginkgo-biloba.

———. "Siberian ginseng." March 2015. Available:http://umm.edu/health/medical/altmed/herb/siberian-ginseng.

Vanderpas, J. "Nutritional epidemiology and thyroid hormone metabolism." *Annu Rev Nutr*. April 2006.

Van Dongen, M., van Rossum, E., Kessels, A., et al. "Ginkgo for elderly people with dementia and age-associated memory impairment: A randomized clinical trial." *J Clin Epidemiol*. April 2003.

Vellas, B., Coley, N., Ousset, P.J., et al. "Long-term use of standardised *Ginkgo biloba* extract for the prevention of Alzheimer's disease (GuidAge): A randomised placebo-controlled trial." *Lancet Neurol*. October 2012.

Vellas, B., and Grandjean, H. "Association of Alzheimer's disease onset with *Ginkgo biloba* and other symptomatic cognitive treatments in a population of women aged 75 years and older from the EPIDOS study." *J Gerontol A Biol Sci Med Sci*. April 2003.

von Unruh, G.E., Voss, S., Sauerbruch, T., et al. "Dependence of oxalate absorption on the daily calcium intake." *J Am Soc Nephrol*. March 2004.

Wailing, E. "Amazing herbs: Discover the benefits of burdock root." *Natural News*. February 2011. Available: www.naturalnews.com/031524_burdock_root_herbal_remedy.html.

Walker, N.W. *Fresh Vegetable and Fruit Juices*. Arizona: Norwalk Press, 1936; 1978 (rev.).

Wang, B.S., Wang, H., Song, Y.Y., et al. "Effectiveness of standardized *Ginkgo biloba* extract on cognitive symptoms of dementia with a six-month treatment: A bivariate random effect meta-analysis." *Pharmacopsychiatry*. May 2010.

WebMD. "Ashwagandha." Available: www.webmd.com/vitamins-supplements/ingredientmono-953-ashwagandha.aspx?activeingredientid=953&activeingredientname=ashwagandha.

———. "Cinnamon." Available: http://www.webmd.com/vitamins-and-supplements/lifestyle-guide-11/supplement-guide-cinnamon.

_____. "Elderberry fights flu symptoms." Available: www.webmd.com/cold-and-flu/news/20031222/elderberry-fights-flu-symptoms

_____. "Goji berries: Health benefits and side effects." Available: www.webmd.com/balance/goji-berries-health-benefits-and-side-effects.

_____. "Holy basil." Available: www.webmd.com/vitamins-supplements/ingredientmono-1101-holy%20basil.aspx?activeingredientid=1101&activeingredientname=holy%20basil.

_____. "Lavender." Available: www.webmd.com/vitamins-supplements/ingredientmono-838-lavender.aspx?activeingredientid=838&activeingredientname=lavender.

_____. "Reishi mushroom." Available: www.webmd.com/vitamins-supplements/ingredientmono-905-reishi%20mushroom.aspx?activeingredientid=905&activeingredientname=reishi%20mushroom.

_____. "Vitamins and supplements lifestyle guide." November 2014. Available: www.webmd.com/vitamins-and-supplements/lifestyle-guide-11/supplement-guide-cinnamon.

Weinmann, S., Roll, S., Schwarzbach, C., et al. "Effects of *Ginkgo biloba* in dementia: Systematic review and meta-analysis." *BMC Geriatr.* March 2010.

Weisburer, J.H. "Lycopene and tomato products in health promotion." *Ex Biol and Med.* November 2002.

Wilde, D. *Train Your Brain.* Bloomington, IN: Balboa Press, 2013.

Williams, M. "Immuno-protection against herpes simplex type II infection by *Eleutherococcus* root extract." *Int J Alt Complement Med.* 1995.

Winther, K., Ranlov, C., Rein, E., et al. "Russian root (Siberian ginseng) improves cognitive functions in middle-aged people, whereas *Ginkgo biloba* seems effective only in the elderly." *J Neurological Sci.* September 1997.

Woelk, H., Arnoldt, K.H., Kieser, M., and Hoerr, R. "*Ginkgo biloba* special extract EGb 761 in generalized anxiety disorder and adjustment disorder with anxious mood: A randomized, double-blind, placebo-controlled trial." *J Psychiatr Res.* September 2007.

Wong, C. "Is lucuma a superfruit?" *About Health.* November 2014. Available: http://altmedicine.about.com/od/herbsupplementguide/a/Lucuma.htm.

Wood, P.L. "Neuro-degeneration and aldehyde load." *J Psychiatry Neurosci.* September 2006.

Wood, W., Tam, L., and Witt, M.G. "Changing circumstances, disrupting habits." *J Pers Soc Psychol.* June 2005.

Wylie, L.J., Kelly, J., Bailey, S.J., et al. "Beetroot juice and exercise: Pharmacodynamic and dose-response relationships." *J Appl Physiol.* August 2013.

Xie, L., et al. "Sleep initiated fluid flux drives metabolite clearance from the adult brain." *Science.* October 2013.

Xu, C., Zhang, J., Mihai, D., and Washington, I. "Light harvesting chlorophyll pigments enable mammalian mitochondria to capture photonic energy and produce." *J Cell Sci.* January 2014.

Zelman, K.M. "The truth about coconut water." *WebMD.* 2010. Available: www.webmd.com/food-recipes/truth-about-coconut-water.

Zhang, L., Mao, W., Guo, X., et al. "*Ginkgo biloba* extract for patients with early diabetic nephropathy: A systematic review." *Evid Based Complement Alternat Med.* February 2013.

Zhang, L.Y., and Feng, Y.P. "Effects of dl-3-n-butylphtalide (NBP) on life span and neurological deficit in SHRSP rats." *Yao Hsueh Hsueh Pao.* 1996.

Zhang, M., Robitaille, L., Eintracht, S., et al. "Vitamin C provision improves mood in acutely hospitalized patients." *Nutrition.* May 2011.

Zhong, Y., Wang, Y., Guo, J., et al. "Blueberry improves the therapeutic effect of etanercept on patients with juvenile idiopathic arthritis: Phase III study." *Tohoku J Exp Med.* November 2015.

Index

Library and Archives Canada Cataloguing in Publication

Prussack, Steve, 1968-, author
    Juice Guru : transform your life by adding one juice a day : boost vitality, increase longevity & stay slim / Steve & Julie Prussack.

Includes bibliographical references.
ISBN 978-0-7788-0529-8 (paperback)

    1. Fruit juices. 2. Vegetable juices. 3. Cookbooks. I. Prussack, Julie, 1969-, author II. Title.

TX811.P78 2016   641.87'5   C2015-908527-6